Developmental
MANAGEMENT

THE RISE OF NEC

B

Developmental Management

General Editor: Ronnie Lessem

Charting the Corporate Mind
*Charles Hampden-Turner**

Managing in the Information Society
Yoneji Masuda

Developmental Management
Ronnie Lessem

Foundations of Business
Ivan Alexander

Greening Business
John Davis

Ford on Management
*Henry Ford**

Managing Your Self
Jagdish Parikh

Managing the Developing Organization
Bernard Lievegoed

Conceptual Toolmaking
Jerry Rhodes

Integrative Management
Pauline Graham

Executive Leadership
Elliott Jaques and Stephen D. Clement

Transcultural Management
Albert Koopman

The Great European Illusion
Alain Minc

The Rise of NEC
Koji Kobayashi

* *For copyright reasons this edition is not available in the USA*

Developmental
MANAGEMENT

The Rise of NEC

HOW THE WORLD'S GREATEST C&C COMPANY IS MANAGED

KOJI KOBAYASHI

WITH A FOREWORD BY
PETER DRUCKER

Copyright © Koji Kobayashi 1989, 1991

Originally published in Japan by Diamond Inc., Tokyo,
under the title *Strategy and Decision Making – My Years with NEC Corporation*.
English translation rights arranged with Diamond, Inc.,
through Japan UNI Agency Inc. and Hutton-Williams Agency.
Koji Kobayashi is hereby identified as author of this work
in accordance with Section 77 of the Copyright, Designs and Patents Act 1988.

First published 1991

Blackwell Publishers
3 Cambridge Center
Cambridge, Massachusetts 02142, USA

108 Cowley Road, Oxford, OX4 1JF, UK

Library of Congress Cataloging in Publication Data
Kobayashi, Koji, 1907–
    The rise of NEC: how the world's greatest C&C Company is managed /
Koji Kobayashi: with a foreword by Peter Drucker.
    p.   cm.
    Translated from Japanese.
    ISBN 1–55786–277–X
    1. NEC Corporation – History.   2. Electronic
industries – Japan – Management.   3. Electric industries – Japan –
Management.   I. Title.
HD9696.A3J363112   1991
338.7'62138'0952–dc20
91–10496 CIP

British Library Cataloguing in Publication Data
A CIP catalogue record for this book is available from the British Library

Typeset in Ehrhardt 11/13pt.
by Hope Services (Abingdon) Ltd
Printed in Great Britain by
T. J. Press Ltd, Padstow, Cornwall

This book is printed on acid-free paper.

This book is dedicated to all those seniors who endeavored to make NEC a great corporation. And to my wife, Kazuko, who showed me her unstinting understanding and forbearance.

Contents

Foreword

by Peter F. Drucker

Dr Kobayashi was one of the first friends I made in Japan – all of thirty years ago, on my very first trip to his country. I ran a seminar that July 1959 in Hakone; I was quite late for dinner the first day because I had been trying unsuccessfully all day to telephone to Tokyo and Osaka – the calls never got through. When I finally gave up and went into the hotel's dining room, the only place left was next to one of my seminar participants whose name, however, I did not know.

"I am Kobayashi," he said; "You look a little upset. Anything the matter?" I told him that I had been trying from nine in the morning until after six at night to get my two phone calls through. He chuckled and said: "If NTT has its way and we follow what the American Telephone Company advises us to do, it'll be another ten years before these calls go through on direct dialing. They want us to lay cables the way they have done in the US.

"But there is a quicker way – I am pushing it. We can do what the American Army did during the Pacific War and put microwave relays on every mountain top. It's never been done for a large population and NTT resists it. But I am building a demonstration line. If it doesn't work I'll be out of a job. But if it does, you'll be able to dial direct anywhere in Japan within three years." When I came back two years later there were microwave towers all over Japan and I could dial Osaka directly from Tokyo – and another year later, directly from Hakone.

The most recent time I saw Kobayashi-sensei was on my last trip to Japan, four-and-a-half years ago, in the autumn of 1986. He was kind enough to supervise the translation of my book *Innovation and Entrepreneurship* into Japanese – as he had done for several of my earlier books – and I called on him to express my gratitude. He kindly invited me to dinner at the NEC guest house and we had a relaxed evening together talking about all the changes in Japan and in the world since we had first met. I told him that my Japanese publishers, Diamond-sha, had just given me a wonderful birthday party on my 77th anniversary. He said: "I have just given myself the best present for my 100th birthday. I have asked the scientists in NEC's research lab to give me a communications-computer that can handle spoken language in several languages, and can translate instantaneously so that a Japanese speaking his language in Tokyo will be heard in English by an American listening in Los Angeles, and vice versa. And they'll give it to me." I was impressed. But I said politely – knowing that Kobayashi-sensei is two years older than I am – "I hope you'll be around to use that computer-phone in the year 2007." "Oh," he said with a laugh, "I'll watch our scientists wherever I'll be in twenty years – and they know it."

Ever since I first began to visit Japan, that is, for thirty years, I have heard complaints, especially from Japanese scientists and teachers, of how the Japanese educational system stifles creativity and independence and how it produces timidity, conformity, and imitators. And then I say to myself: "And how then do they explain Kobayashi-sensei?"

Very few CEOs in history have presided over a company expansion that can match the forty-fold growth of NEC over the twenty-five years during which Dr Kobayashi has led it. Critics will say that he was lucky – and, of course, these were years of unparalleled expansion in Japan altogether and in telecommunications and computers in particular. But there is an old saying "Luck favors the prepared mind." There are plenty of companies in Dr Kobayashi's own industry that did not grow and prosper despite the explosive growth of telecommunications and computers; the best example is the company which, when Dr Kobayashi started, was the largest single shareholder in NEC, the International Standard Electric Company and its once powerful parent company. It is now almost totally out of telephones and computers. I can testify that Dr Kobayashi, even thirty years ago, that is well before he became president, had the vision that built NEC.

On that first evening we sat together after dinner and talked for hours. He became interested in me when I made a chance remark to the effect that my consulting work with the American Telephone System had convinced me that telephones and computers were parts of the same system. Dr Kobayashi states that it was not until almost twenty years later that he began to talk of "C&C" – Computers and

Communications – as an integrated system and a basically new force in economics and world view. Maybe he did not use these terms during our first conversation in Hakone, in July 1959. But he surely already had the vision. And though I am not a technical man it was quite clear to me then that he knew and understood the yet-to-be-invented technology needed to create the integrated worldwide communications and computer system of which the tele-transistor-computer he has ordered for his 100th birthday would be the capstone that makes communications and understanding truly a global system. And since I am a little younger than he is, I do hope that I will be around then to be able to use this wonderful instrument to congratulate him on his achievement – as a scientist, as a business leader, as a practical visionary.

Preface to the English Edition

The Japanese edition of this book was published in May 1989 under the title *Koso to Ketsudan (Strategy and Decision-Making – My Years with NEC Corporation)*. While the original text referred to financial data up to the end of fiscal 1988, this edition incorporates new figures covering developments to 1990 on topical issues.

I have often been asked what prompted me to write this account of my experiences as chief executive officer at NEC Corporation. My invariable response is that I hope my thoughts on corporate management may serve as a starting-point for the next generation of top managers as they set about developing concepts of corporate excellence for the twenty-first century.

Forecasting future trends cannot be done in isolation from present realities. On the other hand, people are too prone to believe that a company whose present overwhelming excellence has brought it to a peak of prosperity will always continue to be strong. The coming age, however, is one in which strength can change to weakness virtually overnight. There is no time like the present, I believe, for top management to start seeking out the skills that can prevent this from happening. At every turn corporate managers will find their abilities and resourcefulness put to the test.

The business climate in Japan may differ from that in which the readers of this book operate, but one cardinal rule of management is shared by business people the world over – the need to detect future trends while pursuing solutions to present problems. It is in this light that I submit this record of my management experiences during the quarter of a century I served at the helm of NEC Corporation for the appraisal of thoughtful readers everywhere.

Two unshakable convictions have sustained me as I have steered my way through turbulent times searching for the tides of impending change. First, a company that makes things must never lose sight of the fact that creating new products is the source of its strength; and second, it must have a vision and a philosophy behind its business activities.

Since 1977, when I first advocated the concept of C&C, the integration of computers and communications, NEC has committed itself to the information industry. Even back in the 1970s I strongly believed not only that the unprecedented breakthroughs achieved from the merger of computer and communications technologies would continue to play a central role in the scientific and technological advances of the years ahead, but also that C&C would exert a profound influence on industry, society, culture, and every other sphere of human endeavor by forming the infrastructure to handle that indispensable component of modern life, information. It is a source of enormous pride to me that I was able to articulate and propose a business strategy, that has the potential to contribute so much to make people's lives richer and more truly human.

Many people have helped to bring this book to completion. My special thanks go to Jean Hoff for producing an English translation that is even more readable than my Japanese original; to Gillian Bromley, Judith Harvey and Rhona Richard of Blackwell Publishers for overcoming the distances separating Japan and Britain and expediting the editing process; to the many NEC employees who gave me their invaluable suggestions while I was writing the book, and especially to Kiyoshi Yamauchi, who assisted me in preparing it for publication. I also received constant cooperation from Mineo Iwamochi of Diamond, Inc., the publisher of the Japanese edition; Tatsuko Nagasawa of Japan Uni Agency, Inc.; and Christopher Hutton-Williams of Hutton-Williams Agency. To all of them go my undying thanks.

Koji Kobayashi
March 27, 1991

Preface to the Japanese Edition

The idea of writing this book came to me in 1985. That was the year of EXPO '85, an international exposition of science and technology held in Tsukuba, just north of Tokyo. But most of my readers will remember it as the fortieth anniversary of the end of the Second World War and a major turning-point in the Japanese economy.

Nineteen eighty-five was a year of momentous and dramatic changes in the economies of both Japan and the United States. In that year the US ceded its status as the world's foremost creditor country, a position it had held since 1914, and slipped into the ranks of net debtor nations. By contrast, Japan, which after the war had been forced to start over again quite literally from nothing, capped its astonishing transformation by becoming the leading creditor country with the world's largest trade surplus.

NEC Corporation was founded in 1899 as Japan's first joint venture with a US company. During the immediate postwar period Nippon Electric Company, as we were then called, survived several business setbacks and increasingly grew in strength as society returned to normal. In the early 1960s, not long after the publication of a government white paper on the economy declaring that "the postwar period is now over," NEC finally freed itself from its dependency on International Telephone and Telegraph (ITT), with whom it had capital and technical tie-ups, and set out on its own independent course. In January 1962 it succeeded in exporting to the United States the technology for its independently developed microwave communications system and cable carrier transmission equipment. It was also one of the first companies in the world to enter the then revolutionary field of satellite communications technology.

Just about this time several faint signs foreshadowing the advent of a knowledge- and information-intensive society were beginning to appear. In 1962 a book entitled *The Production and Distribution of Knowledge in the United States* by Professor Fritz Machlup was published by Princeton University Press, and in 1964 an article based on this work appeared in the American business journal *Fortune*, written by one of its editors, Gilbert Burck. It would be no exaggeration to say that prompt recognition of the business opportunities inherent in this new approach to information and knowledge led to the birth of today's NEC Corporation.

At present NEC has consolidated annual sales of 2.7 trillion yen, twenty-five plants in twelve foreign countries in addition to those in Japan, and a total of 163,000 employees at home and abroad. Under the banner of C&C (the integration of computers and communications) it has been strengthening its strategic tilt toward the development of a new information and communications industry that is neither just a communications business nor just a computer business, and slowly but surely these efforts are producing results. Yet not many people know what NEC was like twenty years ago, or how it developed into what it has become today.

This book is a first-person account of the experiences of one corporate manager from the time he assumed the management of NEC Corporation, and the visions he had for its future. I hope it will be read as an actual case study of how a Japanese company that had once been a quasi-official supplier to the Japanese government resolved to entrust its future to these visions and, without losing sight of the megatrends of the time, succeeded, through dedication and hard work, in transforming itself.

Since 1985 I have revolved these ideas around in my mind, snatching time from odd moments at work to write them down. With much the same feeling of trepidation as a student writing an examination paper, I have carefully recorded these business chronicles of the events of the past twenty-five years just as they occurred, from the day I became president of NEC in November 1964 to the present time. The book was not originally intended for the general public but was written for the edification of executives at NEC; as a result parts of the book are still somewhat rough and in many places the expressions may seem a bit stiff. But because I have written about what I actually thought, felt, and then put into practice, exactly as it happened, I ask the reader's indulgence.

There is a widely held view that revolutionary new technology – in other words, innovation – determines long-term economic trends.

This view stems from the fact that technology has inextricably incorporated itself into the economic structure of the modern world. But it is also true that the groundwork must be done first, to allow any technological innovation to take root; and a certain amount of time must elapse before it becomes a permanent fixture in the lives of ordinary people.

This is certainly the case as far as C&C is concerned. I am often asked, "Mr Kobayashi, how did you think up the concept of C&C? When did it first occur to you?" I am not able to give a definite answer as to where or when the idea first came to me, but in an article on digital technology and the advance of automation published in an engineering magazine back in 1959 I made the proposal for a vast digital system that would integrate the two technologies of computers and communications. As I mentioned earlier, NEC started up as a maker of communications equipment. Even though we entered the computer field in 1954, for a long time communications systems continued to serve as the staple of our business. I was not content, however, to project a future corporate image that would confine NEC to either the communications or the computer business alone. The form that the integration of computers and communications would take was already firmly implanted in my mind.

Although I have advocated a new information network that will integrate computers with communications, taking the next step and establishing this concept as a commercial venture will, I believe, take a very long time indeed. Twelve years after I formally proposed my C&C concept to the world in 1977, the corporate structure necessary for the C&C business – technology development, manufacturing, marketing, and personnel development – has been put in place within the company. NEC now stands on the frontier, poised to develop the vast potential market for C&C. But we will probably have to wait until the twenty-first century before C&C assumes its role as the new global infrastructure for human society and human activity and begins to create a new civilization. Be that as it may, the prospects for C&C are enormous and very promising.

I have always thought that, if left to chance, the lifespan of a corporation is only about sixty years. Once any corporation has reached its peak it begins to move steadily downhill. A glance at the world's giant corporations shows many instances of companies that have fallen prey to takeovers or seen their business ebb away sixty years after their founding. NEC originated as a joint venture between the American company, Western Electric, and local Japanese capital. More recently it was affiliated with ITT, to whom Western Electric's interest in NEC was transferred in 1925. But by 1965 NEC had freed itself from this affiliation and begun to grow as an independent company. Counting from this period, NEC today is a company in its thirties, still very much in its prime – but we must not be complacent. Before today's wave recedes we must catch the wave of the future and let the winds of change breathe new life into the business. Nor should we imagine that tomorrow's business will be a simple linear extension of past trends. We must draw lessons from the past, then elaborate on them to prepare for the future. Changes in Japan's position in the world, changes in industrial structure, the emergence of an advanced electronics industry, the expanding demand for software, increasing globalization – in all these areas the times we live in no longer permit us the luxury of a conventional response.

When I took the helm at NEC as its chief executive officer I made a list of the matters that I felt required my urgent personal attention. These were (in no particular order):

- A primary orientation toward the knowledge and information industries;
- development of the "point to area" management system, i.e. development of a decentralized organization with a horizontal rather than a vertical chain of command;
- establishment of a corporate identity;
- choice of the C&C strategy;
- a quality-orientated business;
- emphasis on semiconductors and microelectronics;
- entrance into the information services business at an early date;
- establishment of software operations;
- the concept of setting up decentralized plants in rural areas;
- the global expansion of the company's business.

In what follows I have written as much as I could remember on each of these topics. It is often said in Japan that a decade ago is ancient history, and many of the events recorded here took place more than twenty years ago. But because I had to deal personally with all of these operational matters, the details came flooding back to me as I wrote, and I remembered them as clearly as if they had happened only yesterday.

I would like to take this opportunity to express my thanks to my old friend Peter Drucker, the American economist and leading authority on management, who when he heard that I was writing this book contributed a foreword full of kind words of friendship. My gratitude goes as well to Hideo Fujishima, Mineo Iwamochi, and Tokuya Hirahara of Diamond, Inc. for their many useful suggestions. I would also like to thank all my colleagues at NEC who gave so unstintingly of their time, gathering documents and supplementing my recollections or correcting errors of fact, but especially to Kiyoshi Yamauchi, who has worked so diligently to prepare the final manuscript for publication. It is thanks to all of their efforts that this book has been completed.

If these recollections of the practical experiences of a businessman are of some assistance to the young people who will be the leaders of tomorrow's industrial world, I can know no greater happiness as an author.

Koji Kobayashi

I

Taking up the Presidency

Taking the Reins

November 30, 1964 was one of the most unforgettable days of my life. That morning, the company stockholders' meeting was followed by a meeting of the Board of Directors, at which I was elected President of NEC Corporation.

Just two days earlier I had been called into the office of the president, Mr Toshihide Watanabe. As I stepped into the room, quite unexpectedly Mr Watanabe announced, "Kobayashi, you're our next president." I was at a loss as to how to respond; that night I stayed awake late, thinking about the duties I was about to assume. After the war I had been appointed a vice president of NEC, and with the passage of time became a senior vice president, then an executive vice president, and, finally, a few years earlier, a senior executive vice president. In all these positions there was always someone just above me. I was well aware that although I did not have the final say in the decision-making process, I did not have the final responsibility either. These experiences gradually gave me some insight into the nature of ultimate responsibility in the management of an independent corporation.

During the long, sleepless hours of that night, the realization sank in that ultimate responsibility for managing NEC now rested solely with me, and that it was vital that I take charge immediately and make my intentions to do so clear to the entire company right from the very beginning. Waiting until I felt better prepared or more sure of myself would only make the transition more difficult. To be frank, this decision was not so much a matter of logic but as an act of courage.

It was these thoughts, and this resolve, that underlay my first pronouncement as president, delivered to the press conference held after the board meeting of November 30 to announce the change of command, and my first address to employees of the company immediately thereafter. After a speech by Mr Watanabe announcing his retirement after more than seventeen years in office, I rose to outline my aspirations to "make NEC into an international corporation."

As I need hardly remind you, since its founding in 1899 NEC has been primarily engaged in manufacturing for Japan's communications services, in areas such as the telephone and telegraph. Because our company was founded as Japan's first joint venture with a US firm, one of NEC's chief characteristics has been its international flavor, although if the truth be told, the period of dependence on a foreign firm and passivity in foreign relationships was a long one. It was only during Mr Watanabe's presidency that NEC developed sufficiently to stand on its own two feet as an independent Japanese company.

When I consider my own mission and duties as president in the light of NEC's historical development and in view of Japan's continuing efforts to establish a more open economic system, I am firmly convinced that we need to move vigorously into the international arena and develop NEC into a top-ranking company in the eyes of the world. What is more, I am determined to do so.

To cite one example of our efforts in this area, a satellite communications earth station built by NEC was instrumental in transmitting live television coverage abroad of the Olympic Games, which were held in Tokyo last month. Today, when technological advances are being made by leaps and bounds, we at NEC, where growth has always stemmed from technological prowess, have been involved since the planning stages in opening up the age of satellite communications, the most advanced technology of them all. In addition to communications, our other mainstays are computers, perhaps the most important electronic product, and electrical household appliances, which make life more convenient for ordinary families. I hope that in the days ahead we will continue to show all-round strength in these areas.

These are some of my resolutions as NEC's new president. Because I still have much to learn about improving external communications I ask for your support in the days ahead.

When the press conference was over, I returned to NEC's head office to make the official announcement of the change of command and give preliminary instructions to all the executives working there. Mr Watanabe opened the meeting by saying,

In June 1947 during the confusion of the postwar period I succeeded President Nagao Saeki and have served as president of NEC for eighteen calendar years. In that time we have passed through the reconstruction period of the late 1940s and early 1950s, responded to the emergence of the electronics industry during the past decade and have now reached the stage where we can be confident of future growth. Ever since I reached the age of sixty-five, I have thought about withdrawing one day from the front ranks. Now at last that day has come.

After thanking Mr Watanabe on behalf of all the employees for his many achievements and his long years of service, I declared to all present my resolve to assume ultimate responsibility for all the company's undertakings and to run its business operations to the best of my abilities from that day on. Having spoken to all the staff above the rank of branch supervisor, the next day I toured the company's four main plants, giving speeches similar to the one I had made at head office. But here, because each plant was an actual production site, I expanded the staff circle to include group leaders so that my message would get back to the rank and file working on the shop floor. I also tried to speak personally with everyone who attended, believing that this would be an opportunity to improve mutual understanding at all levels in the company.

I recall one incident that took place during these conversations at the Sagamihara plant, and which gave me a strong sense that many NEC employees felt an unarticulated mixture of high hopes, uneasiness, and curiosity about their new president. A long-serving group leader said, "I am in total sympathy with your ideas and intentions, and we are all delighted to hear them; but if you listen directly to the views of everyone from the top executives down to the lowest new recruit, how can you conduct the business of a large-scale corporate organization and still maintain order within the company?"

Tuning in to the Times: NEC in the 1960s

I remember 1964 as if it were only yesterday, but the present generation of young people who are now two or three years out of college and beginning their careers were just being born about then. So for the convenience of my readers I will give a very brief account of the general state of NEC in 1964 and the position we occupied in the Japanese industrial world during the early 1960s.

As mentioned earlier, at this time NEC was primarily a maker of communications equipment. We had annual unconsolidated sales of about 70 billion yen and employed approximately 23,000 people at our head office and four main plants in and around Tokyo. Although the general public tended to regard us as an electrical machinery maker, we were ranked in business circles as Japan's leading producer of communications equipment. NEC, Oki Electric Industry Company, and Fuji Communications Equipment Manufacturing Company (now Fujitsu) were generally acknowledged as the big three, the major suppliers of equipment for Japan's telecommunications services. Sometimes Iwatsu Electric Co. (primarily a supplier of telephones) or Hitachi (primarily a supplier of telephone exchanges) would be added to the list to round out the "communications big four," a popular expression in those days.

Within the general industrial category of electrical machinery, companies of different backgrounds could be classified by the nature of their businesses: there were manufacturers of electrical household appliances, the driving force behind the electrification boom of the late 1950s and early 1960s, as well as traditional heavy electrical machinery makers who concentrated on making generators and motors. But even in those days it was already becoming difficult to maintain a single type of business and rigid classifications, and all these companies were then beginning to come to grips with the question of diversification and consolidation. As I will discuss later in more detail, even NEC was not only manufacturing telephones, switchboards, and carrier transmission equipment but was also in the process of expanding into the promising related areas of computers and consumer appliances.

Japanese society as a whole, as reflected in the economic and industrial circles of the time, was midway through the period that has been aptly described as "the golden sixties." Japan was in the midst of an era of high economic growth symbolized by "income doubling," the catchphrase of the Ikeda Cabinet which had come into office in July 1960. Deliberately setting out to match this idea of "doubling," NEC was increasing its capital at a similar tempo, going from 2 billion yen in 1956 to 4 billion in 1957, 8 billion in 1960, 12 billion in 1961, and 12.5 billion yen in 1963 by issuing American depositary receipts (ADR) in the US and subsequently raising capitalization to 20 billion yen in 1966, and 30 billion yen in 1969.

As for the role of the Japanese economy in international society – a topic much discussed in those days – the liberalization of capital and trade had begun in earnest; when Japan was officially admitted to the Organization for Economic Co-operation and Development (OECD) in April 1964, the country's basic task was thought to be the establishment of an open economic system. Nineteen sixty-four was also the year the Meishin Expressway opened between Nagoya and Osaka, the long-awaited Shinkansen Bullet Train began operations, and Tokyo successfully hosted the eighteenth Olympic Games.

This account may suggest that all we had to do was ride the tide of the times and everything would be smooth sailing thereafter; the actual situation, however, was quite the opposite. Dark clouds were beginning to appear on the horizon indicating that the period of economic expansion popularly known as "the Iwato boom" was showing signs of fatigue. That "golden" year also produced the highest number of bankruptcies of any since the war. A recession in the electrical household appliance industry had led to a pile-up of unsold stock and a deterioration in the corporate performance of some of Japan's leading electrical machinery manufacturers; changes in top management had been made in some cases. An even more symbolic event was the "window dressing" incident and eventual bankruptcy of Sanyo Special Steel Company. It is all very well to extol the virtues of high-level growth and want to have your products in great demand, but in this case goods shipped by the company had had their vouchers removed and were treated as sold, although in fact they were still somewhere in the distribution process. This incident was significant not simply because a blunder had been made that cast doubt on the management's stewardship. Such crookedness was thought not to be confined to Sanyo Special Steel, and that suspicion in itself came as a severe shock to prudent managers, preventing them from dismissing the incident as a matter of no immediate concern.

So while on the whole the 1960s were indeed a golden decade, a convergence of various factors was giving rise to a sense of unease, an awareness of danger looming that seemed to those of us in the business world to be increasing from moment to moment. This is a point worth emphasizing – though as far as NEC's business was concerned, fortunately we continued to make a good showing and had no particular shortcomings that we needed to worry about. But I was aware that countless problems and tasks were piling up, yet despite these pressing concerns no action was being taken on *this* matter and *that* one was being left to take care of itself. During this period my own sense of impending crisis intensified. This was my thirty-fifth year with NEC, which I had entered back in 1929; and I was fifty-seven years old.

The Origins of NEC

It was against this background of both expansion and anxiety that I assumed the presidency of NEC in 1964. To enable what follows to be more easily understood, I would like here to add a word or two about the origins of NEC Corporation and some of its special characteristics. In considering these special characteristics – the unique features or circumstances that made NEC different from other companies – it is necessary to keep in mind the following three points. First, up until 1985 Japan's public communications system was state-operated. In that year, however, Nippon Telegraph and Telephone (NTT) Public Corporation underwent a radical reform and was privatized and reorganized as Nippon Telegraph and Telephone Company. The old public corporation itself had originally been part of the government communications services, a branch of the prewar Ministry of Communications (the predecessor of today's Ministry of Posts and Telecommunications) and had been transformed into a public corporation only in 1952. This organization has consistently ranked as NEC's most important single customer. To use an expression that is obsolete today but was a popular term in the nineteenth century, NEC was a *goyo kojo*, a quasi-official plant providing goods to the government.

Second, NEC had been founded as a Japan–US joint venture. The Nippon Electric Company had been set up by Western Electric, the manufacturing arm of AT&T, as its plant for the Far East market. Although Western Electric later transferred its interest in NEC to International Telephone and Telegraph (the nominal shareholder was International Standard Electric, a subsidiary of ITT), we continued to have close ties with that company in terms of capital and technology. I would like to stress here that no relationship exists today between NEC and the original parent company; but back in the early 1960s those ties were still in place.

The third point concerns NEC's relationship with the Sumitomo Group. In the early 1930s, faced with both the worldwide economic depression and the emergence of nationalism in Japan, NEC, as a foreign-financed company, found itself beset by management difficulties. As a way out of this dilemma, NEC's foreign investors entrusted the running of the company to the Sumitomo *zaibatsu* with whom they had had dealings in connection with the manufacturing of electric cables in the mid-1920s and whose management staff they regarded highly. (The system of *zaibatsu* – a commercial–industrial combine whose central holding company was owned by a controlling family – was broken up after the Second World War.) For a time, beginning in 1943 in the middle of the Second World War, NEC was even called the Sumitomo Communication Industries Company. That same year, when the managing director system was abolished and replaced by a presidential system, the company's first president was Takeshi Kajii, the former manager of the Installation Department of the old Ministry of Communications who later became the first head of NTT Public Corporation. After the war, in November 1945, the company revived its former name, preempting the Occupation decree prohibiting the use of names associated with the prewar industrial combines. Both Nagao Saeki, who succeeded Kajii as president in 1946, and my predecessor, Toshihide Watanabe, were originally executives from Sumitomo. I was the first president to rise through the ranks of NEC itself.

2

First Priorities: Management Reform and "Zero Defects"

Even on that first day as president, by the time I was able to return to my office after a busy round of inspection tours within the company and meetings with important clients and the relevant government agencies, the matters that I felt I had to attend to seemed to be piling up inexorably. I wanted to let some fresh air into the company; I wanted to establish a corporate structure capable of withstanding violent waves of change; I wanted to implement a system that would make better use of our employees' abilities. All of these items seemed to intertwine and go racing through my mind: the first order of business was to establish my priorities and decide where to begin. Moving ahead blindly without defining priorities would only lead to internal confusion. It was self-evident that a plan of action was needed that would not disrupt the functioning of NEC's corporate activities. The route I chose can be summed up by the expression "start from the top," and so I began with the structure of top management.

Restructuring Top Management: "Point to Area"

I had announced to the entire company that sole responsibility for management rested with one single person – me, the company president. But though I had become president I had not simultaneously been endowed with unlimited abilities to deal with any matter whatsoever. Herein lay a crucial dilemma.

In a pyramid-type corporate hierarchy the chain of command starts at the base and moves upward through several layers of control until it culminates with the company president at the apex of the pyramid. If the chain of command consists of general managers, department managers, section managers and their assistants or deputies, then on up to the senior staff – vice presidents, senior vice presidents, executive vice presidents – the multiplicity of levels involved is fraught with problems. But the biggest problem of all was precisely the fact that all these levels of responsibility converged on one single point. If all authority was concentrated in a single individual – the company president – how could he possibly perform the duties expected of him? How could a vast organization continue functioning in an orderly fashion under such a system? My first task as the new president was to come up with a solution to these inherent problems and contradictions.

The first thing I did was to determine what the new areas of responsibility would be for the ten executives who had been appointed to the Board of Directors on November 30, 1964, and communicate my decisions to them and to the eight other directors who remained in post. I also decided to change the way we conducted our Corporate Management Committee meetings. Until my new system was firmly in place I proposed to hold committee meetings for half a day twice a week. To clarify what had been decided at these meetings and how the decisions had been reached, I had the general manager of the Corporate Planning Division serve as secretary and take minutes of the proceedings. These would be read at the beginning of the next meeting as a way of confirming and perpetuating records of all previous proposals. Such a system, I felt, would ensure that the meetings did not degenerate into mere discussions.

At the Corporate Management Committee meetings that December, I devoted most of my energies to formulating the future structure of top management. In plain language, what this involved was that every executive should serve as the *alter ego* of the company president in the area of responsibility assigned to him. In other words, if the structure of management is likened to a circle, the president occupies the point at the center and the executives are situated around the circumference and compose the surface area of the circle as a whole. Under this system each executive has a clear understanding of his own position within the top management group and what his responsibilities are.

The president also escapes from the limitations of his position and is able to fulfill his function as the pivotal axis around which the corporation revolves.

The success of the system depends on *trust* and *information*. The relationship between the president and each of his executives is one of trust; and the preservation of this trust demands that each side provides the other with the information each needs. Thus, my view of top management is based on three key concepts: *delegation of authority, trust, and information*. The Corporate Management Committee would serve as the forum for this exchange of information, and great importance was placed on its proper functioning.

Once I had consolidated the form and function of my management team – in those days I used the expression "top management group" – the heart and mind, as it were, of the corporation, and only then, I would go on to tackle other tasks. In whatever I did, even my most ordinary actions like asking for reports or simply walking down the hall, I could feel that the employees were secretly watching me, wondering what I was going to do or say next. I therefore made it clear within the company that for the present I was limiting my reforms to the organization of top management and would adopt a complete hands-off policy for everyone below the rank of vice president so that ordinary employees could go about their work confidently without worrying about what was happening and how it was going to affect them. This decision was directly related to my plans for corporate reform "from the top down," which I will discuss later.

New Year 1965: A Statement of Intent

By now there were only a few days of the year left. At the beginning of each new year it was a tradition in our company for the president to make an address and exchange New Year's greetings. I decided that starting in 1965 this speech would no longer be a mere formality; I would rename it my New Year's Directive and use it to make a meaningful statement of my views and launch my reform program.

Rather than discussing my very first presidential directive at length, I include the text of it here. Although more than twenty years have passed since I delivered it, I believe that the address gives some insight into the situation in which NEC then found itself as well as into my thoughts and aspirations as its new president.

". . . The Best Company in the World"

As the year begins I would like to wish all of you a Happy New Year, to thank you for your efforts during the past year, and to convey to you some of the ideas I have been thinking about recently.

Looking East and West

As you have already read in newspapers and magazines, 1965 will be an extremely important year. The economic outlook, most analysts feel, will be one of little or no change during the first half of the year and a slight upswing in the second half. The Japanese economy quickly feels the effects of economic conditions in the US, however, and although the American economy has continued to maintain high level growth over the past forty-odd months, it may drift downward in the latter half of the year.

In Europe, the sterling crisis has Britain sitting on a powder keg, but a loan of 3 billion dollars from the International Monetary Fund has brought some respite. The fact that this enormous sum was raised in the time it takes to make a single telephone call should be looked on as one sign that we are in the midst of a "time revolution." In the European Economic Community the notable inroads of US capital are becoming the area's biggest concern. Every month plants are being built throughout Europe with US funds. If we are not careful, the same thing might happen in Japan as well. Another important consideration is that because of a thaw in US–Soviet relations we can no longer afford to limit our attention to the United States; from now on we will have to keep our eyes on both East and West. The possibility of trade with China and the Soviet Union is becoming an extremely important issue, both economically and politically.

Although the overall tone of the Japanese economy remains unchanged, the economic growth rate will be even slower than it was last year. We can therefore expect that as competition between companies intensifies, the situation will increasingly become a matter of the survival of the fittest.

Assessing Performance at Home

Given this general climate, our most important concern is Nippon Telegraph and Telephone Public Corporation. Orders from NTT during fiscal 1964 are expected to reach 35.1 billion yen, an 18 percent increase over the 29.8 billion yen of the preceding year. NTT's construction budget for fiscal 1965 is 336.9 billion yen, 20 percent higher than its 1964 budget of 280.9 billion yen. If NEC receives 40 to 42 billion yen worth of orders from NTT in fiscal 1965, our total output will be close to 85 billion yen. Because future orders are expected to increase every year until the number of telephone subscribers nationwide reaches the 20 million mark, the urgent task facing us is to establish a system to absorb this demand. NTT has high expectations of our company because only with our support will they be able to achieve their new five-year plan. If NTT voices any complaints or criticisms, we should not mistake this for anti-NEC sentiment but should interpret it rather as a direct result of the lofty expectations they have of us.

In the electrical machinery sector, heavy electrical equipment has been down since the fall of the year before last, and since last summer electrical household appliances have also begun to decline. As a result the big companies are trying to move into our area of communications and electronics. This has undeniably led to a drop in corporate performance relative to the year before last and a deterioration in our efficiency of fund operations. Let us look at our sales growth rate.

fiscal 1962	15.3%
fiscal 1963	13.3%
fiscal 1964 (first half)	11.4%

The ratio of profits to net sales for the same period was:

fiscal 1962	8.4%
fiscal 1963	8.2%
fiscal 1964 (first half)	8.3%.

Bank borrowings increased by 7.9 billion yen in 1963 and by nearly 5 billion yen in 1964.

Although our actual expenditures are what we expected, actual sales and other revenues have fallen far below budget expectations, and we are counting on a recovery in the second half of the year. Furthermore, external criticisms from NTT and others have been fierce. We have also received strong complaints from NHK [the state-run television network] and the private networks about our broadcasting equipment. The situation on all sides is far from reassuring.

Let us consider some of the reasons that have led to this state of affairs:

- partial paralysis of our organizational activities;
- weak marketing;
- an unfocused corporate image;
- a tendency to invest human resources without any specific goal in mind;
- conventional thinking on the part of middle and upper age groups;

- lack of vigor and managerial awareness on the part of management;
- confusion of corporate and private roles;
- rampant demagoguery;
- excessive concern about what superiors are thinking.

These and other problems have accumulated to the point where they require immediate solutions. My responsibility as company president is to formulate those solutions.

Presidential Resolutions

In order to fulfill my duties as president, I believe that I must make some clear decisions right at the beginning of the year. The nature of these decisions is as follows:

I want to develop NEC Corporation into the best company in the world, the one that offers the best products on the world market. If we are to succeed I will need the sincere cooperation of all of you.

First, we need to think more about how to make the most of our personnel.

Second, I want each level of management to be more profit-minded, to be more single-minded in the pursuit of corporate profit. Business is essentially a ruthless game – as the saying goes, out of money, out of love. We must therefore improve our ratio of shareholders' equity so that we may decrease our total debt-to-equity ratio. [Our shareholders' equity at that time was only about 20 percent, very low by American standards.] This objective must be accomplished even if it takes ten or fifteen years. It is not a matter on which we can demur.

Third is the question of internal reform. This must begin close to home, with those who have the authority and power; in other words, with top management. Although the minimum necessary modifications must be made to the structure at the top, these changes will not affect the workers in the front lines.

Fourth, I plan to implement fully the division system enacted in April 1961. By bringing our corporate image into focus, improving and upgrading our product line, consolidating the three functions – marketing, engineering, and manufacturing – that make up each division, and other reforms to corporate structure, I want us to display the mobility and all-round strength of dynamic management.

Fifth, I want to strengthen our business skills and promote marketing. This will require even closer cooperation between our marketing and engineering staffs.

Sixth, I want to put greater emphasis on industrial engineering and bring down costs.

Seventh, I want to upgrade our manufacturing equipment.

These are the ways I have resolved to establish our company's leadership in the business world. Achieving the top position will involve:

- Raising our sales growth rate above that of other companies.
- Ensuring that the ratio of profits to net sales does not fall below the industry average.
- Increasing our order rates from NTT and other government agencies over last fiscal year's levels in all equipment areas.
- Greatly expanding our orders from overseas.
- Pioneering new areas of demand in the private sector.

The New Management

I would like to explain the new shape of top management. First, let us consider the company president's span of control. Under the old system, the president was expected to exercise direct control over forty-four or forty-five different areas, far too many for a single individual. I plan to cut that span to about one third. How do I propose to go about doing that? In principle, my thinking on the matter can be summed up by the phrase "from point to area": The top management group composes the surface area of a circle, at the center of which is the company president. Even though he occupies a single point his influence emanates out over the entire circle; thus the adoption of this system can raise management efficiency.

An organization has a line and a staff. A company's profits arise from its line operations; the staff is there to support this line. Responsibility for the head office administration staff will be delegated to the senior executive vice president, who will exercise general control over personnel, finance, and property. There will also be a head office operation staff with separate staffs in charge of research and development, manufacturing, and marketing operations; in addition, a special staff unit will be in charge of big projects where those three functions are inseparable.

Responsibility for line operations is assigned to each executive. Because even greater teamwork is required when responsibility is divided up in this way, I am strengthening the role of the Corporate Management Committee. This committee will be my top management group: it will provide me with advice and serve as the focus of company teamwork. I want to improve the levels of coordination and cooperation within the management organization by giving this committee as active a role as possible.

Top priority is making the most of our personnel. I call upon all of you in positions of authority to show affection and consideration for the people who work under you. You must realize that the essence of leadership is to bring out their talents and allow them to employ their abilities to the full. Try to cultivate the personnel under you and make use of them in ways that will instill in them an enthusiasm for their job and a determination to do it well.

The root meaning of the English word "education" is to "draw out" another person's abilities; thus, education is not meant to make people fit into predefined patterns, nor does it mean exerting excessive control over them and making them afraid of you or forcing them to retreat into their shells. Scrupulous care must be taken that you do not suppress the development of your subordinates' individual abilities in any way. What is important is to create a pleasant workplace – to establish a good environment where the ingenuity and originality of all employees are given full scope so that they can work happily to the best of their abilities. *A properly employed workforce is the ultimate source of corporate growth.*

Next, I would like to point out some shortcomings in management attitudes. Because these indicate a lack of application it is important to adopt what I call "conscious management" and devote our full attention to management matters. I often hear people make a distinction between managers with an engineering background and those from a non-engineering background, but I don't think there could be a sillier way of dividing responsibilities than this. Some people are, of course, experts in the field of engineering or in other fields. But most staff members majored in a subject at college for only four years, not long at all compared with the time they've spent in their jobs. In view of that fact, isn't the excuse that something is outside someone's area of expertise merely camouflage for lack of initiative? If there is a job to be done, no matter what it is, it must be tackled with *fight and flexibility*.

One of the dangers of lifetime employment and the seniority system is that those who work in the same place for a long time tend to become oblivious of the bad habit of confusing corporate and private concerns. We must be able to distinguish clearly between what belongs to the company and what is ours as individuals, to recognize whether what we are doing is being done for the company's sake or for our own personal benefit.

Zero Defects

So that each and every NEC employee can participate in efforts to improve the company, I am proposing a ZD movement. ZD stands for "zero defects"; in other words, this will be a total quality control campaign to eliminate mistakes and root out the source of errors. Successful implementation will lead to a lowering of costs and be useful in streamlining our business operations. I want to give each employee the opportunity to reflect on the number of cases – by no means small – where some trifling error made by a single person has had a ripple effect throughout the whole company and led to unexpectedly large losses.

The ZD movement is intended to eradicate such mistakes and increase corporate profits; but because it will make supervisors respect their subordinates' opinions and implement their proposals it is also aimed at *instilling a sense of teamwork throughout the company*. Last summer when I was visiting Hughes Aircraft Company in the US, I saw the ZD slogan and thought that I would like our company to adopt it too. I am now making preparations to launch the ZD movement this coming April.

To conclude this account of my thoughts and wishes for the New Year, I would like the following phrases adopted as the company's slogans: "Make NEC the best company in the world;" "Offer the world's best products;" "A cheerful workplace;" "Better teamwork;" and "Zero Defects."

Equipping Japan for Competition

On this note, I left for the United States to make my first visits as president to the US firms with which NEC did business, and to fulfill an agreement to act as guest speaker at the 11th National Symposium on Reliability and Quality. The invitation had come from Dr Jack A. Morton, vice president of Bell Telephone Laboratories; when I asked him what I should talk about, he said, "Nowadays Japanese products are universally admired for their good quality and low price. There must be some kind of secret behind this. Why don't you talk about that?" This came as something of a surprise. The good quality of Japanese products? For years the byword for Japanese goods had been "cheap but shoddy." This speech, then, gave me the opportunity to speculate about what had enabled Japan, a small country with limited natural resources, to get as far as it had. I concluded that the sole support for Japan's efforts had been the "brain power" of the Japanese people. The question of what Japan would need to do in the days ahead to keep up with the giant US economy was constantly in my mind.

A striking image came to me as I pondered this problem on the flight home. The US could be likened to a large spinning top. Even when it revolved slowly, it maintained stability and did not fall over. Japan, on the other hand, was like a small top; it could only make up for the difference in size by increasing the speed at which it revolved.

But if the speed increased too much, it would fly out of control. Somehow I had to step up the pace at NEC without spinning the company out of control.

Phase Two: The Division System

Proceeding as I had planned "from the top down," return to Japan was my cue for tackling the second stage of my arrangements for reorganizing the company's internal structure.

NEC had instituted a division system back in April 1961. For many years prior to that our two main plants, the Mita Plant and the Tamagawa Plant, reflected the clear distinction between head office and production plant on the company's organizational chart. All the major function areas, such as administration, personnel relations, and finance and accounting, as well as a number of marketing divisions, had been centralized at head office. When the Tamagawa production plant was completed in 1936, I was transferred there from Mita, and after the war I became plant manager. I had therefore always looked at the company from the perspective of a plant engineer and had tasted my fill of bitter problems in dealing with the head office and the marketing divisions. My sincerest wish was to create conditions that would allow everyone to work to the best of his or her ability.

Under the division system set up in 1961, the organizational reforms had been half-hearted and the respective status of the plants had not essentially changed. My own belief was that a division without marketing functions was a division in name only. I had stressed that point whenever organizational reforms were discussed, but unfortunately NEC's management philosophy at the time was excessively conservative, and my views had not been adopted. Because it did not do its own marketing, a division made products but had no responsibility for selling them. And because what the customer wanted could only be ascertained through marketing, the division was unable to recognize consumer trends rapidly enough and to respond accordingly. The barrier that existed between those who made the goods and those who sold them sometimes led to recriminations on both sides. I had experienced the problem at first hand, and I believed that a solution was of the utmost importance. The only hope, I thought, lay in the implementation of a true division system.

My basic premise was that each operating division should be a single unit

containing all three functions – engineering, manufacturing, and marketing.
These would be our line divisions. The various divisions in the head
office would fulfill staff functions, and the combination of the two
would constitute the corporate structure of the organization as a
whole. Each operating division would be a profit center, and its
general manager would coordinate its engineering, manufacturing,
and marketing functions and assume direct responsibility for its
activities. The reorganization of the entire company around the
division system was the task I had to face as the second phase of my
plans.

Preparing the Ground: Presidential Communication

Before I could tackle this series of changes I needed the understanding of all those involved. Without their cooperation I could
make official pronouncements about a new organization, but nothing
would function the way I hoped. As a means of promoting mutual
understanding within the company, as soon as I became president I
adopted and implemented an informal method of communication,
which I called the "president's memo." These memos, which
contained my thoughts on topics ranging from marketing to the
relationship between the divisions and head office, were discussed
first with the Corporate Management Committee or at meetings of
the company executives before being written down and distributed to
the appropriate staff members to read over carefully and digest their
implications. The recipients sometimes had a hard time following my
train of thought about the nature of the new organization and drawing
the logical conclusions from it, and were disconcerted by the liberal
sprinkling of unfamiliar English-language management jargon such
as "line operations," "coordination," "orientation," "marketing,"
"channels," "service," "staff," "group," "product line," "project,"
"span of control," "program," and "profit center." Given the newness
of both the ideas and the terminology, this gap in understanding was
perhaps inevitable. Nevertheless, after frequent repetitions I finally
managed to get across a satisfactory explanation of the principles and
structure of the kind of organization that I wanted.

Establishing Integrated Operations

When this preliminary stage was over, I ordered a companywide
restructuring to go into effect on May 13, 1965. Although as a general

rule each division would have its own engineering, manufacturing, and marketing functions, separate marketing divisions would remain, especially for areas that involved particularly large customers. Line operations would consist of fourteen operating divisions, the central research laboratories, three development laboratories, two marketing divisions, an overseas division and a temporary construction division. The head of each division would have the same authority and responsibilities as the head of an independent company.

The fourteen operating divisions would be divided into four groups according to the nature of the technology involved and the lines produced. Each group might be compared to a holding company with division heads reporting directly to the executive in charge of their respective group. In planning each group special consideration was given to the concept of "span of control" to ensure that the area involved was in fact manageable by a single individual, who would function as a kind of *alter ego* for the president of the company. Over the years, keeping pace with the growth of NEC's business, the division system has undergone frequent revisions and modifications, but this was the genesis of the basic concept.

Toward Dynamism and Flexibility: The Primacy of People

My organizational philosophy is very different from the bureaucratic views that prevail in government agencies. There the underlying presupposition is that first, the organization exists – the positions within the organization take priority and assigning people to fill them is a secondary concern. My view is just the opposite. People come first. You have certain expectations about what they can do, put your trust in them, and let them do the work. In other words, the first step is assigning a person to the job: and drawing up an organizational chart is only possible when all the personnel assignments have been made. I pushed ahead with the basic structure of my new management system, and about six months after I assumed the presidency it had begun to take shape. Today the division system is taken for granted in Japanese management circles, but in those days a function-oriented organization based on a pyramid-type hierarchy was common. One of my models in the course of this reorganization process, though I did not always mention it at the time, was the division system at General Electric, as outlined by GE president Ralph J. Cordiner in his book *New Frontiers for Professional Managers* – although there the operative word was "decentralization." A recent rereading of that book confirmed my feelings that it is a classic study by a corporate manager in this century. I also looked to another pioneer of the division system in the US, Du Pont.

Another major feature of my reform program was to compress several levels of the pyramid hierarchy first into something resembling a gentle slope and ultimately into a flat disk. I called this *"plateau" organization*. The levels of supervision within each organizational unit were reduced to three in head office – general manager, section manager, and branch supervisor – and four in the divisions, where the post of department manager comes between those of general manager and section manager. Almost all the intermediate positions were eliminated. I left the draft circulating and approval system (*ringi*) in place, but simplified the procedure by restricting the number of circulation points.

I called upon everyone in the company to be "more dynamic and more flexible," concentrating in those two terms all my aspirations for the company – *an end to rigidity, freedom from fixed ideas, better communications between area and function levels, and greater individual initiative*. I called the series of measures that began with my "point to area" top structure and ended with the implementation of the division system my "management reform program," to get away from the tendency to speak of it as a "management shake-up," which – even though the program did contain some drastic elements – was a term I preferred to avoid. It was this reform process that laid the foundation for the zero defects program.

Introducing "Zero Defects"

Although I was convinced that my management reform program should take effect "from the top down," I was not happy about asking the vast majority of employees to wait several months before calling on their support. I therefore set myself the task of devising some plan that would involve ordinary employees in NEC's restructuring process.

The rank and file expected the new president to address them and give them some sort of orders. The nature and timing of those orders were crucial. The perfect opportunity was the speech I gave at the beginning of my very first year as president, which – as recounted earlier – I concluded by calling for the introduction of a ZD (zero defects) movement.

Where did the ZD concept come from? I came across it in the summer of 1964, when, touring a Hughes Aircraft plant near Los Angeles, I noticed a strange symbol on the employees' clothes and pasted on doors and along the corridors. I immediately asked what it was, and was told it stood for "zero defects." Zero defects had begun in the United States as a program to improve the production process in the missile-making division of Martin Marietta Corporation. Robert S. McNamara, then US Secretary of Defense, had given the program his enthusiastic support and had had it adopted by all defense-related industries. Ever since that visit to Hughes Aircraft I had wondered whether there was not some way that I could put the idea into effect at NEC. Then, only a few months after my return to Japan, I was made president of the company. Here was the opportunity.

Having announced my plans to introduce a ZD movement, I now faced the task of deciding on the best way to implement it. If I just said "ZD," neither the staff nor the employees would have any idea what I was talking about: I needed someone to help me promote the idea and bring it to fruition. I therefore called in Kunie Yoshikawa, who for many years had worked in product testing and inspection in the Manufacturing Control Division, and asked him to take charge of launching the program. He was greatly in sympathy with the proposal and agreed to take on the assignment but wanted more time to work out the details. I readily agreed to his request.

Both as the initiator of the plan and as company president, it was my responsibility to give the employees some concrete ideas about the zero defects movement. I did so in the following presidential directive.

Ever since I announced the launching of a companywide zero defects movement in my New Year's address and in the house organ, *NEC Life*, interest in and enthusiasm for the program have been mounting throughout the company. I am therefore giving the following instructions for companywide implementation on May 10.

Our mission at NEC is to provide the market with the best products available in the world today and to consolidate the reputation we have cultivated over many years as a leader in the communications and electronics industries. To produce the world's best products all our employees must not only have first-class technical skills; they must also be careful to avoid making *even the most trifling errors* that may cause product defects. Because the elimination of defects will both improve NEC's product quality and decrease its costs, I am confident that it will help us consolidate our position as a global leader in the increasingly competitive communications and electronics market.

The presence of defects indicates that the quality of workmanship in making a product was substandard: in other words, errors have been made during the production process. Since there are many potential causes for error, the goal of "zero defects" can only be achieved when those causes are discovered and eliminated. Simply speaking, the ZD movement is a campaign to make products that have zero defects by doing the work right the first time. Its aim is to make every employee aware that each finished product is the direct result of his or her individual efforts so that he or she can guard against making mistakes and eradicate the source of errors.

Errors cost us dearly. Because NEC manufactures advanced communications and electronics systems, the ultimate in today's technology, trifling mistakes may easily cause major product defects that can seriously threaten the company's future. It is not true that errors or mistakes are unavoidable. But they are most likely to be generated by those who *believe* that errors are unavoidable, and conversely they can be eliminated by those who make a deliberate effort to be more careful.

The ZD movement will produce significant results if it is introduced systematically on a companywide basis and if everyone – from workers on the production line to engineers and office workers all the way up to the chief executive officer – works together to eliminate product defects and supply first-class products to the world market. Because the movement also aims at making each employee aware of and take satisfaction from the fact that his or her individual efforts are contributing to the company's corporate growth, I expect it will help create a highly motivated workforce.

A Zero Defects Steering Committee will be established to promote the ZD movement. This committee will prepare the groundwork for ZD activities, plan specific implementation methods and schedules, and deal with all other matters necessary for launching the movement.

Maximizing Employee Involvement

The companywide launch of the ZD movement officially took place in 1965. The staff volunteered to study the conditions under which the ZD program was used in the United States and formulate policies to promote it at NEC in order to create a receptive atmosphere for the ZD movement within the company.

As I noted above, the ZD movement was inaugurated not only to eliminate errors but also to make ordinary employees feel that they each had a part in NEC's corporate concerns. The aim was to instill in every employee the desire to come to grips personally with corporate reform. What I hoped for above all was that all our employees would become aware that they were personally responsible for quality and that these individual efforts toward perfection would find expression in the products we offered our customers. I expected the movement to last for a year and had no intention of continuing it indefinitely.

My own views on the subject were colored by my unhappy experiences with quality control in my early days at NEC. Quality control then was something known as "statistical quality control," a method based on complicated mathematical and statistical formulas and debated by experts with no regard for customer satisfaction or the actual products themselves. I wanted to take full advantage of the new ZD trends, unimpeded by these mistaken existing views on quality control. So I did not limit the ZD movement to the plants where NEC's products were made, but made a point of arousing an enthusiasm for zero defects in all our employees, whether they were directly or indirectly involved in the manufacturing process – including, for example, those employed in warehouse control or our business offices, and even the telephone operators, typists, and receptionists.

"Zero Defects" Catches On

One day after the movement had finally been launched, I had a visit from Kakuzo Morikawa, chairman of the Japan Management Association. He had had similar plans in mind for some time and had come to ask for NEC's prior consent before the association embarked on a nationwide ZD program. Of course, I had no objection to such a proposal: on the contrary, I was delighted to be of help in developing a program for all Japan's industries, and gave the association my full cooperation and support. In time, the movement spread and became firmly established all over the country in the form of small-group quality control activities, a truly happy development.

Although the ZD movement at NEC was supposed to last only for one year, demands for its continuation were so strong that it is still in effect more than twenty years later: indeed, it has grown over the years. Since 1981 we have sponsored the NEC International ZD Convention and have seen the ZD movement spread and expand among NEC affiliates not only in Japan but throughout the world.

3

Entering the Communications Era

Communications: The Key to Advancement

As noted in chapter 1, all NEC employees took great pride in the behind-the-scenes role the company played in the live trans-Pacific television transmissions of the Tokyo Olympic Games in October 1964. The signal was transmitted from Kashima Satellite Communication Earth Station, part of the Ministry of Posts and Telecommunications' Radio Research Laboratories, using satellite communications ground station equipment manufactured by NEC. To receive the signal in the US, Hughes Aircraft had rebuilt the Point Mugu Naval Air Station north of Los Angeles. This "space" relay of a television broadcast was a tremendous topic of conversation in those days.

The events leading up to this occasion could be traced back to October 1957 and the successful Soviet launch of Sputnik, the world's first man-made satellite. In July 1962 the US National Aeronautics and Space Administration (NASA) launched the AT&T communications satellite, Telstar 1, which succeeded in beaming television pictures live from Paris to the United States. I happened to be on a business trip to the US at the time, and saw the scenes from France on the television set in my Chicago hotel room. This success was hailed as a great achievement; but, far from greeting the news with joy, I felt disappointed, because Japan, which did not have an artificial satellite of its own, would have no part to play in opening the age of space communications.

On my first trip to the United States, in 1937, I was profoundly impressed by the words of the supervisor who was giving me a tour of a telephone office. "Our mission as telephone operators," she said, "is to make telephone connections between any two places in the US within three minutes." At the time this struck me as the ultimate goal of all of us engaged in the communications business. In Japan in those days to make a telephone call from Tokyo to Osaka – a distance of about 300 miles – took an entire day from the time the request was made to the time the call was put through. It took half a day just to telephone the Mita head office only nine miles away from the Tamagawa plant in Kawasaki where I worked, and once I had placed the call I was tied to my desk. Needless to say, I did not have a telephone at home.

After the war I made frequent trips to the United States and often had lively conversations with American passengers sitting next to me on the plane, during which I invariably asked one question: "I am always astonished at the vastness of America," I would say. "What is the driving force behind its development? What is the key to American success?" Perhaps the question appealed to their sense of pride; at any rate, the vast majority gave me an answer along the same lines: the key to America's growth was progress in transportation and communications. As I thought over the changes in American history from the days of the stagecoach to the oil pipelines then being built, I pondered the implication of those words, and realized that indeed, transportation and communications were the mainstays of social development in a vast country like the United States. Moreover, if it were true there, then it would also be true for the rest of the world.

Thirty years before Telstar – almost sixty years ago today – I was engaged in building a nonloaded cable carrier telephone system between Japan and north eastern China. After the Second World War, Japan and the United States were linked by submarine cable and by shortwave radio communications, but I kept thinking that there must be a more convenient method and cherished the thought that one day I might help to develop and build a revolutionary new global communications system. The launching of Telstar, however, seemed to shatter my dreams of playing a personal role in this development.

Satellite Developments with Hughes Aircraft

On my way home from Chicago in 1962 I stopped in at the head office of Hughes Aircraft in Los Angeles. Hughes was one of the companies with which NEC had business links and was deeply involved with the introduction of the Japan Defense Agency's E4 fire control system and the Badge air defense system. When the topic of Telstar came up, Lawrence A. Hyland, the vice president of Hughes, realized how disappointed I was. To cheer me up, he said, "I have something good to show you," and led me to a room in the plant where there was a wooden mock-up of a synchronous satellite that Hughes Aircraft was planning to develop. He then introduced me to the young engineer who had conceived the idea for the satellite, Harold A. Rosen, and told me the story of its development. The basic principle behind this revolutionary concept was to launch a satellite into orbit 22,300 miles above the equator, where it would move in the same direction and at the same speed as the earth's rotation. Because it appears to be stationary when seen from earth, it is sometimes also called a geostationary satellite. If three of these satellites were launched into orbit over the equator above the Atlantic, Pacific, and Indian Oceans, it would be theoretically possible to create a communications link among all the continents on earth. Hyland then turned to me and said, "NEC has excellent communications technology, especially in the microwave area. Why doesn't NEC team up with Hughes' satellite technology to develop a worldwide satellite communications system using synchronous satellites?"

NEC's satellite business began with satellite communications ground stations, and then advanced into the area of developing and manufacturing electronic equipment aboard the satellites themselves; by the mid-1970s it had grown into the space development business. In November 1963, several months before the completion of the Ministry of Posts and Telecommunications' Kashima Station in May 1964, Kokusai Denshin Denwa Company (KDD), Japan's international communications carrier, opened the country's first satellite communications experimental ground system at Juo in Ibaraki Prefecture, with high-sensitivity receiving equipment supplied by NEC. This was NEC's first venture in the satellite communications area. Our receiving system contributed to the success of the first television broadcast relay between the US and Japan using the satellite Relay 1 on November 23, 1963. I shall never forget the historic moment when the television news broadcast announcing the tragic assassination of President John Kennedy was carried simultaneously in the United States and throughout Japan.

In August 1964 NEC and Hughes Aircraft simultaneously announced plans to begin joint development of a satellite communications system in the US and Japan. At the time of the Tokyo Olympics the communications satellite Syncom III (short for synchronous communications) was launched over the Pacific and used to relay television transmissions of the games.

That same month also marked the start of Intelsat, an international commercial communications satellite consortium, which in time officially adopted the synchronous satellite. The actual management of Intelsat was in the hands of the US communications satellite company, Comsat. In December 1965 NEC and Hughes Aircraft succeeded in developing an automatic random multiple access system that enabled ground stations to communicate with each other via satellite at any time. We called the system STAR (satellite telecommunication with automatic routing) and invited Joseph V. Charyk, president of Comsat, and Allen E. Puckett, vice president of Hughes Aircraft, to Tokyo for ground simulation experiments. The system received high praise.

Technology as a Sales Weapon

NEC's timely entrance into the field of satellite communications was undeniably aided by several pieces of good luck, such as our relationship with Hughes Aircraft and the timing of the Tokyo Olympics; but the main reason for our success was that *NEC already possessed the world's most advanced technology in the area of radio communications*. Any detailed account of microwave communications technology at NEC would have to trace its development back to the war years and the immediate postwar period, but it would be safe to say that it had been primarily fostered during the construction of television relay lines throughout Japan in the 1950s.

Immediately after the war Allied General Headquarters forbade research and development of microwave communications in Japan, but as soon as restrictions were eased in 1946, young engineers turned enthusiastically to developing the field. NEC began basic research in the area in the belief that multiplex radio communications was the system of the future. Our first success was the installation of a microwave circuit between Sendai and Aizu Wakamatsu for Tohoku Electric Power Company, using the pulse time modulation (PTM) method.

In 1951, when plans were being made to introduce commercial

television broadcasting in Japan, there was some debate about the so-called "mountaintop method," proposed by President Matsutaro Shoriki of the Yomiuri Shimbun Company, which would use microwaves to relay a broadcast from mountaintop to mountaintop. We at NEC favored a new frequency modulation method and recommended this system not only to NTT Public Corporation but to the regional electric power companies and Japan National Railways. Ultimately this method was adopted.

Among NEC's noteworthy technical successes was the development of an over-the-horizon radio communications system that used radio wave diffraction based on the lack of uniformity of the dielectric constant in the atmosphere. NEC engineers Masasuke Morita and Sukehiro Ito discovered and developed this high-sensitivity receiving system appropriate for weak radio wave communication and succeeded in building an extremely economical communications system, which attracted great attention both in Japan and abroad. In January 1962 we supplied this technology, and technology for our carrier transmission system, to ITT.

Building on the reputation of our proprietary technology and the business base we had established in the domestic market, NEC decided to enter the international market with what it considered its most promising product line, microwave communications systems. This was the area in which NEC was most competitive, and because it could also be used in space, it enabled us to enter the new field of satellite communications.

In the hopes of making even further advances in our microwave communications equipment, NEC tackled the challenge of developing a solid-state system. But our plans did not turn out as expected, and it was only in 1964, after much trial and tribulation, that we were successful. We could now proceed with plans to replace electron tubes wherever possible with transistors and integrated circuits, miniaturizing them and making them more economical and more reliable. We quickly became the world's leading exporter of microwave communications systems, winning orders for a 16,800-mile system with sixty-five stations in Mexico; a 2,300-mile system with eighty stations in Brazil; a 2,500-mile system with ninety stations in Australia; a 1,200-mile system with forty stations in India; and a 1,200-mile system with eighty stations in Iran.

Breaking into the Overseas Market

After the successful ground simulation experiments with the STAR system in Tokyo, NEC and Hughes Aircraft opened an experimental satellite communications earth station in Hot Springs, Arkansas, in May 1966. The success of public tests carried out there gave a great boost to subsequent orders for commercial satellite ground stations. Our very first commission from overseas came from Mexico in 1967 to enable that country to provide international television coverage of the Mexico Olympics the following year. In June 1968 we received an order for a ground station from Peru, which we finally succeeded in opening despite adverse conditions and numerous difficulties. As a result, Peru was the only country in all of South America to witness the Apollo 11 spacecraft land on the moon the following year. In Japan NEC supplied the main equipment for the second ground stations at both Kashima and Juo in March 1968 and at KDD's Yamaguchi ground station in 1969. Winning the orders for each of these ground stations enhanced NEC's reputation and took me one step closer to the fulfillment of my hopes and dreams for the creation of a global communications infrastructure.

Redefining the Business Area

NEC's entry into the satellite communications area proved an excellent base for public relations both inside and outside the company – first, because NEC was taking a pioneering role in communications, in an area that had not previously existed, let alone been explored; second, because intercontinental broadcasting made possible by satellite communications gave new prominence to the unity of the globe and would lead to the international expansion of NEC's business; and third, because it offered NEC the chance to prove its ability to handle the world's most advanced technology in both engineering and marketing terms. Thus, even though 1965 was a dark year of economic recession, my appointment as president had its bright side because it coincided with the dawn of the new space age and all the hopes that went with it. The fact that I personally had played a significant role in NEC's entry into this area had privately given me a great sense of confidence.

As technology and markets evolved, I found myself constantly trying to define the direction NEC should now take. Each year the American business magazine *Fortune* published a list of the top-ranking companies in the United States and throughout the world (in those days NEC ranked about 170th in terms of sales volume among industrial companies outside the US, giving a brief explanation of the nature of each company's business with its entry. NEC had traditionally been classified under "electrical equipment"; after due deliberation I chose instead the words *telecommunications and electronics*. "Telecommunications" went beyond the category "telephone and switching equipment," another typical description of NEC's business; it was a comprehensive concept that covered cable transmission systems as well as various types of radio communications and broadcasting equipment. In short, it included all types of communications equipment supported by advanced telecommunications theory and technology.

The other word, "electronics," had come into general use with the spread of television, but strictly speaking it referred to all equipment produced by means of electronic technology. The outstanding example was computers, but the word encompassed all products based on electronic devices – electron tubes, transistors, diodes, and other semiconductor devices as well as whatever was composed of these parts. In sum, I wanted to draw attention to the fact that NEC made not only communications equipment but also computers, transistors, and integrated circuits.

From Communications to Information and the "Knowledge Industry"

How would this new self-description affect perceptions of NEC's role and position in the economy and in society? Communications serves the function of conveying people's thoughts and messages either by transmitting sounds or by sending data or codes; in other words, anything capable of containing meaningful content or, to put it another way, "information." Just as the different means of transportation carry people and goods and move tangible objects, the function of communications is to carry intangible *information*. That was the key word; that was what needed to be emphasized. Computers processed information; communications equipment transmitted it. Even radio and television were no more than a means of receiving and reproducing information. Reexamining our company and our industry from the perspective of social and economic roles, it was clear that no company was better suited than ours to handle information, in all its aspects. This approach was beginning to gain ground in certain sectors of the company: we were switching our sights from communications to information.

Information and knowledge are intimately linked concepts. The November 1964 issue of *Fortune* magazine carried a special feature under the headline "Knowledge, the Biggest Growth Industry of Them All." The concept of a "knowledge industry" captured my attention. The criteria for participation in this industry – communications equipment, office equipment, and information equipment – seemed to leap from the page. Because communications and computers were singled out as the prospective supports for promising new businesses, the article stimulated and encouraged me in my vision of NEC's future.

It was becoming clear that information was taking its place alongside energy and material goods as one of a country's industrial resources, and was joining people, property, and money as a prime requisite for any business. When faced with the question of how to define the two words, "information" and "knowledge," I avoided a strict distinction, relying rather on the usage of Fritz Machlup, who, in his book *The Production and Distribution of Knowledge in the United States*, had defined the word "knowledge" in very broad terms. From my staff I learned of the unique views on the information industry of Tadao Umesao, then an assistant professor in the Faculty of Science at Kyoto University. Some felt that his ideas on the future were even more significant than those of Professor Machlup. Shortly afterwards, Professor Umesao's new book, *The Methods of the Knowledge Industry*, appeared: it attracted considerable attention, but its contents were somewhat thin on the topic of the relationship of information to electronics.

Although researchers in the telecommunications area with whom I had long been involved had delved deeply into the technical manipulation of electric signals, they seemed to have an unspoken rule not to go any deeper into the heart of the message that these signals embodied. Knowledge and information theory, however, came squarely to grips with the significance of the embodied message itself. Machlup concentrated on the economic side of knowledge, or the work of knowledge from his perspective as an economist; his views were limited by his statistical approach. Burck's comments on the knowledge industry were a revelation to me. I even gave speeches within the company on the topic, though I did not go so far as to relate it directly to our day-to-day business.

In 1966, when NEC's internal reforms had more or less reached completion, I decided after much thought to abolish our Nuclear Energy Research Laboratory, which had been founded in the expectation that a nuclear-related business would be a promising venture for the future. But I had now recognized that NEC's market niche was in the information sphere; so, as nuclear power is part of the energy sphere and has nothing to do with information, I transferred control over the facility and the personnel employed there to the Tokai Laboratory of the Sumitomo Atomic Energy Company.

These comments on knowledge and information are related not only to the question of NEC's corporate identity, but also to my proposal ten years later for the integration of computers and communications; though, I must confess, many problems remain, awaiting more comprehensive research. Nevertheless, what I have written here about the knowledge industry is essential for any understanding of NEC and its management in and after the second half of the 1960s and should be taken as my then current thinking on the subject.

Projecting an Image: The "Three Cs"

Because NTT had traditionally been NEC's chief customer, the company had had little need for public relations, and our dealings with the market for ordinary industrial or consumer use were weak. My predecessor, Toshihide Watanabe, had been a modest man of the old school, who had tried to stay out of the limelight. For that reason NEC and its head office in Mita were not well known to the general public. Since expanding the market for NEC's products from one centered on NTT to one that included private industry and the overseas market was becoming my basic strategy for greater corporate growth, I was increasingly aware of the need to make NEC and its activities more widely known. After I became president I made a point of meeting and talking to journalists. Invariably, the first question I was asked was about my background as an engineer, which always aroused curiosity: A company president usually came from a business background in accounting or law, so a previous career in science or engineering was considered a departure from the norm. The next question was about my aspirations as president. This was tantamount to asking me to outline my future image of the company and the areas I expected to concentrate on as its chief executive officer, and was my opportunity to raise awareness of the company's activities.

I usually replied with the "three Cs." The first C stood for *communications*, the company's traditional area of expertise. Second came *computers*, the champion product in the field of electronics. Then came *controls* for the various kinds of automation equipment that we made. Sometimes I would add a fourth or a fifth C for electronic components or consumer products, the electrical household appliances which were then the domain of an NEC subsidiary, the New Nippon Electric Co. Although this manner of speaking was a convenient way of explaining the company's business, it boomeranged on me when many of the employees who worked in other areas of the company complained that the fields they worked in – educational equipment or medical electronic equipment, for example – did not begin with a C.

I include here a presidential memo from that time which sums up my thinking on these matters.

NEC's Evolution into the Communications Age

The information in this memo sums up my present thoughts on the aims of this organization. I am circulating it in the hopes that it will deepen your understanding of NEC and its new structure and help you formulate a more accurate assessment of these matters as you pursue your activities both inside and outside the company.

NEC: Japan's First Joint Venture

Upon revision of the Commercial Code of Japan in 1899, NEC was founded as the first joint-stock company to be created here with foreign capital. Because 54 percent of the start-up funds came from the American company Western Electric, NEC, to use contemporary terms, was Japan's first joint venture. As you know, Western Electric is the equipment manufacturing arm for the Bell System, whose mission is to supply communications equipment to American Telephone and Telegraph

(AT&T). Since NEC's founding the primary mission of our company has also been to make communications equipment for our number one customer, formerly the Ministry of Communications and now NTT Public Corporation – Japan's counterpart to AT&T. Western Electric is the foremost manufacturer of communications equipment in the world, and as its offspring our company has a glorious heritage. That is why we have sometimes been called "the Western Electric of the Far East." Today, some sixty years after our founding, NEC still maintains cross-licensing agreements for important patents with Western Electric.

Upgrading the Telephone Network with NTT

Before the war almost three-quarters of our sales were to the Ministry of Communications – in other words, to NTT. Even today nearly half our sales are still to the NTT Public Corporation, which remains our number one customer.

In 1953, the year after the state-run communications service was converted into a public corporation, NTT embarked on its first five-year plan to upgrade telephone and telegraph equipment; it is now in the third year of its third five-year plan. In the intervening period our country's communications services have made great strides both quantitatively and qualitatively. But as of January 1, 1964, Japan ranked nineteenth in the world in terms of equipment diffusion, with 8.7 telephones per hundred of population – only one fifth the rate of the top-ranking country, the United States, with 44.3 telephones per hundred.

Three years ago, at the time our American Depositary Receipts were being issued, I traveled around the United States attending meetings concerned with the prospects for new equity issues. When I was asked whether Japan's plans for the future of its communications services were not too grandiose, I pointed out that our country's level of development in the area of communications was still relatively weak compared with other areas like steel and shipbuilding, where Japan had reached international stature. By explaining our need for and the inevitability of expansion in this area, using the comparison of international diffusion rates just mentioned, I was able to dispel their doubts.

With the completion of NTT's fourth five-year plan, which will begin in 1968 and end in 1972, the number of telephones in Japan will have increased from today's figure of 7.3 million to more than 20 million. Because construction plans will continue to grow each year by 15–20 percent, the communications equipment area will remain the mainstay of NEC's business.

New Trends

Although historically our company's traditional strength has been the manufacture of communications equipment, for a period during the war we were forced into munitions work. After the war, however, when it became necessary to restore Japan's communications facilities, NEC reverted to its original role as a communications equipment maker.

In the early 1950s, new trends began to blossom within the company and their growth is now being steadily nurtured. One of these has been our entry into the overseas marketplace; another is the pioneering of private sector industrial demand. During this period, which coincides with the earliest stages of the growth of the electronics industry in Japan, we added the new area of electronics to our traditional area of expertise, communications.

The slight decrease recently in the percentage of our consolidated sales held by NTT is in fact attributable to an increase in the percentage of sales for the export market and the private sector: sales to NTT continue to grow in absolute terms. The importance to our company of the communications equipment area and of sales to NTT is expected to remain unchanged.

Facilitating Communication

Because the main roots of our business remain in the communications equipment area, the mission of our company is to develop and supply the means that will enable people to communicate their ideas and talk freely to one another, any time, anywhere. This goal is being steadily achieved in the advanced countries of Europe and North America and will soon be reached in Japan as well. Although we have hitherto supplied the means of communication mainly within our own country, from now on we must try to accomplish these same goals on a global scale.

That this lofty ambition is now on the verge of fulfillment is thanks to the astonishing development of satellite communications technology, which operates in space and complements existing relay technology using submarine cable. Already at the time of the Tokyo Olympics, the successful trans-Pacific transmission of live television pictures using the Syncom III satellite was living proof of the enormous potential of this technology.

Three years ago our company joined forces with Hughes Aircraft, the world leader in the area of communications satellites, to develop a space communications system. NEC is making steady progress in establishing and opening up a worldwide market for these services, through the Communications Satellite Corporation (Comsat) in the United States and the Interim International Telecommunications Satellite (Intelsat) consortium. We are now awaiting the visit of vice president Allen E. Puckett of Hughes Aircraft, and Joseph V. Charyk, president of Comsat, to observe the random multiple access system that we have succeeded in manufacturing on a trial basis in the Satellite Communications Development Department of the Radio Communication Division. We are also in the process of installing this system at the joint experimental ground station for satellite communications that we have set up with Hughes in Hot Springs, Arkansas, on a site conveniently situated for satellites in orbit over both the Atlantic and Pacific oceans.

The Four Cs

The unflagging technological development of new methods, devices, and modes of production has become a huge springboard for the amazing leaps being made in electronics and communications. The importance of technology in NEC's business must be repeatedly emphasized. *Technology is not simply the pursuit of novelty*; it has to match market trends, then take them one step further, to develop and offer products that will fulfill the desires and satisfy the hopes and aspirations of our customers.

A quick glance at our company shows that we have about forty or fifty product areas. The most important of these are:

1. *Communications*, including broadcasting-related equipment for the mass media. The social role of communications can be compared to the nervous system in the human body: It serves the function of assisting people to understand one another by providing them with the means to communicate their ideas. This function is symbolized by the hotline between the Kremlin and the White House. Because communications can increase understanding and trust between people, it promotes peace, the most important concern in the world today.

2. Electronic data processing systems, in other words, *computers*. The computer is the technological counterpart to the brain in the human body, and, for that reason, it is sometimes referred to as artificial intelligence. Although computers are not yet capable of replicating the mind's creative activities, the speed and accuracy of their data-processing functions are far superior to the human brain in the areas of memory, computation, and sorting.

Today, the dizzying pace of social change has produced what is sometimes called a "time revolution." In an age where there is literally no time to lose, the speed of data processing will dramatically increase human capabilities and supplement the activities of the human mind. The usefulness of computer-based data-processing methods will continue to expand rapidly with the development of new input–output devices and the practical application of new methods of data communications.

The computer business of our company has its origins in the development of electronic data-processing techniques based on communications technology. In this respect, we differ from companies like IBM, where computers developed out of office equipment. In the years ahead, when computers will come to be linked up with data communications, I believe our strength in having both these technologies will come into its own.

3. *Controls*, such as industrial and instrumental controls, which have been brought into prominence by the development of the feedback principle in electronics. Their role is increasingly important in all areas, but especially in manufacturing where these controls will one day make various types of automation a reality.

Automation fulfills a function similar to that of the arms and legs of a human body and can be expected to spread widely throughout all areas of industry. Already our company's products are beginning to be used for communications controls, electric power controls, automatic controls for the Shinkansen bullet train, ship automation, and numerical controls for machine tools.

4. *Electronic components*: a necessary part of the devices and systems in all of the areas just noted. If we continue our analogy to the human body, we can see components as the cells of which these devices and systems are constructed, or perhaps the food that sustains their operations. Progress in component technology – from the vacuum tube to the transistor to thin-film circuits and, finally, to integrated circuits – has resulted in qualitative and quantitative increases in the function and performance of these devices.

NEC's corporate image might, then, be said to rest on the four Cs of communications, computers, controls, and components. Of course, our company has other business areas that do not fit into these four categories, for example, electronic defense systems, medical electronic equipment, electron beam machines, educational equipment, and electrical household appliances, to name only a few. None of these would have thrived, however, had they not been branches springing from the sturdy roots of the common technologies represented by the four Cs.

Product Development

The reorganization into divisions has clarified the operational line functions of the company. At the same time I have also tried to clarify the functions of our three research bases – the central research laboratories, the development laboratories of each operating group, and finally the engineering units of the divisions themselves.

The mission of the central research laboratories is to develop the technologies that will become the common basis for the manufacturing done at our various divisions: in other words to develop basic technologies for communications and electronics and serve as the source of technology for the product development carried out at the division level. It thereby provides the divisions with support for ideas that have a strong potential for technological development.

The development laboratories of the three operating groups are responsible for developing the technology for products that have a definite purpose and that will become the basis for new business activities several years hence.

Furthermore, the technology and product development system in our company is structured in such a way that any proposed improvements to marketing plans or production technology or any other support functions can be readily communicated from the staff divisions in charge of those areas.

The Giant Redwood and the Dwarf Bonsai

Turning to the economic environment within which our business exists, the size of the Japanese economy gives it a certain fragility. Japan can be compared to a small spinning top that must constantly revolve at high speed or topple over. The US, on the other hand, because of the great size of its economy, is like a large top: it can revolve slowly without danger of collapse. This difference in size and stability produces corresponding differences in the ways the two countries regard economic growth.

To put the comparison another way, the US economy can be likened to a giant redwood tree, while the Japanese economy is like a dwarf bonsai growing in a bowl. The bonsai, like any other tree, puts down roots in the earth, flowers, and bears fruit; but a problem lies in the shallowness of those roots. A bonsai is extremely delicate and needs constant care and attention. If it receives too little water or too strong a wind, the tree is soon damaged and shrivels up. The redwood's roots go deep into the earth and storms make little impact on it.

Japanese corporations, both in their business dealings generally and especially in the area of research and development, therefore cannot function on a par with US concerns and must consequently make special efforts to overcome the inherent competitive disadvantages of their national environment.

Energizing the Company

Given this background, we face the very thorny problem of how to energize the company without losing our identity, so that we can overcome the limits of size and challenge these giant competitors worldwide. The organizational restructuring that has recently taken effect and is now being fleshed out has been planned with this end in view: its salient features are as follows.

First, we have established a line/staff system. This system clarifies where the actual operation of business is conducted (line divisions) and where the necessary expertise to support it can be found (staff divisions).

Second, the divisions responsible for the company's business operations have been refined into a more straightforward system. This is to enable us to carry out a firm and steady development of the four Cs, described above, that make up our company's business sphere.

Third, each division is attempting to establish and define its own strategic image in order to set out its own guidelines on how it should run its business.

Fourth, the new system has made it possible for the structure of top management, which could be called the central core of the corporation, to deal rapidly and appropriately with the many and varied problems that constantly arise. This reform involves expanding the chain of command outward from the company president, who occupies a single point at the center of the managerial circle, to the executives who compose the area of that circle, each acting as the president's *alter ego* in his particular domain. This "point to area" approach avoids a rigid chain of command, yet at the same time allows for all corporate responsibility to be focused on one person, the president. It also has the necessary flexibility to allow us to respond to any changes that may occur, whether inside or outside the company.

But ultimately – and this is the fifth point – a corporation does not achieve results through the dedication of its top management alone. All of you in charge of line operations must see to it in your respective posts that NEC will continue to grow as a result of your diligent and constant efforts to make our products and our company the best in the world and to make the new zero defects program a success.

The internal management system of our company, which can be summed up by these five points, has already been discussed in detail many times. But if we are to be successful in achieving and expanding the aims of the organization, you must be able to fathom the relation between NEC's historical background and the current international climate in which our company is placed as outlined in this memo. Without this insight any understanding is superficial and incomplete.

4

Strategies for Expansion

Security and Growth: NEC and NTT

No outline of NEC's business would be complete without a discussion of the NTT Public Corporation's first five-year telephone expansion plan, which began in 1953. Takeshi Kajii, the first president of NTT after it became a public corporation in 1952, had also been president of NEC during the war, and is one of the people responsible for the technological development of Japan's communications industry. Faced with the task of rebuilding and refurbishing Japan's telecommunications facilities after the war, it was Kajii who not only made the basic decision to introduce and assimilate the best new technologies from throughout the world but also provided the inspiration and direction for those involved in this giant undertaking. The actual tasks confronting him were to install a direct dialling system connecting all Japan's major cities and to eliminate the backlog of requests for telephone service. By the time the fourth five-year plan had been completed in 1972 the backlog had been reduced to zero, and the goal of a nationwide long-distance direct dialling network was in sight. At the time I became president of NEC, NTT was in the second year of its third five-year plan.

NTT's construction budget was divided between equipment and cable. The electric cable industry supplied the latter; the development and delivery of equipment was primarily the concern of NEC. Because the size of NTT's budget increased at an annual rate of 12–13 percent, assuming that approximately half our total sales were to NTT, then NEC could also expect an annual sales increase of 12–13 percent. NTT made it a rule to buy at cost, although it permitted a profit margin of a few percentage points above the cost price. Doing business with NTT did not result in big earnings for NEC, then, but it always guaranteed us a certain amount of profit. These assured profits contributed to NEC's business stability.

As I mentioned earlier, the companies that supplied equipment to NTT were known as "the communications big four." In particular, this phrase referred to the four companies who provided NTT with the crossbar switching equipment for its nationwide direct dialling network – NEC, Oki Electric Industry, Fuji Communications Equipment Manufacturing Company (Fujitsu), and Hitachi. Broadly speaking, communications equipment consisted of three different areas: telephones and other communications terminals; cable and radio transmission equipment for sending electric signals; and the switching equipment that switched and connected the circuits. Of the four major suppliers, NEC held the lion's share in crossbar switching equipment and virtually monopolized the two major areas of transmission equipment, carrier transmission systems and microwave radio communications systems. NEC's overwhelming strength in transmission equipment reflected our role in the development of these two technologies and our subsequent achievements in these areas. Iwatsu Electric Co. was added to the big four as a supplier of telephones. The electric cable industry was represented by four major makers: Sumitomo Electric Industries, The Furukawa Electric Co., Hitachi Cable, and Fujikura.

NTT was instrumental in the postwar expansion of NEC's manufacturing capability. Since our company's founding, one floor of the Mita building had housed the head office, and all the remaining floors constituted the Mita plant, which made telephones and switching equipment. The emergence of radio communications in the late 1920s and the need to make our own vacuum tubes had led to the construction of the Tamagawa plant, which began operations in 1936. Thus, before the war, Mita and Tamagawa had been the company's two leading plants. Our first new large-scale facility since the end of the war, the Sagamihara plant, which began operations in November 1963, was built to accommodate the need to mass-produce the crossbar switching equipment required for NTT's construction plans. It thus developed out of the same business line as the Mita plant.

When NEC had entered the computer field in the early 1950s, computer engineering had sprung up in the Tamagawa plant – or, to be precise, among the engineers responsible for transmission technology. NEC's second large factory to be built since the war, the

Fuchu plant, was built primarily to produce computers, and began operating in September 1964. Employees here were conscious of their role as pioneers in a new field, and the atmosphere was charged with the excitement of challenging the unknown. The Yokohama plant, where operations began in December 1969, was our third new big plant in the postwar period. It was built to handle expanded production of radio communications and radio-related equipment, which, like computers, had previously been made at the Tamagawa plant.

The total size of NTT's five-year expansion plans had been 302.1 billion yen for the first five-year plan, 725.5 billion for the second, and 1,787.5 billion yen for the third, which was in progress when I took the helm at NEC. Although the size and scope of this project were extremely large, if NEC decided to base its own expansion plans on those of NTT, our growth rate would not deviate significantly from the rate of increase for NTT's five-year plans. However, since the early 1960s the Japanese economy had been experiencing a period of high-level growth. The growth rate for mining and manufacturing industries as a whole was around 19 percent, or about twice the growth rate of the gross national product, which was then around 8 or 9 percent. (A statistic frequently cited in the press at this time was that if the Japanese economy continued to grow at an annual rate of 7 percent it would double in size in five years.) Although NTT's budget was obviously growing faster than GNP, it was not growing anything like as fast as the industrial average, as reflected in the mining and manufacturing production index. Electrical household appliance companies, for example, had an annual growth rate as high as 30 percent. No one in his right mind would have considered a growth rate of only just over 10 percent satisfactory for NEC. Our ambition in the early 1960s, then, was to maintain an annual growth rate of 20 percent, well above the mining and manufacturing production index.

This had obvious implications for our relationship with NTT. During the administration of my predecessor, Toshihide Watanabe, NEC's expansion plans involved branching out into the private sector and the overseas market. When I became president I made no changes in this basic policy line. Although from time to time I warned against underrating the importance of NTT in our eagerness to branch out into new areas, our main objective had to be cultivation of both the private sector and an overseas market to supplement demands from NTT. NEC's entry into satellite communications was a significant and high-profile step: But if our satellite communications commitment was like the visible tip of the iceberg that receives the full radiance of the sun, the unchanging demand from NTT was like the submerged body of the iceberg, vast but hidden from view.

A Billion Dollar Company

By extrapolating from the current tempo of growth, it was possible to project a future size for NEC. As a more or less attainable goal, and because it had a good ring to it, I decided we should become a "billion-dollar company" (at an exchange rate of 360 yen to the dollar). This would give us the size needed to rank alongside General Electric, Western Electric, RCA, Siemens, Ericsson, and other companies on the *Fortune* list. We might not be in the same league as a corporate giant like AT&T, but we would be well qualified to endure the rough seas of the international market and make our presence felt both at home and abroad.

NEC in the early 1960s had sales of around 80 or 90 billion yen a year. Given an annual growth rate of 20 percent, how many years would it take to reach 360 billion yen, and what should NEC do to achieve that goal? The actual calculations did not take much time to figure out. If sales to the private sector and the overseas market expanded rapidly enough, it would be possible to attain our goal by March 1973, when NTT had completed its fourth five-year expansion plan. By my rough estimate, if we could multiply our annual sales at the time I became president – 70 billion yen – by five, we would reach one billion dollars.

Building on Strength: Into Computers

In terms of historical pedigree NEC's central product line was electronics; so, when it came to diversifying into new areas, we naturally turned to the commercialization of the computer. One shining milestone in this process had been the NEAC-2201 computer displayed at the Automath exhibition during the International Information Processing Conference in Paris in June 1959. This was the first public unveiling of an all-transistor computer, the pride and joy of NEC's engineering team. At that time IBM's model

650 was well known on the world market, but IBM did not make the switchover to a transistorized computer until its model 1401. NEC had publicly displayed its own transistorized model ahead of IBM.

Although the NEAC-2203, the transistorized model for commercial use that followed the NEAC-2201, won high praise as an outstanding Japanese-made computer, annual sales for NEC's computer business before fiscal 1960 did not exceed 200 million yen. As a matter of fact, I had doubts about whether we could succeed on our own in the computer business against the world's great powers in that area. Though we could build the computer itself, I did not have complete confidence that we could mass-produce all the peripherals – a trouble-free printer, for example.

Tapping Foreign Expertise

In the late 1950s and early 1960s, during my years as senior vice president, executive vice president, and finally senior executive vice president, I had held responsibility for all technological matters in the company. Seeking ways both to raise our own technology to American and European levels and to discover new areas, I had been active in searching out and introducing significant foreign technology in order to maintain and strengthen NEC's technological position. The common characteristic of most of the leading foreign computer makers, from UNIVAC or IBM in the US to Machines Bull, Olivetti or ICL in Europe, was that they had all begun in the office equipment area. In short, their machines were essentially typewriters or accounting machines to which had been added calculation and memory functions. The antecedents of almost all the Japanese computer manufacturers, on the other hand, were in communications equipment or heavy electrical appliances. At NEC the engineers in the transmission area with which I had long been associated had originally been the mainstay of our computer operations. I knew that whereas we had long experience with telecommunications, many unknown factors lay in wait for us in the computer area. In many respects the business was on a different plane altogether from making television sets. IBM's sales approach, for example, was not to sell equipment outright but to lease it to users.

I therefore began to suggest the possibility of a technical tie-up with one of the leading foreign computer makers. Soon afterwards, other Japanese companies in the computer business began consolidating their ties with foreign companies – Hitachi with RCA, Toshiba with GE, and Oki with UNIVAC (Sperry Rand). We decided we wanted to team up with a company that offered a particular strength, and, after due consideration, we chose Minneapolis-Honeywell Regulator Company (now Honeywell Inc.). Honeywell had started out as the world's leading maker of automatic controls. It entered a joint venture with Raytheon to develop a mainframe computer, the Datamatic 1000, which it had subsequently taken over and converted into its own computer division; at this time it was making a successful entry into this new area, its leading product being the H-800 mainframe.

I had specific reasons for favoring an agreement with Honeywell in computer technology. First, NEC's real strength lay in the area of small and medium-sized computers, and it did not have the capacity to develop all computer areas, including the larger sizes, simultaneously. Computer companies of the future, however, would have to offer a family series including all types of machines from the smallest to the largest. *By importing the technology from Honeywell we could supplement the machine types we were deficient in and acquire the expertise to deal with the entire range of machines in the future.* The second reason was software. The strength of IBM lay in its large stock of software and applications technology. As far as hardware was concerned the gap between us was not all that great, as NEC's ability to develop its own transistorized computer had shown. But we were still weak in terms of software, and we could cover this weakness by cooperating with Honeywell.

After the technological agreement between the two companies had been signed in July 1962, we proceeded to produce a large computer of the Honeywell type for the Japanese market, and soon Honeywell succeeded in developing a new and superior small computer. This was the parent machine, later called the model 200, for our NEAC-2200 series, which was to launch NEC's computer business into orbit. As a result of this success, NEC concentrated on developing its own large computer, which was sold as the model 500 in the NEAC-2200 series. With this model we achieved our "one machine" design concept for a family series in five different sizes. The NEAC-2200 series dominated the domestic market in the latter half of the 1960s.

Computers and Communications: A Link from the Beginning

It is worth noting here NEC's basic approach to the computer business. In 1960, for example, we developed a seat reservation system for Kinki Nippon Railway Co., based on the NEAC-2203, which provided on-line connection between a central computer and several terminals for making reservations and issuing railway tickets. In other words, we succeeded in creating an on-line information-processing system that combined data processing with data transmissions technology. In 1964 NEC developed and delivered a seat reservation system for Japan Air Lines, also using the NEAC-2230. NEC's on-line real-time system would subsequently extend to other business uses in areas such as deposit management, production control, and sales management. Once the business had begun to evolve along these lines, the Electronic Equipment Division, which had taken charge of NEC's computer operations, was divided in April 1964 into two independent divisions, the Electronic Data Processing Division and the Data Communication Division.

At the end of 1967 we perfected Japan's first time-sharing system using the model 500 of the NEAC-2200 series, which had been developed in May 1965. Called the MAC system, it was used at Osaka University, which was located on four separate campuses. In developing this multi-access system we had learned from the success of a similar system used at the Massachusetts Institute of Technology – sowing the seeds of a close relationship with MIT that has lasted to this day – but the model 500 itself was the result of NEC's own development efforts. A third-generation machine, corresponding to the IBM system 360, it was the first computer in Japan to use integrated circuits for its logic element and soon became the mainstay of NEC's lineup. Although these efforts came at the very beginning of the data communications age, our communications expertise, technologically augmented and applied to an ever-widening range of uses, became an inextricable element in the success of our computer business, which continued on its steady course.

Looking Abroad: Telecommunications in the US

Competition among Japanese computer companies was beginning to heat up; but I remained convinced that our priority must be to concentrate on the world market. One issue brought into focus by this strategy was the different nature of the public communications business in Japan and in the US – the most important overseas market.

Unlike their Japanese counterparts, public communications services in the United States were operated right from the start by private enterprise, dominated by AT&T. Telephone operating subsidiaries of AT&T were located in each part of the country and ran the actual communications operations for that area. Western Electric, NEC's original partner, was the manufacturing division, which delivered the necessary equipment to AT&T and these operating companies; it too was fully owned by AT&T. The division in charge of research and development was Bell Laboratories. The whole complex, embracing these three divisions for operations, manufacturing, and R&D, was called the Bell System.

In Japan NTT (now a private company, but at that time a public corporation) was in charge of operations; manufacturing was done by a number of private firms; and research and development was carried on by NTT Electrical Communication Laboratory and the research and development divisions of the individual manufacturers. NEC occupied a position in Japan equivalent to that of Western Electric in the US.

The Conglomerate Approach

In 1925 the foreign subsidiaries of Western Electric had been acquired by ITT (nominally International Standard Electric Company), which therefore became the American holding company for NEC. After I became president, I would visit New York to report on our operating results to ITT, which remained our largest single stockholder until 1971, although it was gradually reducing its holdings during the 1960s. The president of ITT at the time was the highly respected Harold S. Geneen. Naturally, I had a great interest in how ITT would develop in the future and wanted to learn whatever I could. Under Geneen's leadership ITT had begun to adopt a special growth strategy that was producing striking results. Journalists referred to this corporate concept as the *conglomerate*.

Although we both agreed that communications-based companies must respond appropriately to the coming information age, when I asked Geneen what he thought about getting into the computer business, he immediately replied that computers ate up money and offered too small a return on investment: he had no intention of getting involved with them. How, then, was he planning to cope with the increasing importance of information, I asked. His response was that the only answer was the conglomerate. I could not fathom the logic in that approach. ITT had already acquired Avis Rent-a-Car and was proceeding to take over hotels and food businesses. I was at a total loss to understand how this was a response to the information age. Geneen explained it to me this way. When information from all over the world reaches people's eyes and ears, they will want to travel and see for themselves, so the hotel business will boom. When they stay at a hotel, they will have to eat, so the food business will prosper. Whether they are there for business or for pleasure, they will need transportation: that is where the car rental business comes in. They can rent a car when they need it and return it when they are finished. Accidents may happen, so the insurance business will grow.

That was more or less the reasoning behind his lecture. It was a totally unexpected idea, but there was a certain coherent logic to it. It was not as if ITT would buy any sort of business merely because it seemed likely to make a profit. Geneen even suggested that NEC join with ITT and begin to buy hotels and car rental agencies in Japan. But though Geneen was certainly proving that this was a management strategy for high growth and good returns, I did not feel it was a direction I wanted NEC to take. I discussed the matter with one of my many American friends, who gave me a clear assessment of the situation. *There are two possible types of corporate management and corporate managers*, he said. *The first is the book-keeping type, of which Geneen, with his background in corporate accountancy, is a good example. The second is what might be called the industrial development type – building upon the foundation of one particular technology.* The fact that I was not in sympathy with Geneen's approach, I decided, was because my own philosophy of management belonged to the industrial development school.

Around twenty years ago there was great interest in the emergence of conglomerates such as TRW and Litton Industries. ITT was a corporation in the same line of business as NEC, not only related to our parent company but also in those days our leading shareholder. Because it was the American firm closest to NEC, I paid close attention to its business development. But I was clearly aware that we were going our separate ways into totally separate worlds.

NEC took the orthodox route, perhaps. We decided to become a "billion dollar company" through internal growth built on our own traditional technological base. Even the limits of business diversification were gradually defining themselves. The criterion for pioneering new spheres was not just their potential profitability; they must share similar technologies, customers, and markets with our existing operations. Our entry into the computer field might be called diversification, but it was based on an area that was inextricably tied to our main line of business.

Small is Beautiful: Semiconductors

One day in June 1965, not long after my divisional reorganization program was more or less complete, a draft proposal from our semiconductor operations arrived on my desk. It was a request for an investment of 2 billion yen in plant and equipment, and took me completely by surprise. Sales by our semiconductor operations had been 3.8 billion yen during the previous fiscal year. An investment of slightly more than half that amount in plant and equipment was a large sum of money for NEC in those days. I immediately referred the proposal to the Corporate Management Committee, asking them to investigate it thoroughly and then come up with a company policy on the electronic components business. This sort of problem was not something that could be dealt with within a single division: it was the role of the Corporate Management Committee to consider such an issue within the framework of the entire company and discuss all its possible ramifications.

In order to expand our business we would clearly have to expand the equipment and floor space needed for manufacturing. Common sense suggested that if you wanted to double production you had to double your floor space. But first we needed to consider whether the company had the financial resources to accept all the proposals for new equipment that the divisions could be expected to submit. If a whole series of these proposals were submitted to the Corporate Management Committee for discussion, even with detailed explanations attached by the departments that submitted them, a committee member lacking sufficient knowledge to discuss their relative merits would have no basis on which to make an appropriate recommendation. This could have potentially dangerous consequences, and I therefore tried to make it clear that while the Corporate Management Committee was a key forum for the exchange of ideas and information, it was not the place where final decisions were made. All official decisions should be made following the format of the traditional circular letter (*ringi*) decision-making process.

NEC's semiconductor operations had started out within our Tamagawa plant. In 1958 we had built a brand new mass-production factory there, which was yielding steady results. In January 1965, to accommodate increased demand, the new Nichiden Takahata Works at Takahata in Yamagata Prefecture was opened; the manufacturing of mass-produced transistors was transferred there, allowing the Tamagawa facility to specialize in the production and development of more advanced devices.

The special characteristic of NEC's semiconductor operations that distinguished it from the semiconductor businesses in other companies was that it developed components for communications and other types of industrial equipment rather than for domestic products such as radios and televisions. As in the case of computers, where we had been the first to make the switchover from vacuum tubes to transistors, we were pioneering the process of replacing the electron tubes in all our communications equipment with solid state devices made and supplied by the semiconductor unit, which had originated as a branch of our electron tube operations.

For all our products, miniaturization – packaging increasingly higher performance in ever smaller units – was becoming a major challenge and a technological trend. In both the carrier transmission equipment area, which I had run for many years, and the radio equipment area, which was then becoming our star product line, circuit panels containing the different components that made up the heart of the system were becoming smaller every year. In the semiconductor area we were not only miniaturizing electron tubes, we were also in the process of developing new high-performance products such as diodes and transistors. We had recognized the promise of silicon-type semiconductor devices at an early date and decided to focus on the planar type. On this point we differed from the semiconductor divisions of other companies, most of which used germanium transistors for household appliances. Fortunately for us, the American company Fairchild, which held the patents for the planar technique, decided it did not have the reserves to enter the foreign market and consented to give NEC exclusive licensing rights to the process in Japan. However, the rights to the Kilby patents for laying out circuits on a single piece of silicon were claimed by Texas Instruments, which planned to use its superiority in this area to launch out directly into overseas operations. It was reluctant to give Japanese firms the licensing rights to its patent, and at the beginning of 1964 submitted a request to the Japanese government to set up a Japanese company. After more than a year had gone by without getting the necessary permission from the Japanese government, Texas Instruments had the subject brought up at the US–Japan economic ministers conference in Kyoto in May 1965, where John T. Connor, US Secretary of Commerce, pressed for early approval. The subject was widely covered in the newspapers and attracted the attention and concern of the Tokyo stock market at Kabutocho. As a result, integrated circuits – ICs – entered Japan's vocabulary.

The time was not yet ripe for the IC business, however. This was the period of the emergence and popularization of color television, the golden age of the transistor. Young junior high school graduates from the countryside, affectionately known as "transistor girls," were flocking to the Tokyo–Yokohama area to work in the Keihin industrial belt. The Japanese economy then was entering the zenith of high-level growth based on the heavy industrial and chemical sector. The heyday of the IC business, later known as microelectronics, was yet to come. Nevertheless, the proposal for new plant and equipment for our semiconductor operations was in essence raising the question of whether NEC would embark on the manufacturing of ICs. We did, of course: this decision is worth noting as Japan's first commitment to the IC business.

Designing Expansion: Decentralization

Repeated requests for the construction of new plants about this time prompted me to gather my top staff together and deliver the following warning: If our sales double or triple in the next five years, the orthodox view is that we should increase our plant size commensurately to accommodate the increased demand. But given the trend toward miniaturization, projections for future floor space needs based on multiples of the existing area may prove a serious miscalculation, for not only are the sizes of the devices shrinking to one half or one third their present size, their performance is also increasing. Similarly, we must take automation into account in calculating the number of workers we will need. An extremely dangerous situation may result from an oversimplified approach to expansion. I want you, I said, to recheck every point carefully and work out new plant construction plans for the entire company.

The tight labor market for young workers was then becoming a direct obstacle to the construction of new plants. As mentioned earlier, investment in plant and equipment and a massive commitment of manpower were the motive forces behind Japan's high-level growth. In the late 1960s, while the future importance of knowledge-intensive industries was beginning to be recognized, growth was still to a marked degree the result of labor-intensive mass production, and the percentage of GNP occupied by the knowledge industry remained small.

The supply of young workers was drawn mainly from the farming and mountain villages in the countryside, which were steadily being depopulated. The formation of the Tokaido megalopolis, the corridor along the Pacific coast extending from Tokyo to Osaka and Kobe; the increasing concentration of population in the cities; the building of a huge seaside industrial zone in the Tokyo–Yokohama area – these were the main demographic–industrial features of the time. It was against this background that I announced my decision in September 1968 to build the present Yokohama plant to handle the expansion of our microwave and satellite communications businesses, which had hitherto been carried out in the Tamagawa plant; and it was while studying the Yokohama construction plans that I came up with the concept of decentralized plant location on a nationwide scale as my basic strategy for setting up NEC plants in the future. I realized that soon the limited supply of both land and skilled labor would make it difficult to plan for large-scale plants in the greater Tokyo metropolitan area. Commuting and housing conditions would add to the difficulties. From now on the company would have to go to where the labor supply was. Most workers would probably welcome being able to work in the place where they had grown up.

Fortunately, most of the products NEC dealt with were small and light and could be easily transported. Around the time of the 1964

Tokyo Olympics, long-distance transportation in Japan had made dramatic improvements in terms of both the geographical area covered and the variety of means available. The communications infrastructure also posed fewer impediments, thanks to progress in NTT's nationwide direct dialling network construction plans. What motivated me most was that telecommunications was essentially a means of overcoming spatial distances. If we could convince the country as a whole, and our customers in particular, of that fact, they would buy and use our products, and our company would be established on a firm footing. It seemed only logical that NEC should act in accordance with this proposition.

I therefore proposed a plan to build regional plants in three different categories, divided roughly according to size. Regional characteristics and geographical conditions would be taken into consideration in determining which plant size would go where. The first type, type A, would have around 1,500 employees; type B would employ around 1,000; and type C about 500. As a further refinement, we would not call them just "plants" but would organize each as an independent corporation with a corporate name consisting of "NEC" and the appropriate place name. A type A plant would be called after the name of the region, and types B and C after the name of the prefecture.

In tandem with the establishment of these regional plants we laid plans to expand our nationwide sales network. Locating manufacturing facilities throughout the country, bearing the company name and offering employment opportunities to the local residents, would, we hoped, increase familiarity with NEC and have a synergistic effect on our marketing policy. The strategy would also prove highly effective for corporate public relations.

After Yokohama in 1968, the only other large-scale plant we built in the greater Tokyo region was the Abiko plant in Chiba Prefecture, where we encountered many difficulties in acquiring land. That plant was completed in 1982 as a model office automation center and serves as a technological hub for cable communications. In addition we have facilities in Otsuki and Yamanashi City in Yamanashi Prefecture; because these are so close to Tokyo they are not independent corporations but NEC's own plants.

Establishing Regional Self-Sufficiency

As each local NEC company was an independent corporation, so naturally each had to have its own executives. Having full-time executive officers – president, executive vice president, senior vice president, etc. – living in the local area was desirable not only to provide sound management with direct knowledge of local conditions, but also because it would increase the sense of pride, responsibility, and self-confidence of the people who held those positions. Each of these companies has the function of supporting one or more of NEC's manufacturing divisions; as NEC Corporation wholly owns each of them and handles their sales, we came to call them "regional manufacturing subsidiaries."

By 1972, when Prime Minister Kakuei Tanaka first proposed "restructuring the Japanese archipelago" in order to disperse industrial development away from the Tokyo–Osaka industrial belt, NEC's regional subsidiaries already extended throughout the country from north to south, and our decentralization plans were beginning to bear fruit. I rank NEC's plant decentralization program along with the division system as the two basic principles upon which my management strategy is based.

Into the World Market

In fiscal 1966 NEC's foreign sales exceeded 10 billion yen for the first time. Because total sales for that year had climbed over the 100 billion yen mark to 102 billion yen, the export figure of 10.7 billion yen gave us an export rate of 10.5 percent.

To put this in the context of our annual performance since fiscal 1964, the year I became president, our unconsolidated sales that year totalled 71.4 billion yen, of which 9.4 percent – 6.7 billion yen – were from exports. In 1965 sales were 85.6 billion yen and exports 6.9 billion yen or 8.1 percent of the total; in 1967 sales were 113 billion yen and exports 11 billion yen or 9.7 percent; and in 1968 sales were 149.5 billion yen and exports 28.5 billion yen for an export rate of 19 percent.

The figures for fiscal 1968 rocketed NEC from fifty-eighth to twenty-seventh in the export rankings for Japan published in *President* magazine. Back in those days export growth was regarded as a valuable contribution to the Japanese economy. In 1964 I was awarded the Meritorious Services Award for Export Promotion by the Prime Minister of Japan, and NEC was recognized every year for its contributions to exports by the Ministry of International Trade and Industry.

I was confident that because communications coverage inevitably transcended national borders to interconnect the entire world, communications systems would constantly evolve until a global network had been completed and perfected. By seeking markets overseas and creating a presence for itself in the international arena, NEC was building on a foundation of bright future prospects.

Overcoming the Constraints of the ITT Link

As I have already mentioned, NEC's basic strategy for future development was not to limit ourselves to the communications business within Japan but to tap Japanese private sector demand for industrial electronics and enter the overseas market in electronics and communications. When we had actually begun exporting, however, one serious limitation kept getting in our way. After the war, when NEC had resumed relations with ITT, we had signed a technical agreement covering almost the whole spectrum of communications equipment and parts, one of the conditions of which was a restriction on our export territory for the products we manufactured using ITT technology. This would now have to be regarded as one of the disadvantages of the technical tie-up; the other side of the coin, as it were.

Believing that if we increased our own technological prowess to the point where we could offer our proprietary technology to ITT we would be able to modify these conditions, we worked diligently to this end. The export to ITT of the technology for our over-the-horizon microwave communications system and carrier transmission equipment in January 1962 was the breakthrough. Until that time the products that NEC could export had been limited to areas where ITT did not have competing technology; and even with product lines that were not subject to the territory clause, whenever we succeeded in putting in a bid in the highly competitive international market, we faced many unexpected ordeals in the areas of pricing and methods of doing business. Realizing that only through this process could we learn what it took for our products to be competitive internationally, I called on the entire company not to be content with the Japanese market but to acquire the expertise to bring our exports up to international standards.

Targeting the Developing Countries

Since almost all the advanced countries had their own manufacturers of communications equipment, NEC decided to target the developing countries first. Historically, the market in many of the Third World countries was dominated by companies from the advanced countries that had once been their colonial masters. We would only be able to win contracts in these countries by offering better technology at a better price. The export totals cited above were achieved only after much trial and error. The one small blessing for NEC was that the forces of nationalism and modernization in the developing countries often took the form of trying to shake off the influence of their former colonial masters, in trade and technology as in other areas.

To provide the developing countries with communications infrastructure; to cooperate with them and accommodate their aspirations for local production as a means of achieving economic independence – if we could fulfill these goals the door stood open for us to establish in those places Japanese companies untainted by colonial history. NEC first set its sights on the developing countries in nearby southeast Asia, including Taiwan, the Philippines, Thailand, Indonesia, and Singapore. Next we turned west to India and Pakistan; then Iraq, Iran, and Turkey; then east to Mexico, Brazil, Peru, Colombia, and Venezuela; then south to Australia and New Zealand. NEC's first overseas company after the war was a joint venture in 1958, Taiwan Telecommunications Industry Company. Our partner at first was Tung Cheng Dong Electric Company, a leading trading company, but we came to feel that the difference in the nature of their business and that of a manufacturing company like NEC was too great; so after some deliberation we changed to Tatung Company in 1966. We began to invest in Taiwan Television Enterprise in 1962 and Pakistan Television in 1965, and established overseas companies such as NEC de México and NEC do Brazil in 1968, and NEC Australia Pty in 1969.

Our market then expanded to the African continent. Back in the early 1960s, when Emperor Haile Selassie of Ethiopia visited Japan, the crown prince and his entourage visited our Tamagawa plant. That visit was the beginning of NEC's business with Ethiopia, which has continued to the present day. NEC has contributed to that country's telecommunications modernization plans by building microwave routes and delivering ground stations, crossbar switching equipment, and broadcasting equipment. In April 1967, NEC received its first order from Morocco for a microwave communications facility. NEC had been specifically asked to submit a proposal by the Moroccan minister of posts, telegraph, and telephones when he had visited Japan the preceding year. We succeeded in ousting the French manufacturer that had been Morocco's traditional supplier and won the bid. This success led to large orders for microwave equipment from other African nations.

In April 1974 I visited Egypt as the head of an economic mission sent by the Japanese government. I met President Anwar Sadat, Vice Premier Dr Mohammed Abdel Kader Hatem, and other government officials and was able to contribute in a small way to the promotion of economic exchange between Japan and Egypt. In January 1979 I toured Egypt, Sudan, and Algeria. I have vivid memories of inspecting satellite communications ground station installations and microwave radio repeater stations built by NEC and visiting construction sites to cheer on NEC personnel working in North Africa. We subsequently expanded our markets to include Libya, Kenya, Zambia, Ghana, Nigeria, Guinea, and Madagascar.

Because the overseas customers NEC dealt with were tantamount to the governments of these countries, it was most effective to have the company president meet with the head of state or the relevant government officials, both as a sign of respect and as a way of strengthening contacts. I therefore familiarized myself with the internal affairs of all the countries with which we did business and tried to visit as many of them as possible in order to deepen my understanding of local conditions. In this way we gradually became skillful at the export business and amassed a growing list of successes in winning contracts. Our basic principle in this move overseas was: *Go to the countries that welcome us.*

Faced with an increasingly tight labor market at home, NEC did not immediately leap into local production overseas, as many Western companies did, but chose instead to branch out into other parts of Japan. But the growth of our exports eventually rendered the need for local production urgent. Of course, there were still great disparities in local abilities to make high-tech intensive products like microwave communications and switching equipment and to master the technologies and engineering embodied in them. The conditions in each country were always different – whether in terms of the circumstances surrounding our venture, or the products we dealt in, or the form they took. What was possible at the local level was operations, maintenance, and repairs; the next stage was assembly. In this way we gradually found ways of accommodating the desire for local production. Beginning by helping to lay the communications infrastructure in the developing countries, we then moved on to export entire plant facilities for broadcasting systems and microwave radio communications systems. After we had succeeded in developing a complete solid-state microwave communications system in 1963, we had defeated our foreign rivals and ranked number one in the world, winning a reputation as "NEC the giant-killer."

Knocking on the Door of America

Our next big ambition was to enter the North American market – but when would the best opportunity come? In the fall of 1965 information reached us that the Pentagon was going ahead with the Kanto microwave project, the installation of a microwave communications network to link US military radar stations throughout the Kanto Plains area around Tokyo. I wanted more than anything for NEC to win this contract. But since this large-scale project was being planned by the American forces in Japan, it was naturally assumed that the necessary equipment would be brought in from America for installation. No matter how many times I approached the authorities the doors remained tightly shut.

Because it seemed to me absurd that the bidding system for the building of a microwave communications network to be used in Japan should exclude NEC, I resolved to approach the Pentagon directly when I visited the US in January 1966. Before I left Japan I wrote a polite letter requesting an appointment with the Secretary of Defense, Robert S. McNamara, who had attracted my attention many years earlier because of his sharp and rational approach to management. Although I was not able to meet with Secretary McNamara, I did meet an assistant secretary. The Pentagon had a "Buy American" rule for military supplies, I learned; and even if it did elect to buy from NEC, its products would have to be 50 percent cheaper than American products to win the sale. Yet after lengthy negotiations

NEC's bid was accepted, and in 1968 we succeeded in winning this large special order worth a total of 5 billion yen. In the final analysis the reason why we won the contract was that *only we, NEC, had the technology that met US military requirements*. Moreover, we completed it ahead of schedule, winning a bonus said to be unprecedented in US military history.

Although this contract was a special case, it gave us the confidence to sell NEC products to the advanced industrial countries. We had opened our first US office in New York in 1963. It began with market research and gradually moved into sales activities. This sales outlet, originally known as Nippon Electric New York, continued to grow, and in 1971 it was reorganized as a manufacturing company under the new name of NEC America.

Competing with the US: Technology Gap or Management Gap?

Whenever I took part in international conferences in the US and joined in discussions about US–European affairs, the focus inevitably turned to something called "the technology gap." I myself was painfully aware of the technology gap between the US and Japan, and so this way of looking at things matched my own understanding of the situation. But in those days nobody thought of Japan when this topic was being discussed; the discussants were, of course, referring to the technology gap between the US and Europe. The root of the European complaints against the US was that the causes of the technology gap could be traced to the development of US technology by the military–industrial complex: that is to say, such technology was not the product of commercial development but was financed by the US government, in other words, by the American taxpayer. The gist of their criticism was that US industry's share in the international market was based on technology it did not have to pay for. But Robert McNamara argued that the gap between the US and Europe was not a technological one but rather one of management. Almost all the advanced technology the US then possessed had germinated in Europe but had been developed in the United States. It was this American ability to foster development that he called "the management gap."

In view of the recent trade frictions between the US and Japan, I cannot help feeling we should take another look at these past discussions of unfair international trade practises. McNamara was called "Mr Computer," and the computer gap was then regarded in Japan as yet another aspect of the discrepancy in management strength between the US and Japan. This was the view of the MIS (management information systems) study mission, also known as the Okumura mission, formed by the Japan Committee for Economic Development (Keizai Doyukai) in the fall of 1967. As the head of NEC, which regarded itself as a computer maker, I had some interest in the commercial use of computers for data processing. But at the time we ourselves were still studying the installation of computers for company use. Moreover, hardly a day went by when we did not feel pressured by the gap between US and Japanese products in the computer area. To put it another way, I freely recognized that this was an area where we lagged behind – to use a favorite proverb, it was a matter of the cobbler's wife going barefoot – and that we would have to wait for the day when we could demonstrate our true strengths.

Discussions about the gaps between the US, Europe, and Japan, a key approach to understanding the worldwide industrial situation in those days, were illuminating for many reasons and a matter of intense speculation for me. Simply to posit gaps between countries in terms of specific levels of national strength to be reached was not only meaningless, it did not inspire any ambition to do so. Instead, we should include in the calculation the growth rates of the various countries: The basis of the comparison should be the angle of elevation at which each country was growing. Even if there was a gap in the existing levels, if we added the factor of time and extended the lines representing the angle of elevation, we ought to be able to see when these lines would meet – and cross. *The angle of elevation analogy would also encourage us to "look up and catch up."*

What sustained me during this period, in fact, was my hope in this angle of elevation for Japan and for NEC – our national and corporate growth rates. The phrase "catch up" had not yet caught on in Japan at the time, but to catch up and overtake the levels of the advanced countries of North America and Europe gradually became a popular slogan throughout Japan. Yet if we were to catch up we had to *learn*, from ourselves as well as from others.

5

Theory and Practice:
Management as Learning

In addition to my strictly corporate duties as president I regularly took the opportunity and allotted the time to make statements outside the company. Such activities were, it is true, part of our corporate public relations efforts; on the other hand, these public statements seldom if ever dealt with NEC itself but focused on topics such as the Japanese economy or Japanese industry. That is to say, I hardly ever on these occasions discussed any of our company's specific undertakings or achievements. I took great care in choosing what lectures and articles I would agree to do because I believed that each afforded me a unique opportunity to learn and to reflect on my role as president. The many experiences arising out of my overseas business trips also proved to be effective learning situations.

The difficulty in taking opportunities to reflect and to gain new insights, of course, was finding the time. The number of documents that I had to glance through each day was really quite staggering. I asked employees writing in-house memos to confine their ideas whenever possible to a single sheet of paper: In a long memo it was often difficult to pin down what the author was trying to say. I also received several English-language letters from abroad every day, although I had limited time to spend reading them. Nevertheless I believed it important to keep abreast of ideas and developments. What books was I reading in those days and what did I learn from my readings? Around that period I wrote a presidential memo on management books, the text of which I insert here.

Learning from General Motors

Our company is in the midst of a management reform program that began the year before last and is forging ahead. I believe it would be worthwhile to examine the position corporate restructuring holds in the evolution of modern management practices. Several excellent books on management have been published recently: One that deserves careful reading is *My Years with General Motors*, by Alfred P. Sloan Jr, who as GM's chief executive officer developed that company into the number one corporation in the world. Other works of this type worth listing here include *A Business and its Beliefs* by Thomas J. Watson Jr, president of IBM, and *Vitality in a Business Enterprise* by Frederick R. Kapell, president of AT&T.

What these books have in common is that the authors of all of them, the CEOs of America's leading corporate giants, frankly and explicitly discuss the struggles their companies faced in attaining their present prosperity and give valuable lessons for the future. Through these works we can become more aware of our own present situation and learn what we ought to do and how we ought to do it in order to grow in the years ahead. I have therefore written down a few of my impressions about *My Years with General Motors*, which I present here to all of you as food for thought.

General Principles

1. The level of corporate management in our company lags more than ten years behind that of US firms. Matters that our company is now treating as basic problems to be solved are ones that GM tackled a generation ago.

2. Although some people have the impression that our ideas on management reform are a direct import of US-style management theory, it is not a matter of American style or Japanese style. What needs to be understood is that our company faces the same sort of circumstances that all advanced corporations have faced during the process of their development and that many of the solutions that they have discovered through trial and error can also be applied to our company.

3. During the past fifty years the trail has been blazed and a well-beaten path laid down for solving several of the basic problems faced by all corporations, and many of these lessons are being codified into rules. Since these rules are logical and apply to any company, it is inevitable that they will be applicable to our company as well.

4. Whether the company is Hughes or Honeywell, it is reasonable to assume that the basic philosophy and methods of corporate management,

with which our company and other Japanese firms are now coming to grips, do not essentially differ.

5. Knowing the history of other companies not only helps us to know these companies better; it ought also to be useful in helping us understand the position of our own company and its weak points and strong points relative to others. While reading *My Years with General Motors*, it is important to consider what light it throws on our own company and the steps we can or ought to take.

6. We can learn from actual real-life examples what sort of problems front-running corporations must inevitably face and which responses are likely to lead to success or failure.

7. Books like this one give us some foreknowledge of what measures our company will need to adopt in the future. Some of these steps we will have to work out for ourselves, but excellent formulas already exist for dealing with several others.

8. While we are in the process of dealing with a particular problem we are apt to lose sight of its relation to the whole or its position in the scheme of things. By reading *My Years with General Motors* we can develop a broader outlook and understand the significance of each of several different problems without losing sight of the main issue.

9. It also makes it easier for us to see what factors we have omitted or overlooked or where we have fallen behind, and to decide what features are amenable to correction or reorganization.

10. *My Years with General Motors* is being widely used as a textbook on management within Japanese companies. Works of this sort should, as a matter of course, be required reading for all those involved in corporate management.

11. Just as soldiers traditionally study strategy, in-depth reading of actual examples of management practices ought to be included along with the basics of on-the-job training. Not only would this raise the level of management by corporate staff, it would improve their skills in developing and guiding their subordinates.

Specific Points

1. The central task facing Sloan in a highly diffuse company such as GM was how to provide it with a single system that would integrate and co ordinate the activities of GM's central administration and its numerous divisions. The book offers a model for our own company to follow in the relations established between the head office, including the staff, and each of the divisions; or, to put it another way, between top management and the actual production line.

2. The book shows in concrete terms the importance of financial

controls and gives actual examples of how they operate. It thus provides many points of reference for remedying our own deficiencies in this area. The book is particularly good on appropriations for capital spending, internal reserves, and inventory control for raw and semifinished materials.

3. As a method of evaluating divisional performance, Sloan sees profit as a function of cost, price, and volume, and gives cogent reasons why return on investment is his primary yardstick. His discussion suggests that the proposal in my New Year's directive for improving management efficiency hits the mark and lends support for its implementation.

4. The division system is now becoming common practice in Japan. This book traces the origin of this system at GM, outlines the process by which it was formed and organized, and helps us to understand how to co ordinate relations among the divisions in respect of products and parts.

5. The book shows how to win the mass market by formulating a product policy and a pricing policy, adopting measures that will respond flexibly in times of economic upsurge or slowdown, and setting up a distribution system.

6. On staff–line relations in the areas of research, engineering, and development, we can take many hints on how to operate effectively without inviting confusion. The book also discusses the distinctions between matters that are the concern of central office staff and those that belong to division staffs, and shows the economic effectiveness of the former in holding down costs.

7. After distinguishing between the policy-making functions of committees and administrative functions, Sloan explains the need to develop unity of opinion throughout the company and discusses ways to achieve mutual understanding by upgrading the proposal system, the reporting system for divisions and sales dealers, and other information mechanisms.

8. On the subject of grasping changes in the market and responding to them immediately, he not only shows how GM's concept of management and its business philosophy differ from Ford's but also gives actual examples of ways to promote market development.

9. His discussion of the way he operated as CEO and the structure of his top management group made me acutely aware of the need for further efforts and reforms in those areas in our own company.

10. Finally, not being prepared for change and lacking a plan to cope with it can destroy a company. An organization, no matter how well prepared it may be, does not run automatically; it only provides the operational framework. In the last analysis it is always individuals who must make the decisions and take responsibility.

My Years with General Motors convinced me that there is no end to the work remaining for us to do. As I noted at the outset, this list of points that

I found instructive or noteworthy is simply a guideline for your own personal study. I believe that the possibilities of what you can learn from this book and the ideas that you can take away from it are limitless, and I am confident that you will do so. I understand that this sort of study activity is already being carried out by some people within the company, and I earnestly hope that it will develop spontaneously into a company tradition.

Sifting the Literature; the Importance of Culture

In the main I preferred books written by business executives: I did not want to be overwhelmed with theory. I have already mentioned the book by Ralph J. Cordiner, the head of GE. There were, however, several books by academics from which I profited greatly, such as *The Practice of Management* and *Managing for Results – Economic Tasks and Risk-Taking Decisions* by Professor Peter F. Drucker.

Of all these works, one book came as a revelation to me. This was *Personal Relations in a Vertical Society* by Chie Nakane, then an associate professor at the University of Tokyo. This book, which I read soon after it appeared in 1967, explained the criteria Japanese use to create a social order and the vertical relationships that bind this order together. One of these criteria is ranking on the basis of seniority. I had been intent on building a streamlined and efficient corporate structure; now I was forced to reconsider my ideas. Power and position alone are not enough to make a corporate organization run efficiently: others operate on a more emotional level. Many passages in the book reminded me of things I had forgotten and cast light on previous experiences. *I realized that business would not run smoothly if I used only a Western rationalistic approach. I must not lose sight of the fact that the Japanese lived by a different set of emotional responses, which had evolved out of a tradition and cultural landscape completely different from that of the West.*

Although much discussed, the theories of Marshall McLuhan did not strike a responsive chord in me. Because his ideas dealt with media trends they aroused a lot of interest among people in the broadcasting business, but I did not feel that they had the same resonance as Machlup's ideas on the knowledge industry. As for Herman Kahn's economic predictions, I was both attracted and uneasy, wondering how anyone could possibly be so optimistic. I found nothing strange in the idea that by the next century Japan would have a *per capita* GNP of $10,000 because the twenty-first century was then still in the distant future. But I found it hard to believe that Japan had that much potential. The Japanese gross national product had just passed that of West Germany and reached $200 billion. My own feeling was that it would be no easy matter in the days ahead to raise that to $300 or $400 billion.

A Test Case: The First Overseas Establishment

On August 26, 1969, I took off from Haneda Airport for Brazil. This was my sixth overseas business trip already that year and my third visit to Brazil since I had first gone there in October 1966. From Japan, Brazil really is the other side of the world, the gateway to the vast continent and Latin American culture. Only a few centuries ago no white man had lived here: now some Japanese were about to open a manufacturing company. Not many years earlier such a plan would have been inconceivable.

NEC had already fulfilled an order for a microwave communications trunk line to connect the major cities of Brazil. We had also accepted a request from the Brazilian government to provide the necessary expertise to maintain, repair, and locally produce radio communications equipment, switching equipment, and carrier transmission equipment. Originally, North American and European companies had controlled the Brazilian market. Indeed, it was that domination which had formed the background against which NEC, with no past history of involvement, had been invited to Brazil. Since our policy was to go where we were welcomed, even though it was a foreign country where the language was unfamiliar, in November 1968 we established NEC do Brazil, a wholly-owned subsidiary capitalized at US$660,000, in São Paolo and began to build a factory at Guarulhos, a suburb of that city. The factory had now been completed and was about to begin operations, and I was on my way to attend the opening ceremonies.

The new factory was located on the east side of the Dutra highway, facing the street. The red NEC logo stood out clearly against the chalk-white building – a beautiful sight to behold! Inside, the assembly lines were in place to produce crossbar switching systems, and the components manufacturing shop was also ready for action.

At the opening ceremonies on September 4, the words of welcome from the local authorities were followed by speeches expressing their hopes for its future growth. As the representative of the parent company, I made an impassioned statement about the importance we in Tokyo accorded to improving Brazil's communications infrastructure and to the contributions this local company would make to that process. At the same time I expressed our sincere gratitude to the local government and the city officials for their cooperation. I did feel a bit self-conscious about one point, however. The entire area of the plant was only 18,000 square feet, and it would employ only 150 people. The place was too small to be considered a normal plant, but I declared my hopes that from these modest beginnings it would one day grow into a large factory with 100,000 square feet of floor space and 2,000 employees. In fact, by the end of 1989 it employed 3,500 employees in a building containing 360,000 square feet of floor space.

The opening ceremony for the microwave communications circuit that NEC had supplied had been scheduled for September 2, but something had interfered with the Brazilian President's schedule. Not only was the opening delayed, there were even assassination rumors. The university and several public buildings in São Paolo showed signs of recent damage from terrorist bombings. Yet although one could not overlook the uncertainties of such "country risks" as fluctuations in currency rates, public unrest, military dictatorship, and nationalism, Brazil is a country of which much is expected in the twenty-first century, and NEC looked forward to the day when we could establish an appropriate foothold there. NEC do Brazil was our very first overseas establishment and for me one of the most important of the foreign subsidiaries established during my presidency. Success or failure in Brazil would have profound implications for future NEC expansion.

Exchanging Ideas: Growth, Character, Perpetuation

I returned to New York via Rio de Janeiro. Just being back in an English-speaking country, being able to read the newspapers again, made me feel as though I had returned home. I pondered once more the importance of being able to understand the local language, and sympathized deeply with our employees in Brazil who had to cope with the language problem every day.

The next morning I visited Bell Laboratories in Murray Hill, New

Jersey, electronics mecca and one of the world's leading research centers, with a staff of 4,500. Here I was warmly welcomed by President James B. Fisk, my old friend Dr Jack A. Morton, and Dr William H. Doherty. Two years earlier they had shown me their picturephone, the television telephone that they were developing. This time, too, they presented me with an array of technological goodies – an electroluminescence display, an updated version of the picturephone, and a bubble memory containing 500 million pieces of memory elements in one cubic inch. The sequel to that story came when I returned home and announced to the NEC research team that Bell Laboratories was in the process of developing a bubble memory. Imagine my surprise to learn that six months earlier a young NEC researcher had presented a research report on bubble memories at an international conference. Depend on NEC researchers to come through, I thought.

After lunch I returned to the New York office to meet Stephen F. Keating, the head of our computer partners Honeywell. We exchanged ideas about developing a new series of machines and discussed trends in the US and European industrial world: then I set off for a party at six o'clock at the Hotel Pierre for NEC's important American customers.

The next day I went to Chicago for the first time since my visit two years earlier as part of a government mission to the midwest. As a result of that mission NEC had established a new base in Chicago for our consumer appliance business, and this was a follow-up visit. At the same time I paid a courtesy call to Magnavox Company in Fort Wayne, about forty minutes away from Chicago by helicopter. NEC's consumer electronics division, New Nippon Electric, now NEC Home Electronics, was exporting TV sets to Magnavox on an OEM (original equipment manufacturer) basis.

From Chicago, as from New York, I could easily telephone to Tokyo to keep up with all that was happening during my absence. After a two-night stop there to recover from jet-lag, I headed for San Francisco, the main stop on my itinerary for this trip. I had seldom been to San Francisco, because few of the companies NEC did business with were located there. I was going this time for the fourth International Industrial Conference (IIC) on September 15–19. Nearly 700 leaders of industry from all over the world would be gathering for this conference, which convened every four years in San Francisco under the auspices of the Conference Board and the Stanford Research Institute. I had been invited to attend and to participate in a panel session on "The Job of the Chief Executive Officer," alongside representatives of the US, Germany, and Brazil.

At the opening ceremony David Rockefeller, president of the Chase Manhattan Bank and star of the US financial world, gave the keynote address. Janus-like he looked back over the 1960s, which were drawing to a close, and ahead to the coming 1970s. He posed the question whether economic growth was an adequate yardstick to measure social progress and argued that the fundamental issues of the times, including world population growth and the North–South problem, stemmed from the social estrangement between the rich and the poor. It was a high-minded speech delivered in a cool and dispassionate manner, his tone of delivery in sharp contrast to the disturbing topics he examined.

Two points about this conference deserve special mention. The first arises from the questionnaire sent by the conference sponsors to all participants, the world's top executives, the results of which were summarized in a report. Particularly noteworthy was the response to the question, "What is the ultimate responsibility of a chief executive officer?" The answers boiled down to three issues: "growth," "character," and "perpetuation." The other concerns Fletcher Byrom, who presided over the panel I was on and later gave me a small pamphlet containing words of advice to his successor when he left the presidency of Koppers Company. He called this his "commandments," the nine rules that all executives ought to know:

1 Hang loose.
2 Listen for the winds of change.
3 Increase the number of interfaces.
4 Keep your intuition well lubricated, but
5 make sure you know where the information is buried.
6 Use growth as a means of getting and keeping good people, and use those people as a means of achieving continued growth. The two are interdependent.
7 Avoid like the plague those specialists who are only specialists.
8 Set your priorities in terms of the probable, rather than the merely possible, but
9 make sure you generate a reasonable number of mistakes (because rectifying them will keep you on your toes).

The reason these words impressed me was that Byrom, a CEO who had evolved what was considered a progressive business philosophy even by US standards, regarded as completely natural many ideas that we Orientals hold. This made me realize that Americans worried about the same sort of management problems that concerned a Japanese like myself. His fourth commandment in particular was completely unexpected. American executives like Robert S. McNamara and Harold S. Geneen got hold of the figures, analyzed them shrewdly, and adopted the best plan from the choices available. That was the method of scientific rationalism, which I had assumed to underlie the American approach to business. However Byrom's approach closely resembled the essence of ancient Oriental philosophy. The five days of the International Industrial Conference seem to have existed for that single insight. I was delighted to have learned such a valuable lesson.

My trip did not end with the IIC. I skipped the last day of meetings and left San Francisco immediately after my panel was over to go to Los Angeles, where a party had been scheduled to celebrate the opening of NEC's Los Angeles office. (The reception was on Sunday, a day which normally would have been avoided, but we had wanted to have an informal party to which especially close friends would be invited.) That afternoon I met Dr Lawrence A. Hyland of Hughes Aircraft, who invited me to visit him the following day at his ranch. He would come to the hotel the next morning and pick us up (my wife had accompanied me on this trip because of all the social engagements). I readily accepted his warm invitation: Indeed, I was very curious about what US executives did to relax, how they made use of their leisure time to refresh their sources of energy. I was fascinated to hear that some American executives raised racehorses or spent every Sunday building houses, which they later sold. The IIC executive report contained detailed statistics about the professional life of the world's leading chief executives, their ages, careers, and areas of expertise: my visit to Hyland's ranch, I thought, would give me the opportunity to learn at firsthand how American executives spent their private moments.

By now I had been away from head office for nearly a month, my longest business trip since I had assumed the presidency five years earlier. Fortunately, the company continued to grow smoothly. The IIC had given me the opportunity to confirm that the course I had adopted as CEO was right on track and, despite the seemingly infinite variety of individual details, did not deviate significantly from the direction other corporate executives worldwide were following.

Technology and Society

Slightly more than one month after the International Industrial Conference, after a trip to Taiwan and barely enough time in the Tokyo office to get my chair warm, I found myself back in San Francisco.

A few years earlier, in 1966, a nonprofit organization called the Japan Techno-Economics Society had been founded, primarily by a group of industrialists with backgrounds in engineering who believed that in the days ahead science and technology would have an increasingly important role to play in the economy and society. Most of its members were drawn either from the government Science and Technology Agency or NTT, or the private firms that did business with them. In 1967 the group, of which I was a member, held a symposium with the very timely theme "Preparing for the Advent of the Postindustrial Society." Because we all shared the belief that the United States was in the vanguard of a new civilization, the group made plans to take a firsthand look at how American industrial society was changing, in the belief that this would be instructive for Japan. At that time, the mass media were predicting that the four most promising areas of industry would be information, education, space development, and oceanic development.

A study group called the Industrial Forecasting Special Research Team was formed. At first I categorically declined the request to lead it, on the grounds that I had no time to prepare and was not qualified to lead such an important mission, but relented when I was told that I would have Yujiro Hayashi and Noboru Makino as my associates so that the burden would not be too onerous. The group that set off for San Francisco on November 3, 1969 composed of more than thirty people from industry, academia, and the media. Professor Kazuo Noda of Rikkyo University acted as the group's adviser and provided valuable support.

The mission visited the think tanks and research centers along the US West Coast, then went to the Cape Canaveral Space Center in Florida, which was at the height of the Apollo spacecraft program. After touring universities and research institutes in the Midwest and along the East Coast, we concluded our schedule with a visit to Washington, DC.

At the Stanford Research Institute, the head researcher explained that American business was moving out of the age of corporate marriages and into a period of corporate divorces. At the Salk Institute for Biological Studies a young Japanese researcher told us that it would soon be possible to determine the sex of an unborn baby. If my memory serves me correctly, that young man was Dr Susumu Tonegawa, who nearly twenty years later was awarded the 1987 Nobel Prize for Medicine and Physiology. Among the *savants* at the Center for Democratic Institutions, a Los Angeles think tank, was one person who, in response to questions by our group, warned that the unchecked development of the computer might one day lead to the domination of the machine over man.

In June Apollo 11 had landed on the moon and had brought rocks back from the lunar surface, which as a child I, like all Japanese children, had been told was inhabited by a rabbit making rice cakes. The advancement of human knowledge, the triumph of science and technology, had been brought via television into the world's living rooms with breathtaking immediacy, and no one could guess at the possibilities that lay ahead ten or twenty years down the road.

The trip recalled impressions of previous visits as well. In 1967 Detroit, the capital of the automotive industry, which was the backbone of US manufacturing, had been the site of widespread rioting. I remembered that when I had visited Lansing, the capital of Michigan, with the Kikawada mission about that time, the governor, who was being touted as a potential presidential candidate, welcomed us with words that contained both envy and irony. The Japanese, he said, had entered the revolving door later than the Europeans and Americans but would be able to pull off the trick of coming out ahead of everyone else. At every place we visited, on both that mission and this, we felt like the second coming of the Iwakura mission that had visited America almost exactly 100 years earlier to discover the sources of Western wealth and power.

What sort of new ideas and outlooks could we expect to learn about in Washington? With a sense of expectancy we visited the Office of Science and Technology, the final stop on our itinerary. Before we left Tokyo we all imagined a rosy-colored future for industry, the key to which lay in systems engineering. Shattering these expectations, the President's adviser on science and technology, Dr Raymond Bowers of Cornell University, began his talk by saying that although the mechanics for space travel could be worked out by scientific or mathematical formulas, the really urgent priority was tackling the problems facing human society here on earth. After discussing the seriousness of these problems, in areas ranging from the cities to the environment, he concluded by saying that "choice" and "assessment" were becoming the most pressing matters in dealing with modern technology. He then passed out a document explaining the National Environment Policy Act, which he cited as an issue of the gravest concern to President Nixon. We could not believe our ears.

After intensive questioning about new trends our group finally asked about the future of computers, as a follow-up on the management information systems mission of three years earlier. Dr Bowers, disclaiming expertise in the field, called on Andrew Aines to respond. Aines explained that computers were indeed an important issue, and while there were many views on the subject in America, his own opinion could be summed up in three words: and on the blackboard he wrote *deus ex machina*.

On our final evening in Washington 250,000 people marched down Pennsylvania Avenue. Police cars were stationed near the Shoreham Hotel, where we were staying. The crowd was demonstrating against the war in Vietnam, calling for peace on earth rather than the conquest of space. We had come to the United States to discover the industrial trends of the next generation. The conclusions we had reached seemed to be symbolized by the events of that day in Washington.

On returning to Japan, we drew up a report and presented our conclusions in the form of the following seven proposals:

1　America may not necessarily be the model we should look to for future development. The time has come for us to set out and plan for a unique course of growth for Japan.
2　To ensure the sound development of the social system we will need to establish and disseminate the practices of technology assessment.
3　To cope with the rapidly expanding role of systems engineering in industry we will need to train systems engineers and techno-economists.
4　We will need to set up think tanks to deal with the increasing complexity of decision-making.
5　We will need to be more heavily oriented toward technology-intensive products to cope with changes in industrial structure.
6　In the area of corporate planning we will need to do away with the *status quo* approach to management by adopting modern planning

methods and an openness to new ideas arising from the individual executive's experience and intuition.

7 In an age of systems engineering the need for new types of small and medium-sized businesses will increase.

When the time came to present our report, as mission leader I was a bit concerned as to how to handle the warnings about the negative aspects of technology represented by the US National Environment Policy Act. That was not the sort of triumphant account of our travels that everyone expected to hear. After some discussion the mission members decided to call a spade a spade and not conceal anything, yet at the same time to maintain a cautious attitude to avoid any confusion that might arise from misreporting or mistaken understanding.

Before going on this mission, I had believed that technology was an effective and useful tool in the development of society; now my eyes were open to the fact that it was a two-edged sword not only capable of delivering great benefits to human society but with the potential for much destruction as well. I do not believe that any mission has been so full of daily surprises and deep impressions as this one was. Even if what I had learned from the mission could not immediately be put into action in the corporate management of NEC, it provided invaluable food for thought when coping with the climate of constant rapid change in the days ahead.

Although the IIC meetings in September and the industrial forecasting mission in November were both opportunities to get close to the heart of America, what I took away from the two experiences was radically different. While the former strengthened my confidence in my management skills, the latter made me painfully aware that 1969 marked some sort of turning point and that the society in which we lived was about to enter a new phase of history. In the months leading up to EXPO '70 in Osaka, the pace of the Japanese economy seemed to pick up speed as if approaching some final culmination to the years of high-level growth. As head of the Industrial Forecast Special Research Team, I had received my baptism of fire, and even though I could not find the appropriate words to describe the undercurrents of the age, I felt a deepening awareness that the world was changing greatly.

6

Corporate Identity and the
Drive for Quality

The Crisis of Progress and the Club of Rome

In April 1971, with the various tasks of the new fiscal year that began on April 1 behind me, I flew to Ottawa via New York to attend the second meeting of the Club of Rome. Although it was April the last traces of snow were still visible. Nearby ran the Ottawa River, posted with "No Swimming" signs because the river was polluted. For the Sumida River in the middle of Tokyo to be polluted was one thing, but I was surprised that the environmental pollution problems I had heard discussed recently in Washington had reached as far as Canada and affected this river in the midst of such beautiful natural surroundings.

Two years earlier, at the International Industrial Conference in San Francisco, I had returned to the Fairmont Hotel after listening to David Rockefeller's keynote address at the Masonic Memorial Shrine Auditorium and was sitting in the lobby when two tall gentlemen pushed their way through the crowd and came up to me. "Are you Kobayashi of NEC?" one of them asked me, stretching out his hand. It was Aurelio Peccei, who had come to the conference from Italy. The other man was Dr Hugo Thiemann, director of the Battelle Memorial Institute in Geneva, Switzerland. In June of that year I had received a letter from Peccei inviting me to join the Club of Rome to study the future. The letter was only a few lines long, and I could not quite grasp what it was all about. Now I had the opportunity to find out. When I mentioned the subject, Peccei launched into an impassioned speech, the gist of which was that as fathers and grandfathers with children and grandchildren of our own we had to act while there was still time to prevent the destruction of the earth, our common home as members of the human race, and this was his aim in founding the Club of Rome. This was a cause I could well appreciate, and I gladly agreed to join. So here I was in Ottawa.

The main reason I joined the Club of Rome and felt deep sympathy with its aims was that I had a profound interest in and concern about the future of the human race; but that was not the only reason. I was also interested in the way European intellectuals from different countries would get together from time to time to exchange ideas and put them into action and felt that the Japanese would have much to learn from this experience. You might say I felt I ought to understand what a club was and how it functioned.

The Club of Rome meetings lasted for three days and centered on MIT Professor Jay Wright Forrester's theory of world dynamics. Discussions focused on five major problem areas, analyzing them through the use of computer simulation and showing in chart form the difficulties the human race would encounter in the year 2020 or 2030. The five variables contributing to the "predicament of mankind" were population, the food supply, natural resources, manufacturing industries, and pollution. If the present population of the earth (which was expected to double in the next twenty to thirty years) was to attain the standard of living now enjoyed by the advanced countries of the West, food supply and industrial manufacturing would have to increase exponentially. The enormous consumption of natural resources that this would entail would lead to a buildup of industrial waste that would pollute the environment and threaten the continued existence of the human race on this planet. Particular emphasis was given to the finite supply of underground deposits of natural resources. The constantly escalating consumption of natural resources to make life in the advanced countries even more affluent could no longer be tolerated. The operative phrase was the overall "quality of life" for all people.

Donella H. Meadows, a student at MIT and a member of Professor Forrester's study group, gave a more detailed analysis. The mound of figures that comprised her data were published the following year as the first report of the Club of Rome, under the title *The Limits to Growth*.

The twenty-first century was then still thirty years away, and I did not feel any particular personal sense of urgency; but measured in terms of the timescale of human history that was not far at all – it was the future of the next generation, that of my children and grandchildren, which we were discussing. Although I personally believed that technological progress so far had contributed to the development of society, I had learned during the mission to the US a year and a half earlier that the ways technology was used in the future would have both positive and negative effects on human society. Some American intellectuals had even taken these views to their logical extreme and now regarded technology with something akin to fear, predicting that it might lead to the destruction of the human race. In the space of two short years the world had watched the rosy-colored hopes of futurology fade to a dismal shade of gray.

Investigating Identity: Innovation and Entrepreneurship

At the end of September that year I found myself in North America once again, this time at a seminar facility called Harrison House in Glen Cove, a resort just east of New York City, to attend the Second Innovation Conference at the invitation of Dr Jack A. Morton of Bell Laboratories. The theme of the conference was "The Crisis of Corporate Identity," and its purpose was to discuss what the world's leading companies must do to meet the challenges of the days ahead. Among the participants from Europe was Dr Gert W. Rathenau, director of research at the Philips Research Laboratories, an old acquaintance with whom I had been on a panel at the Miami Beach conference six years earlier.

The program began after lunch and soon evolved into a free discussion. Somehow or other the focus shifted to zero growth. Dr Morton was the moderator, and suddenly with a grin he turned to me and asked my opinion on the subject as a guest from the land of high-level growth. I immediately responded this way: For some reason you all have been discussing a zero growth economy. I still have not made up my mind whether that will happen or not or whether it would be necessary or desirable if it does. But until only about one hundred years ago Japan experienced a period of zero population growth and almost zero economic growth – the Edo Period – that lasted for more than 250 years. I have even heard that population control was achieved through selective infanticide. This was a time of isolation from the outside world: a period very different from the economic conditions of today.

Scarcely five months after the Club of Rome meetings in Ottawa, at a gathering of a totally different group of people assembled to grapple with leading-edge technology, the main topic of discussion had been set aside, and we had found ourselves discussing zero growth. I could not but feel once again how fast the world was changing.

Before leaving for the conference I had repeatedly asked my public relations staff what sort of things would be said on the topic of identity, but they had not been able to come up with any precise ideas because there is no suitable equivalent for the word "identity" in Japanese. When I had somewhat naïvely asked an American what the meaning of "identity" was, he drew a card from his pocket and said, "This is what we call an ID." To answer the question in my own way I had brought with me a single picture, which I showed at the conference. This picture was an outline of our corporate structure in the form of a tree, showing NEC's management resources and its various business areas (I will discuss the NEC Tree in more detail in chapter 8). Because it is widely accepted that a company's business areas determine its corporate image, it seemed only natural to try to define them in order to show what kind of a company NEC is. Corporate identity later became a widely discussed topic in Japan, but the starting-point of my own thoughts on the subject can be pinpointed at the Glen Cove conference.

Because of their topicality and importance for management, when I returned to Japan from Glen Cove I made a point of giving wide currency to the two main subjects of the Second Innovation Conference – zero growth and corporate identity. But many other subjects discussed there had made a deep impression on me. One of these was "entrepreneurial esprit." Although on that trip I traveled only along the East Coast of the United States, new corporate trends on the West Coast, especially in the field of electronics, were centering on Silicon Valley south of San Francisco, where several venture companies embodying the "entrepreneurial esprit" were beginning to sprout up, including Intel and Amdahl.

I regard entrepreneurship as the force that generates innovation. For that reason there is a difference in nuance between the words "entrepreneur" and "corporate manager." To put it briefly, the behavior that can be expected of an entrepreneur is quite unlike that of an ordinary business executive. The etymology of the word "entrepreneur" itself is close in sense to "promoter" or "impresario." "Innovator" suggests the vision and temperament of an impresario, but as I understood it, the word also implies the capacity for systematic rational thought.

The key term in describing "entrepreneurial esprit" was "risk-taking." But an entrepreneurial venture also had to be "challenging" and "dynamic." An entrepreneur was someone who dared to tackle new areas. I had caught a whiff of this sort of psychological stimulation at the Innovation Conference. Although no direct reference was made there to the beginnings of new ventures or the motivating force behind them, I have mentioned the topic here because they affected my decision to put "quality of management" at the head of the seven goals in our Operation Quality campaign, discussed below.

I first read the works of Professor Joseph A. Schumpeter on innovation when the need arose to prepare for the Innovation Conference. Regrettably, the impetus generated by this conference, which was the source of so much intellectual stimulation, seems subsequently to have petered out, perhaps as a result of Dr Morton's sudden death or the confusion of the subsequent oil crisis. As I had been unable to attend the First Innovation Conference, I had been asked to contribute an essay for a commemorative volume. Because it sums up some of my ideas on management at that time, I include it here.

Building on the Foundation of Technological Development

New Perspectives on Technological Development

Some years ago the "technology gap" was a topic of lively debate, primarily because postwar Japan's high-level economic growth was dependent on the aggressive adoption of new technologies, most of which were imported from abroad, especially from the United States. If Japan was to grow in the future it would clearly have to develop its own technology. The topic also prompted us to reexamine the need to strengthen Japanese management skills, since, granted a technology gap existed, it could be traced back to inadequacies on the part of management to guide technological development and perfect it for industrial purposes. Because Japan was just then beginning to liberalize capital investment, some people advocated that Japanese corporations should build up their international competitiveness, but the "Japan-as-developing-country" complex persisted among others who believed it was still premature to do so.

In 1967, however, Japan's GNP overtook those of Great Britain and France, and that of West Germany the following year, to rank third in the world after the United States and the Soviet Union. Thereafter, discussions about the technology gap and the need for Japanese technological development began to fade, either because the results spoke for themselves or because Japan's inferiority complex was beginning to disappear. The technology gap debate itself had originated in Europe, arising from criticisms about the invasion of US capital there made by members of the Organization of Economic Co-operation and Development, although some argued that the true cause of the gap lay in the conservative strategies adopted by European firms. Even then the Japanese economy, which had been making rapid strides, was beginning to cast its shadow on Europe.

In 1969 the success of the US Apollo project to land a man on the moon gave Japan an "Apollo shock." The Apollo project itself was widely perceived as having been established by President Kennedy to restore American prestige and catch up with the Russians, who had launched Sputnik in 1957. Because we live in an age dominated by technology, no country ever seems to feel that its own technology is quite good enough. The successful Apollo 11 moon mission certainly made us in Japan acutely aware of the need for both large-scale projects and systems engineering. One of the lessons of the Apollo project, it has been said, is that it was the result not of new technology but rather of the skillful combination of existing technologies. Yet, while I recognize the significance of systems engineering, I feel that it is an exaggeration to say that the Apollo project embodied no new technological developments: And as a member of the Industrial Forecasting Special Research Team organized by the Japan Techno-Economics Society, I had the opportunity to visit Cape Canaveral just before the Apollo 12 space launch.

A question of mine to Lawrence A. Hyland, the vice president of Hughes Aircraft, the foremost company in the field of space development, summed up many of these issues: "The expression 'age of discontinuity' has become popular now in Japan. What about in the United States?" Hyland responded: "There is no sense of discontinuity. During the 1940s and 1950s one new technology appeared after another – nuclear power, plastics, computers, jet planes, rockets, solid-state technology, lasers. But since the 1960s people feel that the pace of technological innovation has worn itself out. Until the 1950s one out of every two or three discoveries was a technological innovation; looking back on those days, we were more likely to feel something akin to discontinuity then than we do now."

The 1960s in America has been a period when new technologies permeated society, contributing to social and economic progress and accelerating the rate of change throughout the world. But if technological progress has contributed to advances in American civilization, it has also caused air pollution, constant noise, overpopulation in some places and depopulation in others, and a rising number of traffic accidents. These environmental problems have forced Americans to realize that technology does not invariably contribute to the well-being of society and that unless something is done the situation will soon get out of hand.

At the White House and in Congress, American government officials are coming to grips with the need for an assessment policy to deal with technology. In fact, at the beginning of this year, the President of the United States stated that the greatest problem facing the US in the 1970s was how to cope with pollution. As a result of this experience, our mission came to the conclusion that, although there was certainly much to learn from the United States, present trends in America did not necessarily indicate directions for future development in Japan, and that the time was coming for Japan to define its own image of the future. This was the gist of the report we made when we returned home.

Today, both sides of the technological innovation issue, the benefits and the pollution, have begun to appear all at once in Japan. Because the problems are no less serious than those in the United States, many people here are beginning to feel a strong sense of discontinuity. The situation requires that we take an even more sophisticated approach to the problem than the one we adopted earlier to deal with the technology gap between Japan and the US.

The Role of Technology in Society

For good or ill, the sense of challenging the unknown is very much a part of technological development. Today, when mere high-level economic growth no longer necessarily leads to increased well-being, we are being confronted with questions such as whether the causes of pollution are the results of technological progress or indications of technological deficiencies, and whether pollution problems can be solved by new technological developments. At this juncture I believe we should review our fundamental assumptions about what technology is and what attitude we should adopt toward it.

Technology is a means of satisfying human wishes. If the human race wishes to put an end to pollution, it must either take the steps to do so or devise new methods that will eliminate any potential abuses. Because of inadequate consideration of these issues, some people believe that technology is to blame for most of the types of pollution under discussion today, and that it is therefore up to technology to eliminate these problems. But we must not lose sight of the fact that technology itself is morally neutral; good or evil consequences arise from the way people use it. If the way we use technology causes environmental problems, we must invest the necessary amount of money to correct them. If a boiler needs a smokestack, add a smokestack of the prescribed height. If the smokestack causes pollution, find something to replace it – in other words, devise a method that will make smokestacks obsolete. That is what technology is for.

Because it is not possible to review each and every technology or technological development here, I would like to discuss the most basic and common concerns that we will be facing in the years ahead.

What will Japan be like in 1980, ten years from now? As a very rough guess I would estimate that the size of the economy will be approximately four times as large as it is at present, or, to put it another way, about the same size as the US economy is today. There is one fundamental difference between Japan and the United States, however. That is the disparity between the two countries in terms of size and usable space. The total area of Japan is about one twenty-fifth that of the United States – approximately the same size as the state of California. In terms of usable flatland, however, Japan has less than one fiftieth the area of the United States. Even though the Japanese economy is expanding and becoming more internationally minded, so that not all its economic activities will be carried on in Japan, it cannot escape the high-density issue. A rough sketch of Japan ten years from now projects the equivalent of today's US economy being run by a population half the size of the United States in an area one fiftieth as large.

Given these fundamentally different spatial conditions, we must face the problem of what Japan can do to make its economy run smoothly and bear fruit. Moreover, because we all want more greenery and peace and quiet than we currently enjoy, we must plan to bring back clean water to our rivers and coastal waters, restore the smell of fresh air and the sight of sunshine, and create an uncongested transportation network and homes spacious enough to provide room for recreation and relaxation. To create an economy and a society that fulfills these conditions may mean solving problems one hundred times more difficult per unit area than those currently facing the United States. This is one of the reasons why I said earlier that Japan could no longer regard the United States as a model for future trends.

The current rapid rate of change is one of the reasons behind our present acute sense of discontinuity; and it is not hard to see that the tempo will gain momentum in the days ahead. Nor will such change be limited to statistics such as the GNP and other economic indicators; we must expect it to extend even to human values and lifestyles. The complexity of the situation can be seen from just one of the issues involved: the education needed to cope with this new age. A boy or girl of fifteen today will be a fully fledged member of the working world in 1980. Providing an education to deal with society as we know it today is complicated enough; but what is the best way to train today's young people to prepare them for the ultra-high-density society of ten years from now? Even if we espouse the cause of lifelong education, we cannot halt the flow of time and wait for an answer to the question what sort of education each generation should receive. The type of education in science and technology we must give today to those who will be responsible for tomorrow's technological innovation, and the teaching methods used to impart it, are critical issues that underlie our future technological development.

At one time, working for a large company and contributing to the achievement of corporate goals was a way of life about which most people had no qualms. But in the US today, not only do an increasing number of young people feel no attraction to working for big business, some offspring of the upper middle class, blessed with the opportunity to receive a higher education, lack the ability to handle even the simplest matters necessary for life in society, and many of them are growing increasingly out of touch with the middle class who make up the majority of society. We must be aware that these same tendencies also exist in Japan. If technology is in fact a means of satisfying human desires and the needs of society, we must add to our agenda of important future concerns these issues of basic human behavior that take precedence over purely technological considerations.

From Seeds to Needs

With regard to the types of technological development required for industrial society in the years ahead – for, although its information-intensive aspects will deepen, it will remain an industrial society – various factors demand attention. The methods of achieving technological development are, of course, not necessarily predetermined; fertile possibilities for obtaining valuable results often exist in unexpected places. But because these are by definition unknown and therefore beyond the range of prediction, they cannot figure in any planned approach. The wisest course of action, therefore, is to direct our efforts toward fashioning approaches that will attain results more easily.

The first such approach is to start from social needs. Traditionally, most research and development has sprung from the interests or concerns of the researchers themselves. From now on, however, it will be important to lay down an order of priority and set target objectives based on degrees of social utility. To discover precisely what these are, a social needs survey will have to be systematically carried out. It is often debated whether social needs are the chicken or the egg. This is because the concept of needs has hitherto tended to be limited to superficialities. But if needs are understood in terms of the utility that people seek, then it would be impossible to respond that they are a secondary concern.

This approach, which could also be called "market-creating," is more versatile than the traditional approach, which tended to start from types of technology – what I call "seeds" – and more likely to head in a needs-oriented direction. But if researchers or research administrators are unable to understand the direction society is taking, they will be unable to respond appropriately to its social needs. For that reason we may have to tackle the question: how do we raise the upper middle class's level of awareness of social trends? During the process of Japan's modernization in the slightly more than 100 years since the Meiji Restoration in 1868, and especially with the influx of foreign technology in the postwar period, Japan has tended to acquire the seeds of technology from abroad rather than developing its own. The reason I have long advocated developing a market-creating technology is because I believe in the importance of an approach that gives the ascendancy to "needs."

Although the ability to solve or eliminate problems is a basic condition of a needs-oriented approach, it will also require enormous amounts of money, and this long-term investment may collide with short-term interests or bottom-line profits. But we must solve these contradictions by working our way through them. We must take the view that the very existence of such contradictions contains the seeds of future technological development, and be sustained by the conviction that as long as these seeds exist all problems are capable of solution.

The second approach is through the free use of "soft technology." Up till now, technological development can be said to have been technology-oriented, and most innovations have been based on technologies arising from research in physics or chemistry carried out within the confines of academia. This approach has given rise to new discoveries, but not enough to satisfy needs. It may also help to account for the fact that fewer noteworthy discoveries or inventions have been made recently and R&D results are becoming harder to produce. The Apollo project, it is said, did not make use of any new technologies, but as many as 10,000 inventions arose from it as spin-off effects. Perhaps the reason these new technologies or new products are not called innovations but are regarded as merely by-products is that they are not connected with needs.

The expression "soft technology" is still not a clear or precisely defined concept. Scientists use it in contrast to "hard technology," which involves deductive reasoning, to refer to an approach to technology based on comprehensive problem-solving, including prediction and planning methods and other management techniques that constitute what is known as management science. Thus, it means essentially the same thing as needs-oriented technology. The distinctive new feature of this interdisciplinary approach, in which the findings needed for problem-solving are adopted from various fields, as the situation demands, derives from the fact that it does not treat phenomena as fixed but posits a cycle in which they function as a kind of circular system. Thus it depends on a *biological approach* in that it tries to manipulate products and processes as part of a totality with the environment that surrounds and interacts with them.

The third method is the systems approach. Each unit of a system is composed of many elements. A product or structure that seems to be a totality is in fact nothing more than a subsystem. Even though no flaws may exist in the function, quality, or reliability of the subsystem itself, trouble may arise when it functions, that is, when it interacts with other systems or environmental conditions.

Today the greater part of what is called pollution occurs when something that has no flaws at the subsystem level develops flaws as part of a total system. For that reason, *technological development in the future must take into consideration the relation of technology to the human body, to the environment, and to society, and come up with the optimum solution based on all these factors.*

Preparing the Ground by Management

The period from the end of the war until the 1960s might be considered an era when, from a macroeconomic perspective, the United States assumed responsibility for research and development as part of an international division of labor. Japan readily imported many of these American technological results and achieved economic growth by skillfully modifying them to suit its own circumstances. During the past ten years the annual economic growth rate in Japan has been in excess of 10 percent, more than 40 percent of which is believed to have been due to technological advances.

Japan has been wise to pursue practical results and learn from others wherever there is something to learn, regardless of its national origin. Ours is becoming an age in which first-rate technology cannot be based on a single invention but is necessarily of a composite, indeed, a comprehensive nature. Furthermore, the ranks of Japanese researchers and engineers have been swelling with the result that, except in areas financed by the US government, the technology gap is not as great as it was ten years ago. Indeed, in industrial engineering and a few other fields of technological development, we have acquired real strength and in some instances even surpass the United States. The time has come to tackle development projects that are particular to our own country, to respond to the social needs of Japan. Although such projects will not be restricted to the approaches mentioned earlier, we need to devise ways to use all three of them.

The importance of the role of business in society has been growing in recent years, and the effects that a corporation has on society through its products and business activities are increasing in magnitude. A corporation must strive to acquire profits for its own ends, but it must also fulfill its social responsibilities, and so new management initiatives are also becoming a corporate concern.

First, no industry or corporation can hope to optimize its business operations if it thinks only in terms of corporate interests. For its own health, therefore, every business must make conscious efforts to marshall its energies and fulfill its corporate responsibilities to society at large.

Second, to meet the various challenges arising from radical changes in the business environment we must cope with one new situation after another. Quantitatively speaking, if the economy of Japan as a whole is to multiply by four during the coming decade, some corporations will have to maintain growth rates of eight or sixteen times their present rate in order to compensate for other businesses that will stagnate or decline. Because a jump of this magnitude will be no easy matter, most of these companies will be heavily reliant on technological development and will have to display even greater flexibility than ever before. Thus, management will repeatedly need to undergo reform and self-renewal, beginning with corporate structure.

Third, because the mere growth or expansion of existing concepts or conditions will be insufficient to meet the needs of society, new methods will become necessary. Of course, existing companies will have to change and grow, but there is a limit to the changes in direction or types of diversification that they can make. For that reason we can expect the appearance of new types of institutions and must take positive steps to create and cultivate them. What sort of role should be given to think tanks, for example, in the area of research and development? How should we promote spin-offs from existing companies? To meet needs of a kind never experienced before, we must look to the development of completely new and original corporate structures.

Sufficient attention must be paid to these topics, for they are a prerequisite for promoting future technological growth. Likewise, satisfactory development depends on factors that I have repeatedly identified on other occasions – strategic management, mobilization of personnel, upgrading of data-processing methods, and widespread investment in streamlined production techniques. The problem is not one facing the corporate sector alone; there are many things that must also be done in association with government and the general public.

In considering the various problems that face us in the days ahead, it is easy to lose sight of our basic purpose because the factors are so complex and so numerous. When that happens I believe we should return to our most fundamental feelings as human beings and consider what meaning our actions will have on the future of our children and grandchildren. Go back to the starting-point – that must be our guideline when we are troubled by problems of technology, management, society, or government.

Ours is said to be an age of technological innovation, but we must never forget that technology does not play the leading role; it is only an instrument for people to use, a means to an end. The path to creation or innovation is a continuous process fraught with difficulties, but the joy of the moment when one savors the glory of making a breakthrough is a reward that only the person who has chosen to follow that path can ever know.

To build new things for a new era – isn't this still the true meaning of making one's mark in history?

In 1971, a few months before the Innovation Conference, Japan was hit by the double blow of the so-called "Nixon shocks." The first impact came when US President Richard Nixon announced a *rapprochement* with China without previously consulting the Japanese government; the second when he set in motion an economic package to defend the US dollar that included going off the gold standard and adding surcharges to imports. By December 18, 1971, when the exchange rate stabilized at 308 yen to the dollar, the effects of the second Nixon shock had begun to take shape, but the full significance of this new rate finally became clear only the following spring when we came to calculate our closing accounts for the last half of fiscal 1971. Companies like ours that had grown accustomed to an exchange rate of 360 yen to the dollar throughout the whole postwar period had not grasped the full implications of the Nixon shock when it happened the previous summer, though we had struggled to adjust. At NEC we dealt with an exchange loss of nearly 2.1 billion yen by gritting our teeth and tapping into the surplus earnings we had so carefully accumulated. I resolved to start all over again and reachieve the performance goals that we had attained through steady growth.

Stable Growth in Unstable Times

After I returned home from the Glen Cove conference, the discussions by Japanese economics journalists of zero growth or negative growth were already having repercussions in Japan, and the term "low growth" was coming into common parlance. The consumer movement and group actions initiated by local residents were also beginning to emerge. There was even a "to hell with the GNP" campaign. I felt that Japan could not succeed with low economic growth and disliked even using the term. Of course, there had been something slightly out of the ordinary about Japan's high-level growth during the 1960s, and the fact that it had lasted as long as ten years was nothing short of miraculous. What we needed now was an appropriate level of growth, a sustained growth rate with a minimum of ups and downs. In searching for a term to describe this, I decided we should speak of "stable growth" and started using this expression in all my pronouncements inside and outside the company.

Call it the current of the times or the way the economic wind was blowing, but it was impossible to deny that the world was changing at an unexpectedly rapid rate, and a feeling of gloomy foreboding was becoming widespread. It was against this background that I was appointed to chair the Management Planning Council of the Japan Committee for Economic Development. The council members deliberated about what we should tackle as our main topic, proposing ideas as they occurred to us and discussing them among ourselves. We decided unanimously that we should try to project a model of the corporate image needed to deal with these new and constantly changing social factors. Shortly after the Japan Committee for Economic Development had been founded, immediately after the war, it had drawn up a statement about businesses' social responsibilities. Thus, from the historical perspective as well, the proposal to reexamine this topic in the light of the present situation seemed altogether appropriate to the Management Planning Council. It was around this time that government and academic circles proposed replacing that talisman of the period of high-level growth, the industry-centered GNP, as Japan's sole economic indicator, and made several attempts to substitute some sort of standard of national well-being. This was what was known as the GNW (gross national welfare) theory, and it was yet another factor contributing to our decision to focus our study on an examination of the present social responsibilities of business.

Launching "Operation Quality"

The Management Planning Council deliberated for nearly three years before bringing its recommendations together in a proposal entitled "Toward the Establishment of Mutual Understanding between Business and Society." During this period I personally continued to search for a beacon of light to guide NEC through the rough seas of this turbulent new era. As part of these efforts I tried to apply the approach to problem-solving I had written about earlier as head of the Industrial Forecasting Special Research Team, and make use also of those universal virtues of the corporate world – growth, character, and perpetuation – which according to the IIC report were the responsibilities of the chief executive officer. The search for an appropriate corporate image for the times would also allow the Japanese industrial world to propose a solution to the "crisis of corporate identity," which had been the main topic at the Second Innovation Conference.

Rather than relying on general abstract discussions, I realized that a concrete approach to the question could be found in the corporate history of NEC. When NEC had been established, its motto had been "better products, better service." As manufacturers it was only natural for my predecessors to adopt the slogan "better products," but they had expressly given equal importance to "better service." Clearly they had anticipated the need to get ahead in today's world by striving to do better in both the tangible area of products and the intangible area of service. In my own mind I included the idea of software in the intangible service area.

It had been hard – although I eventually did so – to reject the alternative suggestion to replace the word "better" with the concept of "excellence," which, as you may recall, later became a key word in a seminal US book on business. In the meantime I continued to explore such fundamental questions about a corporation's social *raison d'être* as: Why must a company offer good products and good service? Why is growth necessary for the economy? Why does a corporation need to grow? In the process it became clear that it was not simply a matter of how good a company's products and services were; in other words, it was not just their quality in a material sense. I came to the conclusion that ultimately the criterion was whether or not they contributed to improving the quality of human life. At the end of 1971 I had not yet found a way to give these ideas concrete shape, but because the underlying concept was firmly in place I proposed a quality campaign as the centerpiece of my New Year's directive to the company and included it with the other items I wanted to deal with during 1972.

"Operation Quality" at NEC grew out of an examination of what steps corporate executives needed to take at the micro level of day-to-day business to produce better products and better service. This was the key to a new corporate image that involved the pursuit not just of quantitative results, as in the past, but of quality as well. Operation Quality was a practical program to establish a corporate image which would live up to these ideals. In January 1972 I announced to the entire company that from then on quality would be the guiding principle behind all business conducted at or by NEC.

The seven major points of the Operation Quality campaign were as follows:

1. *Improve the quality of management.* If the quality of management is unsatisfactory, a corporation can have no hope of growth. Especially important is the quality of corporate decision-making and direction-setting. Because every instance of one person making use of the services of another should be regarded as management, every possible effort must be made to improve its quality from the president down to each individual group leader at every level. If employers make the effort to think in terms of their employees, they must always give due thought to what the latter may find annoying. Those who are placed in a position of authority over others must realize the implications of the power they wield.

2. *Improve the quality of products and services.* Although this point is self-explanatory, it should not be considered simply from the technical perspective of quality control. Thought must also be given to making goods that will please the customer. Because products must be consumer-oriented, feedback about users' needs should be a prime consideration. Improving the quality of products and services means checking the entire production cycle, carefully taking into consideration each step in the process from the moment when the raw materials are received, through the planning and development stage,

all the way to manufacturing, sales, use, and even beyond, to the time when the item is discarded.

3. *Improve the quality of the working environment.* Because we spend a considerable proportion of each day at work, the workplace is an important part of our lives. Efforts to improve the working environment will therefore lead to an improvement in the quality of life of our employees. These efforts must spring not merely from reasons of manufacturing efficiency but from a serious regard for human life. When I made the proposal to upgrade the working environment, I was warned that it would probably result in requests from various sectors of the company for money to implement this idea. It thus required a great deal of courage for me as president to make this announcement. But my feeling was that such requests should be faced, and I decided to go ahead.

4. *Improve the quality of community relations.* The often-used English-language concept of "community" does not exist *per se* in Japan, although there is a term that can roughly be translated as "local society." In the case of pollution and other such problems, the feelings of local residents are an important consideration. Once those feelings have been aroused, local authorities are practically powerless, and any subsequent dealings between the company and area residents may result in the same polarization as occurred at Yokkaichi in Mie Prefecture, where an air pollution lawsuit was brought against a group of petrochemical companies. To prevent things reaching that stage we must be extra-sensitive to local sentiment. It is important not to be passive, but to take positive steps to ensure harmonious relations with the local community.

5. *Improve the quality of human behavior.* Although all the previous items deal with the company's responsibilities, the fifth Q is an appeal to the individuals who work for the company to improve their own attitudes and behavior. Instead of just telling them to work hard, it encourages them to improve their skills and assume responsibility for their own work. But it also requires employees to obey the rules and not to do anything to cause unpleasantness to others in the workplace. Management must have the courage to make this demand of its employees boldly and fearlessly. Management itself must behave prudently, but it must also be strict with its employees. Adopting this sort of attitude is for their benefit.

6. *Improve the quality of business performance.* If a corporation operates unprofitably, it will have neither growth nor staying power

and will be unable to pay any dividends. In evaluating a company's performance, operating results ought to be one of the important indicators. We must stress the importance of achieving results and require the cooperation of all concerned.

7. *Improve the quality of corporate image.* If the general public is puzzled about what a company is doing, or if a rumor spreads that a certain company will do anything for profit, it will lose its credibility. It is therefore important that the true nature of a company be correctly perceived by the world at large. Furthermore, within the company itself thought should be given to what sort of corporate image would increase the employees' sense of belonging – their feeling of identity with the company. If employees feel that sense of identity, we can create a highly responsive organization.

Having proposed these seven Qs, I called on all the employees to set their own goals and promote their own projects based upon them. Operation Quality was introduced in that year's business report to our Japanese stockholders and in our annual report in English for our overseas shareholders. I remember how gratified I was to receive letters from top executives at leading US firms who wrote to say they shared my views. In November 1974 I was awarded the Deming Individual Prize for Operation Quality, which was cited as a unique development of the total quality control movement.

Maintaining Global Expansion: The President as Salesman

While we grappled with the problems of adjustment to the new climate of the 1970s, my chosen strategy of targeting overseas markets had to continue unabated. A company like NEC whose business involves exporting systems, networks, and even entire plants often deals directly with governments, which meant that I frequently had to go abroad personally to represent the company.

The first "Nixon shock" – the announcement on April 16, 1971 of President Nixon's impending visit to mainland China – had particular consequences for NEC. After forming his cabinet in July 1972, Prime Minister Kakuei Tanaka went to China on September 25 and signed a joint communiqué reestablishing diplomatic relations between Japan and China. On that occasion NEC pulled off the feat of setting up a satellite communications ground station outside Beijing in only just over a month in order to transmit live television coverage of the Prime Minister's visit. Our business in this area had shown such rapid growth that by this date more than half the satellite communications ground stations in the world had been built by NEC. Nevertheless, the delivery of this particular station was a matter of national prestige. A success here was a brilliant achievement, both because it demonstrated the usefulness of transportable ground stations that could be flown in by air and because it proved that NEC possessed the capability to do this. The scenes broadcast live from Beijing that day remain vividly implanted in the memories of all of us who took part in that project. This ground station was later sold to China at the request of the Chinese government.

NEC's first joint venture after the war had been in Taiwan, however, and even though Japan had followed the US in establishing closer relations with China, we found it psychologically difficult to sever our ties with Taiwan and join hands with mainland China simply because it offered a huge market of one billion people. While other Japanese corporations, from trading companies to manufacturers, were both eager not to miss out on these new opportunities and were being pressed for political reasons to renounce their ties with Taiwan and establish friendly relations with China, I held my ground. However, because of my behind-the-scenes role in the television broadcast of Prime Minister Tanaka's visit, in February 1973 I found myself preparing to enter China at the head of a delegation of Japanese executives representing various fields of technology, including switching equipment, which had been arranged in Japan through the auspices of the Association for the Promotion of International Trade.

The first time I went to the Soviet Union had been in October 1971 when I landed at Moscow airport on my way to Europe as part of a mission to the European Community sponsored by the Federation of Economic Organizations. That was merely a transit stop; the first time I actually set foot in the Soviet bloc was in July 1972 when NEC sponsored a four-day symposium on Soviet technology in Moscow. The process of *détente* was then gradually moving into the economic sphere, and because NEC was in the midst of Operation Quality at the time, I hoped that by setting the improvement of the quality of life as a shared goal we and our Soviet counterparts could overcome our political differences and find some common grounds for understanding. I broached these ideas to the Soviet authorities I met, arguing that though it was vital to create a new civilization where both political systems could freely use the latest technology to develop their economies and make technological progress, the motivation for change had to go back to the starting-point, the improvement of the quality of human life. But this approach was beyond their understanding, and I made no headway. Although I did not pursue the subject any further, I had the impression from this negative response that the Soviet Union remained essentially unchanged: It might talk about change, but it still did not have the flexibility to implement it.

Beginning in the mid-1960s NEC received orders for a seven-route microwave communications network project in Iran. I visited Tehran in December 1967, again in November 1968 as part of a Japanese government economic delegation, in June 1970 on company business, in April 1971 as part of the Iran Economic Mission sponsored by the Federation of Economic Organizations, and in August 1972 to attend a Japan–Iran Committee meeting. During that period Iran was proposing to build an integrated telecommunications system throughout the entire country. NEC and its competitors, Page Communications Engineers and General Telephone and Electronics, both from the US, and Siemens of West Germany, joined forces to form an international consortium, which was given the contract in January 1970.

In September 1973 the Fifth International Industrial Conference was held, once again in San Francisco, and once again I attended. This time the main theme was quite different: the social responsibility of a corporation. Because this topic had been thoroughly discussed in Japan, the sessions had little new to offer me. One evening, during a lull in the proceedings, I received an invitation to a reception at the Consulate General of Ireland. The sponsors of this event, the Ireland Development Corporation, a quasi-governmental agency, explained their interest in getting foreign companies to locate in Ireland and outlined their aims and the various incentives they were offering. When I arrived back in Japan I brought this talk up at the Corporate Management Committee meeting. We had wanted to export our semiconductor products to Europe, but because of various restrictions on the Continent – tariff barriers, import quotas, and other safeguards – we concluded that there were great advantages to local production in Ireland.

In July 1974 NEC Ireland (now NEC Semiconductors Ireland) began local production of integrated circuits just outside Dublin, a venture whose starting-point could be traced back directly to the IIC I had attended the previous year in San Francisco. Thus, NEC pioneered the entry of Japanese IC companies into Europe at a time when concerns about trade friction had almost no effect on our decision to locate there.

These were some of NEC's overseas activities on the eve of the first oil shock. As the first move in our long-contemplated entry into the European market, we established NEC Electronics (Europe) in Düsseldorf in April 1973 as the sales outlet for our electronic devices and household appliances. That June we set up NEC Tele-communications Europe, now NEC (UK), in London to sell our communications equipment. While the new Tanaka Cabinet was moving ahead with plans to "restructure the Japanese archipelago," we were taking active steps to move overseas in order to globalize our business and were in the midst of building up the organization to take that great leap forward.

7

Riding Turbulence: From Oil Shock to the Birth of C&C

In October 1973, shortly after I returned from the International Industrial Conference in San Francisco, a Club of Rome conference took place in Tokyo, the first ever in Japan. About forty Club members and other prominent persons from abroad had been invited and, as head of the executive committee, I was concerned that the meeting should go smoothly and produce significant results. At the UN Conference on the Human Environment held in Stockholm in June 1972 the catchphrase "only one earth" had focused attention worldwide on the earth's finite resources. The publication at about the same time of a Japanese translation of the first Club of Rome report, *The Limits to Growth*, had forced industrial circles and other groups in Japan to pay serious attention to the future of human society. Dr Dennis Gabor, the Nobel prize winner who had written *Inventing the Future* and *The Mature Society*, had come all the way to Japan for the conference. His vision of the future with the advent of the age of hydrogen energy made a deep impression on me.

During the conference the *Asahi Shimbun* had arranged a discussion between me and Aurelio Peccei, the Club's founder, for publication in its newspaper. When the conversation was over the reporter who had acted as moderator asked whether the Club's views on the finite supply of resources might have a ripple effect that would strengthen the position of the oil-producing countries. The question caught me completely by surprise. During the Club of Rome's Tokyo meetings, war had broken out in the Middle East. Rumors were flying that the Arab oil producers were cutting production of crude oil, stopping delivery to unfriendly countries, and raising their prices.

Might not this new attitude have been influenced by the Club of Rome's arguments about limited resources?

Reaction to the Oil Threat: The Problem of Excess Inventory

In view of the current geopolitical conditions I had a survey made of our inventory of materials in order to check how much damage might be done to NEC's future corporate activities. The report revealed a totally unexpected situation that left me both astonished and appalled. Our warehouses, far from being empty, were so overstocked that the company risked going bankrupt under the strain.

Ordinarily the purchase of materials is such a standardized procedure that in a large corporation there is no need for the head of the company to give personal attention to this area of the business. Stock purchasing can be likened to the digestive and circulation systems in the human body, which function out of sight and almost automatically. The need to provide direction or exert control – management, in other words – takes place at higher, or at least more visible, levels. The fact that parts of the corporate body outside my range of vision were not functioning in a healthy fashion was clearly an abnormal situation. Responding to frightening rumors that the oil supply was about to be cut off, our purchasing department had built up a stockpile in a short period of time. Given the profound fallibility of human nature, it did not do to criticize the actions or decisions of the people involved, who had clearly acted out of a strong if mistaken sense of duty. On the other hand, the situation was obviously an embarrassment. Because of these unforeseen circumstances I remember feeling a double sense of surprise. First, the oil shock was not a problem in the distant future resulting from the exhaustion of natural resources, such as the Club of Rome had warned about; it was very much a contemporary problem facing me in 1973. And second, instead of struggling to maintain adequate supplies I faced the opposite problem of excess inventory.

At a General Managers Committee meeting at the end of November I made the following statement:

During the twenty-five years since the end of the war we have succeeded in restoring and expanding the fortunes of the Japanese economy and NEC

Corporation through diligence and hard work. Though no war has broken out, all of the economic conditions that we have so carefully nurtured have totally collapsed. It does no good to complain. We have no alternative but to recall those days a quarter of a century ago when we crawled our way up from scorched earth and start all over again. I am prepared to do so, and I call on all NEC employees to share the same resolve.

NEC made immediate plans to cut back on power costs and conserve energy and material. We also had to deal coolly with our number one problem, which was to reduce our inventory to a healthier level. As I looked back over the previous ten years, NEC's current position was our worst showing since 1964/5. Although we had been headed for recovery in 1966/7 and the year of EXPO '70 in Osaka had marked the climax of high economic growth, the Nixon shocks in 1971 had forced us into retreat. After coping with foreign exchange losses of 2.1 billion yen, we made a fresh start and had finally managed to climb back up again in 1972 and 1973, when our performance suddenly plummeted in the second half of that year. It looked like we would hit bottom in 1974, the tenth year of my presidency, the year I had planned to put the finishing touches on all my plans. Now I was forced to face the pain of starting all over again.

The Quality of Time

That fall I continued to explore ways to proceed with our company-wide expansion plans with an eye on the years ahead. Not only had each of our main plants used up all its extra floor space; labor, power, drainage and transportation conditions were forcing us to enlarge all our regional plants. (This was the second phase in our nationwide decentralization program discussed in chapter 4.) Although we had made provisional plans for the future, worsening business conditions as a result of the oil shock meant that we did not have the capital to cover them all. On the contrary, we were sliding into a situation that would make some retrenchment inevitable. Unless we defined our production and investment priorities, we would not be able to avoid making drastic cuts, and, if the worst came to the worst, we would have to contemplate laying off workers if the company were to be kept going. Faced with these painful choices, we decided to go ahead as planned with the expansion of our semiconductor production facilities. This move would later prove to be the key to NEC's astonishing growth in this area.

While shipments of finished goods remained stagnant, payments to cover the costs of materials exceeded 4 billion yen. Because of the need to improve our cash flow, reducing our inventory, which was approaching 95 billion yen, was a very urgent matter. Furthermore, it was becoming clear that a small percentage of critical parts were not in stock, and this too was interfering with the manufacturing process.

That December I was asked to take part in a government mission to Indonesia and had to spend a few days in Jakarta, Bandung, and Bali. An anti-Japanese movement had flared up, and the neon signs of Japanese trading companies and manufacturers were the targets of attacks by Indonesian students. Criticism of Japan had spread to all areas, even to Japanese golf manners. The purpose of our mission was to clear the way for the visit of Prime Minister Tanaka to southeast Asia, but I had the feeling that any issue whatsoever, not just the oil situation or internal economic conditions, was likely to fan the flames. There is an old saying that "you only feel the heat when it's going down your throat." Looking back at the situation today it is possible to be calm. But in the thick of things, when we had no idea what lay ahead, confusion, uneasiness, and irritation were unavoidable. As demand plummeted, the government's fiscal policies centered on ways to hold down to the level of aggregate demand. In the middle of all this confusion I kept wondering whether my views about the world had been wrong up to now, whether I had made some mistake. Only by reconsidering the situation from a macroeconomic perspective would I be able to understand current trends and reach a sound decision on what course of action to take.

Around this period comparisons were being made between the oil-rich countries of the Middle East and Japan with its limited natural resources. Following the views of the American political scientist Hans Morgenthau, I reexamined the requisites for national strength. Oil lay buried beneath the deserts where nomads lived, but they had so far been unable to transform their deserts into centers of modern civilization. Now at last that opportunity had arrived, but if the world continued to tap these springs, in a few decades the source would run dry. The Japanese complained about the smallness of their land area and their lack of natural resources; but if the factors of pure rain water and greenery were added into the comparison, then the country's stock of resources was not so small. Moreover, any discussions of progress must take into consideration the amount of time involved. That, of course, is what history is all about. Seen from this perspective, Japan in the previous twenty years, or in the previous 100 years since it had opened its doors to modernization, had used its time extremely efficiently.

How to best utilize the infinite variety of the world's natural resources and climatic conditions depends on the intelligence and ingenuity of the people who live in any particular place. The same could be said for individual companies. It does not follow that one has it easy because it is an oil company and acts as a supplier and that other types of business are at a disadvantage because they are consumers. Things change from one day to the next; six months or three years from now the situation may be entirely different depending on what those in charge do and how they do it.

In other words, the resource of time is given equally to everyone. *Everything depends on the quality of how one uses that time, the quality of how one chooses to live.* The thought came to my mind that we must rediscover the quality use of time. In developing Operation Quality within the company I decided to raise the issue of the quality of time. Because it involved no more than stating the obvious, it did not need repeated explanations; by the same token, perhaps it would not produce many conspicuous results. But at least it was useful for cheering up the employees during a difficult period and raising morale by giving them a project to tackle.

After experimenting with various ideas, we came up with several plans, some of which other companies also adopted. Meanwhile, in job areas where we could not cope by simply eliminating overtime, we were forced to adopt a reduced working week and cut back on part-time help. We also studied raising the price of our products. Half of our problems had internal causes. Many excuses had been offered, such as that we had few products that enjoyed wide public popularity, which contributed to our overstock of manufactured goods. I tried to take a clear view of the situation and called on our employees not to ask for what we did not have; the important thing was to sell what we did have. In the meantime, the employees did their best to cope and continued to search for solutions. They gave their full cooperation, realizing that if the company did not survive, their own futures would be jeopardized. I was deeply gratified by their attitude.

The Spirit of Self Help

On the evening of October 18, 1974, I received an urgent message that the most senior of the NEC executive vice presidents, Takeo Kurokawa, had died suddenly after giving a lecture in an employee education course. Since entering the company in 1937, Kurokawa had served by my side for nearly forty years and had coolly and efficiently handled many difficult situations. The sudden news of the death of my right-hand man was a far greater blow to me than the Nixon shocks. This was the death of a colleague who would be greatly missed. With great anguish I had to draw up a new slate of NEC executives to present at the stockholders' meeting on November 30.

What sustained me in such times of difficulty, either in business or in my private life? My ruminations on this question forced me to confront the most primitive levels of human experience. In so doing I recalled that when I had been growing up in Yamanashi Prefecture I had tried to memorize an English-language supplementary reader during the five-mile walk from my home in Hatsukari village to Tsuru Middle School in Otsuki City. The title of that book was *Self Help with Illustrations of Character and Conduct* by Samuel Smiles. Within the company about this time I kept repeating the words "self help," practically chanting them to myself. Someone on my staff found me a battered first edition of Samuel Smiles's book. Not long afterwards I received a letter from a professor at Notre Dame Women's College in Okayama Prefecture stating that some 100 years earlier our forefathers in the Meiji period had learned from Smiles's English classic the lessons necessary for modernization during Japan's sudden rise to power and that special recognition should now be given to this historical fact. I found it very strange that the national power of Britain, where for some reason the book had been completely forgotten, had declined like the setting sun. Still, even if it was too late to revitalize the idea of "self help" in England, I felt it would be a good idea to put this concept to use in Japan during the long dark tunnel of the 1970s.

In the business context self help has basically been taken to mean earning money in order to survive as an independent entity. For a corporation, that meant raising profits to a suitable level in order to fulfill its obligations to its shareholders, customers, employees, and society at large. I was well aware that the general public holds the view that profits are fundamental to business. And, needless to say, corporate management has to make a profit for the company's stockholders. Profits, however, are not earned by simply saying a few magic words; they must be regarded as the end result of certain business efforts. I held firmly to the view expounded by Peter Drucker: Although profit is a necessary condition for the development of a corporation, *the ultimate objective of management is not profit, but perpetuating the business.*

Stockholders or investors not only expect dividend profits; naturally enough, they also hope to profit from the rise in stock prices. On this score, it is doubtful whether the price of NEC stock met our shareholders' expectations until the late 1960s or early 1970s. One reason for this was the fact that ITT was our major stockholder. Whenever NEC stock prices began to rise, ITT would flood the market with the shares it held, and the price would naturally fall. It is worth pointing out that in March 1976, when ITT's holdings were a mere 0.52 percent of all NEC stocks, this situation completely disappeared. By March 1978 ITT's share holdings had been reduced to zero. Throughout my years as president, dealing with ITT was a constant headache, a preoccupation that never allowed me to let down my guard. But, in the end, I believe I was able to deal with everything satisfactorily.

Crystallizing Experience in Writing

Perhaps because I had now held the presidency for ten years, I began to receive suggestions from various quarters that I write a book. One of the most enthusiastic supporters of this idea was the *Nihon Keizai Shimbun*, a newspaper which was carrying a series of autobiographies under the title "My Personal History." Although I was gratified by these suggestions, I continued to refuse for many reasons, the foremost being that I felt I had not yet accomplished all I had set out to do. More than ten years later, I did agree to write "My Personal History," and the twenty-nine installments of my autobiography were serialized in the *Nihon Keizai Shimbun*, beginning on November 1, 1987, and reached 2.7 million readers throughout Japan.

Although I had refused to write this series of articles back in the mid-1970s, my pen had not been idle. I thoroughly enjoyed polishing my thoughts and experienced something akin to catharsis in writing them down. But undertaking to write an entire book in my free moments would have reduced me to a dish-rag. Indeed, I doubted whether it would have been possible to squeeze in the time. One alternative was to collect what I had written over the past few years about my thoughts and actions. That, in fact, had been the form my earlier books had taken. The essays written during my first three or four years as president were published under the title *Meeting the Challenge of the Computer Age*; those written in the three or four years around Osaka EXPO '70 were called *Management Problems for the Seventies*. All the pieces in the next book, a selection of essays written between 1971 and the summer of 1975 which included public pronouncements made outside the company during the early seventies, unwittingly had the same theme – perhaps it might be called a tentative theory of culture. On the advice of the publisher and my NEC staff it was entitled *Quality-Oriented Management*: Whether it is best described as a work on management or an attempt at a theory of culture, it recorded frankly my views during a period of violent upheaval and is a book of which I am particularly fond.

The Realignment of the Computer Industry

In September 1971 I was stunned by some totally unexpected news: the report that RCA had dropped out of the computer business. RCA – Radio Corporation of America – had a long and splendid history, originally as a leader in the field of radio, then as a driving force behind the television boom, and as one of the largest American producers of popular appliances. Under the leadership of David Sarnoff, RCA had outstanding prospects in the blossoming area of electronics during the 1960s. Blessed with a long tradition and a pioneering spirit, it was also one of the world's leading companies in the computer area. The Japanese firm Hitachi had a technical tie-up with RCA and was involved in developing the computer business in Japan. Only a very short time earlier RCA had been ambitiously developing a large mainframe called the Spectra 70, the software for which was said to be compatible with that of IBM. There had been considerable interest in what RCA would do under the leadership of Robert Sarnoff, who had succeeded his father as president. How was one to interpret the fact that after pumping huge amounts of money into the computer business RCA had suddenly suspended development and withdrawn from the field? What conclusions had top management come to about the chances of success in this business? The situation gave rise to endless speculation.

RCA was not the first company to drop out of computers. General Electric was another major US firm that had made a substantial commitment to the computer business, only to pull out in the end. A real force in the electronics area with a long history of experience as well as seemingly limitless technological prowess and management skills, GE had been universally regarded as fully capable of mounting a challenge to IBM. But in May 1970, one year before RCA dropped out, GE had decided to divest itself of its computer operations. The announcement took everyone by surprise; the analysis of the decision in the October 1970 *Fortune* magazine seemed to sum up the true state of things. GE was engaged in three important areas: atomic energy, jet engines, and computers. Continued investment in all three fields simultaneously, even for a company of GE's size, was difficult because of the enormous outlays required for each. In essence, GE had chosen to stake its future on the areas of energy and aerospace.

Repercussions of Withdrawal

GE's withdrawal from computers was a matter of direct concern to NEC. Honeywell, with whom NEC had a technical agreement, had acquired GE's computer division and merged it with its own to set up Honeywell Information Systems (HIS). Moreover, as mentioned in chapter 4, Toshiba had had a technical tie-up with GE in the computer area. That meant that the affiliation between GE and Toshiba had been taken over by the newly formed HIS, which now had licensing agreements in Japan with two companies. Nor did the effects stop with the US and Japan; the establishment of HIS set off an automatic chain reaction in the European computer industry as well. As I recall, it was in 1964 that Machines Bull, the leading French manufacturer of computers and business machines, stopped working on its own computer and entered an affiliation with GE, which came to a similar arrangement in Italy with the computer division of Olivetti. For that reason, the creation of Honeywell Information Systems had repercussions in the US, France, Italy, and Japan, and meant the creation of an international alliance uniting European, American, and Japanese interests.

Renegotiating NEC's Relationships

The technical tie-up between NEC and Honeywell in the computer area had been signed in July 1962. Before long, the ten-year period of that contract would expire, and the time was fast approaching when we would have to decide whether to renew it or not. After the Innovation Conference in Glen Cove I flew to Boston and the Honeywell offices to begin negotiations about the future of our computer venture.

NEC had two aims. The first was to get the conditions of the next contract changed to our advantage – in short, we wanted a reduction in the royalties we had to pay. NEC's technological expertise in computers had risen markedly in the preceding ten years, and we were now close to Honeywell in real strength. An example of this improvement was our model 700 in the NEAC series 2200, a large mainframe which we had developed the year before and for which we were beginning to receive orders. This mainframe, like its predecessor the model 500, was an original system developed entirely by NEC's engineering staff without any direct technological input from Honeywell. Our second aim was to sound out development plans for the new series of machines being planned by HIS to confirm whether any of them would be useful for NEC's computer business in the days ahead. If this were the case, we would indicate our intention to continue with the technical tie-up. To put it another way, I wanted to find out whether they had anything worth buying.

After exchanging memos about our mutual intentions I returned home. Realizing that American business and technological trends in electronics, and especially in the computer area, were changing rapidly, I decided to set up the NEC Systems Laboratory in the Boston area near the HIS office as a way of strengthening its liaison function with Honeywell Information Systems.

Developments at NEC: Technology and Organization

Where was NEC in terms of computer technology during the early 1970s? The first element in our position consisted of trends in NEC's own computer technology dating back to the mid-1950s; the second involved computer technology from Honeywell, and the third was technology of GE origin that had been taken over by Honeywell when

GE had dropped out of the computer business, and stemming mainly from the GE computer plant in Phoenix with additional input from technologies originally developed by Machines Bull and Olivetti.

Yet another stream of NEC computer technology was that behind the NEAC 1200 series of small computers that had its origin in the parametron computer, which had been developed in Japan, with a prior history as a simple and convenient electronic calculator. This model would eventually develop into a small business computer in the latter half of the 1970s, but it was then one of a number of other types of small computers and terminals that formed the cluster of technology surrounding NEC's main computer line. In addition to all these divergent strands we also had to deal with the technology for DIPS, NTT Public Corporation's information-processing system for data communications purposes.

In 1971 NEC initiated a large-scale reorganization of its computer operations, creating two new divisions – the Computer Systems Engineering Division, which was made responsible for developing all types of computers from small office machines to mainframes, and the Computer Systems Manufacturing Division, which was responsible for manufacturing them. We also established new divisions to handle peripheral and terminal devices, magnetic storage devices, and electronic switching equipment, and clarified the spheres of responsibility for each.

Toward Liberalization

The contemporary business climate for computers was evolving rapidly. In July 1970 IBM had announced its system 370. If the system 360 marked the beginning of third generation computers, the system 370 was halfway between a third and a fourth generation machine. Its use of a virtual memory was particularly noteworthy. Furthermore, IBM had recently proposed a plan for "unbundling" its software, with separate prices for hardware, software, and services. In July 1971 the Japanese government, yielding to strong pressure from the United States, had announced a timetable for the liberalization of computers and integrated circuits. At first this was to be a partial liberalization, but in April 1973 the government decided on the bold course of complete liberalization of capital investment and imports by the end of 1975, and the liberalization of software from April 1, 1976.

The Minister of International Trade and Industry at that time was Kakuei Tanaka, who later became Prime Minister. Under him the ministry tackled the task of reorganizing the Japanese computer industry as a way of strengthening it in preparation for eventual liberalization.

These conditions were sparking off many changes. In October 1971, not long after I returned from the abovementioned visit to Honeywell, first Hitachi and Fujitsu, then Oki and Mitsubishi, announced that they were pairing off and concluding technical tie-ups in order to embark on joint development of their respective new series of computers. It was widely speculated that NEC had no choice but to band together with Toshiba, the only other firm left. The fact that our two companies shared the same technical source in the US had made this relationship seem practically inevitable. Although the directions our two companies were moving in did not quite mesh, after some deliberation we came to an agreement on joint development in November 1971.

Meanwhile, independently of the pressures of liberalization, since late 1968 NEC and Honeywell had been exploring the possibility of developing a new series to succeed our existing line of computers. To distinguish it from our current product line (CPL) we called it our NPL – new product line – and began working jointly on ideas for its development. In addition to the many thorny technical problems that needed resolving, there was the further difficulty of deciding how to make use of the GE technology that had been added in May 1970 when Honeywell had absorbed GE's computer division. This complication inevitably affected the progress of our schedule and our development ideas. It was March 1972 before the necessary adjustments had been made and a concept for the new series worked out.

The Computer Business Takes Off

In the midst of the gloomy 1970s, NEC managed to pull off a coup. Everyone inside and outside the company was wondering when we were going to announce our new computer series: On May 23, 1974, the day for us to launch our new family of high-performance computers, the ACOS series 77, finally arrived. To begin with, we announced three types of machines in the ACOS series, systems 200,

300, and 400. Compared with the NEAC system 100, which had been unveiled the previous August and was still on the market, the ACOS system 200 was four times more effective in terms of cost performance, and the systems 300 and 400 were five and six times more effective respectively.

The acronym ACOS meant many different things. First, the initials stood for Advanced Comprehensive Operating System, a reference to the main features of the new series. But that was not all the initials could be taken to represent – All-Round Customer-Oriented System or Advanced Computer System were other possible interpretations. The lucky number 77 was added for good measure. But we had no intention of depending on the name alone. Finding ways to accommodate the users of our previous NEAC computer series as well as the users of Toshiba machines became an important part of our business strategy for the new series. Despite the fact that a tie-up with Honeywell Information Systems existed during the development process, the underlying technology shared by the ACOS series had been developed solely by the new computer series technology research association that NEC and Toshiba had formed in August 1972. Subsequent sales were also to be carried out by NEC and Toshiba respectively.

For that reason, on January 23, 1974, a few months prior to the announcement of the ACOS series, the two companies established a joint concern called NEC–Toshiba Information Systems to co ordinate basic planning policies and marketing activities by the two firms. The original idea had been to start the joint company the previous September, but it had taken six months of consultations for these two erstwhile competitors to reach an agreement. The new company would have authorized capital of 4 billion yen and paid-up capital of 1 billion yen, with NEC contributing 60 percent of the financing and Toshiba 40 percent. Seven of the company's executives (including the president) would come from NEC, and six (including the senior executive vice president) from Toshiba, and both firms would send a statutory auditor. The two companies decided on a single brand name for the new series and agreed to work together to promote the computer business. The joint venture was officially established on March 9, 1974.

Thereafter we continued to add to the lineup of machines in the ACOS series and to develop the operating system. Everything proceeded smoothly. In November 1974 the two companies unveiled the large-scale ACOS systems 600 and 700; the following June we announced the system 500, developed primarily by NEC; and the giant systems 800 and 900 came out in April 1976. With this we had completed the development of the entire series and were steadily improving and perfecting the software.

While the ACOS series was being unveiled, NEC was also making several preliminary moves in anticipation of future developments in the computer business. The first was the establishment of NEC Information Service on September 19, 1974. In those days few people seemed to have a clear understanding of the nature of a data-processing services business, but in time, with the opening of data communications networks and the evolution of value added network (VAN) services, its mission became firmly established.

Another move was the establishment of NEC Software on September 9, 1975, primarily to deal with the development and sales of applications software. Originally, there had been some misgivings within NEC about setting this up as an independent company. Today, the business has grown so much that many companies with similar purposes have been set up in various parts of Japan, of which this was the precursor. Organization as an independent company would later come to occupy an important place in the development strategy of NEC's computer-related businesses.

The Next Wave: Toward C&C

As these businesses were being set up, I was dogged by pressing questions. One, of long standing, concerned trends in electronic switching systems in the communications area. The DIPS information-processing project, which we were helping develop for NTT, was also an important concern. And new trends at IBM also called for close observation: I had heard from the US that they had come up with a concept called SNA – system network architecture. In what direction would the main stream of computer technology develop? Where should NEC set the upper limits for the development of its ACOS series? This was becoming a problem that required immediate solution.

The thought gradually formed in my mind that instead of building a giant computer, it would be more efficient and more practical to have one of our small or medium-range systems 200, 300, or 400 in the ACOS series serve as a main or host computer to which some NEAC system 100 computers or other types of intelligent terminals could be connected as satellites in constellation fashion. This was the concept of distributed information processing network architecture, or DINA for short, which NEC announced in December 1976.

My vision of NEC was not simply one of a computer maker. The shape I had in mind integrated computers and communications – a communications network linking a number of computers, perhaps. In the late 1950s, when I was still only a senior vice president, I had published an article exploring the technical implications of large-scale digital systems which would include data-processing equipment and electronic switching and which would become possible with the introduction of digital technology. As the existence of that article indicates, the concept for this new system had long been tucked away in the back of my mind. I had the firm belief that somehow or other this concept needed to be reflected in NEC's computer business; indeed, that as a technological strategy it would provide the impetus for NEC's great leap forward in the computer world. The Kinki Nippon Railway on-line seat reservation system mentioned in chapter 4 had been the first actual implementation of this new system. Now, with the ACOS series and the DINA concept behind us, I had the feeling that NEC's computer business was about to enter a new phase of development. As the natural extension of these ideas, my concept of what eventually became known as C&C began to blossom and take definite shape.

8

Building the C&C Business

Retrenching to Advance

As a result of the oil shock, NEC recorded a deficit of 0.2 billion yen for fiscal 1974 (the year ending March 1975) on consolidated sales of 475 billion yen. Although sales for fiscal 1975 increased by 11 percent to 527 billion yen, profits that year were a mere 1.7 billion yen. Consequently, beginning in the second half of 1974, NEC was forced to adopt a number of retrenchment measures. We had to face the current situation, I realized, with the same unflinching resolve with which we had recovered from the devastation of the war. There was no sense in "band-aid" measures: To recover from a shock of worldwide proportions we would have to make carefully thought-out plans, and it would take at least two years to get back on our feet again. We therefore took steps to reduce our production levels, cut back on fixed costs, and streamline our management resources.

What this meant in practice was a shorter working week for permanent employees at our five main plants at Mita, Tamagawa, Sagamihara, Fuchu, and Yokohama; cutbacks in the number of temporary workers at our regional plants; considerable pay cuts for company executives; and a 10 percent cut in salary for staff at the level of assistant general manager or higher, effective from October 1974. The year-end bonus normally given to all employees was paid in two installments, one in December, the other the following March. In addition, the annual pay raise in April was deferred for six months for everyone of the rank of section manager or higher; the number of new recruits was cut from 1,300 in April 1975 to 1,000 in April 1976; and personnel were reassigned to sales. NEC had never once resorted to such measures in over twenty years since the period of economic dislocation following the war, but fortunately the labor union was fully aware of the gravity of the situation and gave us their complete support.

Happily, my prediction that it would take "at least two years" to get back to normal was mistaken. Within a year and a half the Japanese economy was on the road to recovery, and business was beginning to look a bit brighter at NEC as well. In fiscal 1977 (the year ending March 1978) we recorded profits of 7.7 billion yen.

Sharing Power: From President to Chairman

On April 30, 1976, at the regular April meeting of the Board of Directors, I announced my decision to resign as president and hand over the position to a younger man. I proposed that senior executive vice president Tadao Tanaka succeed me as president, and that I be made chairman of the board. To complete my new top management slate I also recommended that senior executive vice president Yuzaburo Makino, who was retiring, continue as counsellor, and executive vice president Shinichi Uematsu replace him as senior executive vice president. The formal decision implementing these appointments was to be made at the board meeting held on June 30. On the afternoon of April 30, following traditional procedure in Japan, President-elect Tanaka and I went to Keidanren Hall to announce the new management team to the press.

Although it had been my original intention that the president and chairman of the board would jointly occupy the central position in the new "point to area" system of top management, my predecessor, Toshihide Watanabe, had died slightly more than a year after he had become chairman of the board in 1964. Because the management reform policies that I had set in motion upon becoming president were all reaching a climax at that time, with the chairmanship vacant I had been forced to do everything by myself. Now, however, the increased size of the business, the complexity of the economic environment, and the need for a solid management base all demanded a more sophisticated management structure. For that reason, I decided to become chairman myself and plan for future growth through cooperative efforts with the new president. To deal with the new conditions of stable growth after the oil shock, I had proposed someone with a background in accounting to be NEC's new president and someone with a background in engineering and manufacturing to serve as the new senior executive vice president.

If I and the new president were to work together effectively, however, the first thing we had to do was to clarify our respective areas of management responsibility – not in a legal sense, but in terms of what our actual functions would be within the company. In Japan the chairman of the board is generally a former president who has withdrawn from the front lines of management. I was well aware of that fact, but such a role was not appropriate in my case. After Mr Watanabe had died, I had combined the functions of what, in American management terms, would be called the chief executive officer (CEO) and the chief operating officer (COO), assuming ultimate responsibility for both the long-term management strategy of NEC and its day-to-day business affairs. My prime motive in becoming chairman was to appoint an executive who would take responsibility for ordinary business operations, carrying on along the lines that I had laid down nearly ten years before. This would lighten my own workload, though I would continue to wield ultimate authority as CEO. According to company bylaws, the chairman of the board at NEC exercises "general control over the important basic concerns of the company's business operations," whereas the president exercises "general control over the company's business operations." Although the wording is vague, it implies the difference between the functions of a CEO and a COO. Both the chairman and the president are in the forefront of management and share its duties.

In November 1974 I had set up an Executive Committee to serve as a forum for promoting mutual understanding among top management, sharing information, and improving the quality of decision-making. NEC also had a Corporate Management Committee, which had been established in the late 1940s. Henceforth the chairman would preside over the Executive Committee to "discuss matters pertaining to the highest policies of the company or the fundamental direction of its business operations"; the president would preside over the Corporate Management Committee to "discuss important matters of day-to-day management." Perhaps it would be best to think of the former as a place to explore long-term problems and the latter as a place to raise issues related to ordinary business. The CEO, while delegating authority in several areas to other executives, would still retain "residual responsibility." He might be thought of as the person who is ultimately in charge.

There was one other reason why I decided to become chairman at this time. After I became president I had worked to develop our three business areas – communications, computers, and semiconductors – to the top ranks in their respective fields. By 1976 we had almost achieved this goal, and the future was beginning to look bright in all three areas. For that reason I decided that psychologically it was just the right moment to assume the office of chairman.

Holding Course in the Storms

By the mid-1970s we had reached a crucial stage in the development of our communications, computer, and semiconductor businesses.

The August 1977 edition of *Fortune* gave extensive coverage to our communications equipment business, then entering a difficult period. Very few households in Japan were still in need of telephone service, yet weighting the balance toward the overseas market would mean entering into direct competition with the world's leading manufacturers. Nevertheless, I felt that just a little more effort would get us where we wanted to be – not only the top manufacturer in Japan, but among the top ten in the world.

In the semiconductor business, research and development efforts and massive investment had put us in the lead in the domestic market. NEC had made the decision to enter the semiconductor business back in 1967 because of the problems we encountered with the reliability of the integrated circuits that we had been importing. Although we had taken the first steps toward self-sufficiency, half of the ICs we were using at the time in our computers, communications equipment, and other industrial-use electronic equipment had to be imported from American manufacturers. Because of the low reliability of these imported ICs we were constantly encountering IC malfunctions that were adversely affecting the image of our products. We therefore decided to adopt a through-process system, in which all the necessary parts and/or subsystems would be manufactured by NEC itself.

When we actually began production, however, it soon became apparent that the semiconductor device industry was far more expensive than we had expected. We began outside sales of semiconductors in 1970 and soon ranked second or third in the domestic market. But by 1974 we faced serious problems coping with further investment. At the time of the Nixon shocks in 1971, semiconductor production was down more than 10 percent from the previous year, and our semiconductor operations managed to survive only by having work diverted to them from other plants. Then, just when we thought we were on the verge of recovery with the production of large-scale integrated circuits for the highly promising field of electronic calculators, the first oil shock occurred in 1973, and demand for semiconductor devices plummeted. Despite fears that changes in the market and lack of money would undermine our business plans and prevent us from operating efficiently, we held that the situation called for patience. And so we gritted our teeth and went ahead with plans to invest in plant and equipment.

Capital investment for the entire company amounted to 27.1 billion yen in 1972 and 36.4 billion in 1973, the second highest for any year in NEC's history. Increased investment in equipment for semiconductor production accounted for more than half these sums. Rival companies which had been contemplating expansion decided to cancel their plans; but judging from technological trends, I felt confident that the market would recover. My reading of the situation proved correct. The economy bottomed out, and in 1974, when demand began to revive, our production of semiconductors reached 60 billion yen, shooting us to the top of the domestic market. Massive investment in semiconductors had ultimately led to an increasingly bright future for our company.

But we needed capital to maintain our position as Japan's top semiconductor maker. No matter how you look at it, semiconductors are an expensive proposition. Because the rate of technological change is incredibly fast, manufacturing equipment must constantly be replaced, and if once you fall behind in research and development, it is almost impossible to catch up again. We could not raise sufficient capital in Japan to meet our needs and were racking our brains for a solution when senior vice president Motoo Hirota and associate senior vice president Kenzo Nakamura (now chairman of the board) proposed that we raise the necessary funds in Europe. Credit must also be given to vice president Hisao Kanai for his invaluable assistance at company information meetings in Europe. The convertible debentures sold so well that we were able to maintain our expansion strategy, and by 1984 our output had reached 590 billion yen. *The foundations had been laid for NEC's rise to the world's number one maker of semiconductors.*

Our computer operations, however, were a source of headaches. Although we had ranked first in the Japanese market from 1971 to

1973 – thanks to the success of our NEAC series 2200, Japan's first domestically produced one-machine concept computer line – when the time came to change lines, the announcement of our new series was delayed, and we were forced to yield our lead in market share to another company.

At just about this juncture the United States, which was suffering from a growing deficit in its international balance of payments, was pressing strongly for the opening up of the Japanese market, especially in the area of computers and computer-related industries, to rectify the uneven balance of trade between the US and Japan. Finally, as noted earlier, the Japanese government was to liberalize all aspects of the computer business – capital, imports, and the introduction of foreign technology – from April 1, 1976. To help the industry cope with this difficult business climate, the government decided to target the computer business for development and, as I mentioned in chapter 7 the six Japanese computer makers paired off into three groups.

In my annual New Year's Directive for 1976, I declared that in the coming year we would concentrate the full strength of the company behind planning for the growth of our computer operations. Confident that the goals I had set for the company were being reached, I was ready to entrust the role of chief operating officer to my successor and, as chairman of the board, to devote my close attention to guiding NEC along the strategic course of action that I had mapped out for it.

Clarifying Identity: The NEC Tree

To develop a company and get its business to grow, it is necessary to clarify its corporate identity. In the past companies had had company policies, codes, and slogans – in the case of NEC, a slogan that dated back to its earliest days – "better products, better service." But, as a general rule, most of these maxims belonged to the category of founders' precepts and were quite inadequate for the present day. What was needed was a corporate identity that would sum up the nature of the company's business, suggest the direction in which it was headed, and give a favorable impression of its corporate activities which would help it gain acceptance by society at large.

Around 1966, when I was visiting the office of Lawrence A.

Hyland, the *de facto* chief executive at Hughes Aircraft, he showed me a plastic model of a tree about two feet tall, which was sitting on his desk. According to Hyland, the Hughes Tree, as it was called, showed in three dimensions the interrelatedness of all the business areas in the Hughes company. Because it seemed a good and easily intelligible idea, when I returned to Japan I called in someone from our engineering coordination staff and instructed him to make a version of the Hughes Tree for NEC. A few days later he brought into my office a pencil drawing and a model made in wood: this was the prototype of the NEC Tree.

The strong roots of the tree represent NEC's technological strength. From these roots the switching operations draw nourishment and send forth the first stout branch from the tree trunk. At about the same time another strong, independent branch forks off from the first branch: This represents our carrier transmission business. The next branch represents our radio division; it is followed by the branch for electronic devices, the basis for all our other business operations. Next comes the branch for electronic data processing – in other words, computers. Finally, in order to suggest the growth of new branches, at the top of the tree is a branch labeled "unknown" representing future divisions as yet unnamed. "Unknown" seemed a bit bald, but there was no other suitable expression to indicate future business prospects. Sprouting from the earth as an offshoot of our technological roots is a young sapling depicting electrical household appliances at New Nippon Electric. (I did not feel that making household appliances a separate tree was necessarily appropriate, however, and we later changed its position.) In order for the tree to absorb nourishment from its roots and put forth branches and green leaves, it must receive light from the sun, which represents the marketplace – or, to put it another way, the needs of our customers. Whenever I looked at the NEC Tree I used to think, and talk with others, about what needed to be done to make it develop into a majestic specimen.

After several additions had been made to the original prototype, the perfected version of the NEC Tree was first unveiled outside the company in January 1973, at the beginning of our 1972 annual report in English published for foreign stockholders. Since then English and Japanese versions of the tree have been widely used in both in-house documents and publications outside the company to describe succinctly the nature of NEC's business. The NEC Tree thus serves as a means of informing employees about the current state of NEC's business strategy and as a method of giving outsiders an accurate understanding of the company.

Digital Switching and C&C

Concurrently with the development of the NEC Tree, another idea was taking shape in the back of my mind. When viewed from the perspective of the development process of electronics technology, it was quite an obvious one; but it was just what I needed as a beacon by which to steer the company on a knowledge- and information-intensive course.

In the summer of 1975 the International Ocean Exposition opened in Okinawa, attracting more than 3.5 million visitors by the time it closed the following January. NEC computers and communications equipment had been extensively used at the site. In September, at the Second World Telecommunication Forum '75 in Geneva, sponsored by the International Telecommunication Union (ITU) and the London *Financial Times*, I delivered a speech entitled "A Manu-facturer Looks at the Next Ten Years," outlining my views of the coming decade from my vantage-point as CEO of one of Japan's manufacturing companies. In effect, I said that now the installation of telephone networks had been completed in the industrialized countries we would soon be able to enjoy the benefits that would arise from the "docking" of telecommunications and computers, made possible by the switchover from analog to digital systems in communications lines. Computers would make it possible for communications networks to serve functions other than the trans-mission of information, and the key to this new breakthrough lay in microelectronics. Although this was not the central point of my speech, it was the first time that I had articulated the idea that had haunted me for the past ten years. This basic concept was the integration of computers and communications – "C&C."

The year after this conference an event occurred that came as a real shock to me. In May 1976 the Canadian telecommunications manufacturer, Northern Telecom, sponsored a three-day public seminar at Disney World in Florida and with great fanfare unveiled its digital switching DMS series. Before a large audience containing representatives of the telecommunications field from the US,

Canada, Sweden, and France, one Northern Telecom representative after another stood up and with great fervor declared that the phone of the future would be digital and that only Northern Telecom was capable of putting digital switching equipment on the market. Northern Telecom, which had been somewhat slow to develop a space-division electronic switching system such as the D-10 in Japan or Western Electric's No. 1 ESS, had thrown down the gauntlet to the competition in the area of digital switching.

In its annual shareholders' report published in April 1976, Northern Telecom had put together a five-page special supplement entitled "The Digital World, A New Era in Telecommunications." Somewhat earlier the company president, Robert C. Scrivener, had come to me with the proposal that since Northern Telecom had technological strength in digital switching and NEC in digital transmission, our two companies should team up to build a digital network. I politely refused Scrivener's suggestion because I felt that the time was approaching when I would be able to announce my C&C concept to the world in a clear and compelling fashion. Although I should have foreseen what was coming, when the announcement broke I couldn't help feeling that Northern Telecom had stolen a march on us.

At the time Northern Telecom announced that it was going digital, NEC was selling crossbar switching equipment and space-division electronic switching systems in the US market. After the announcement, however, our American sales representatives began complaining that whenever they paid a call on a customer they would be asked whether NEC had digital switching, and that it was becoming increasingly difficult to make a sale without it. Although our US sales office, NEC America, suggested that it would be wise for NEC to start selling digital equipment soon, I resisted their advice, believing that such a move would be premature in view of the situation in Japan, where NTT was sticking with space-division electronic switching systems. I proposed that we continue to supply the US market with our space-division systems and crossbar switching equipment.

In 1962 NEC had built one of the world's leading crossbar switching equipment plants at Sagamihara, second only to Western Electric's Hawthorne Works. In view of this plant's supply capacity we realized that if our business was to grow in the future we would need to seek markets abroad. The plan to rely on exports to expand our switching business resulted in a huge success in the US for our crossbar switching equipment. But we were unable to achieve the same rate of success with the space-division electronic switching system that we developed next because of strong competition from Western Electric's No. 1 ESS in the US and from ITT's Metaconta 10C and Ericsson's AXE systems elsewhere in the world. In this respect we were perhaps fortunate that the era of space-division switching systems was unexpectedly brief, and that they were soon replaced by digital switching.

NEC Moves Ahead with Digital Technology

At the beginning of 1977 the conglomerate TRW bought out Vidar, a digital transmissions equipment manufacturer which then began selling its new digital switching equipment in the US at absurdly low prices. NEC America's sales staff began to throw up their hands in despair. When their customers asked whether NEC had digital switching they could only say no. Somehow they managed to get by, but by the summer of that year the situation was completely hopeless. No one was interested in buying unless we had digital switching. When the request came again from NEC America that we immediately develop a digital system, we had no alternative but to swim with the tide. At NEC we were well on our way to developing a digital switching system that involved the digitalization not only of the control functions but of the speech path as well. According to a report from our Switching Group, which had been set up in May 1976 to oversee the project, they expected to achieve their objective by the summer of 1977.

In February 1977, I received an invitation to deliver a keynote address at an international telecommunications exposition called Intelcom '77 in Atlanta, Georgia that October. Other keynote speakers would be Björn Lundvall, president of Ericsson, the prominent Swedish telecommunications equipment maker, and Robert Scrivener of Northern Telecom. The main theme of Intelcom '77 was "Telecommunications and Economic Growth," an area of considerable interest to NEC. I had plenty of time before October to prepare; moreover, in April I was scheduled to receive the 1976 Frederik Philips Award from the Institute of Electrical and Electronic Engineers (IEEE) for my contributions to the development and growth of telecommunications and electronics. I had the feeling that the Intelcom exhibit would be the ideal opportunity for NEC to make some sort of new departure. I therefore accepted the invitation and began to explore possible ideas for my speech.

Back in March 1959 I had published an article entitled "Digital Technology and the Advance of Automation" in a special edition of the Japanese journal *OHM*. In it I had argued that the introduction of digital technology would hasten the appearance of digital systems that would include electronic switching and data-processing equipment and that we should look forward eagerly for these promising future developments. The time had now come when the first tangible wave of this technological vision was beginning to impinge on NEC's business operations.

Having made the move from digital transmission to digital switching, if we could succeed in digitalizing every aspect of communications technology this would create a technological common ground with computers, which are themselves based on digital technology. In the computer field, as the idea of distributing the data-processing functions of the computer slowly caught on, the spotlight fell on a configuration involving the use of online systems. At the end of 1976 NEC had announced the DINA concept, perfecting a system that separated information-processing functions from the database and then connected them together via a digital communications circuit. The idea of integrating computers with communications was just the new departure I had been looking for to boost NEC's sagging computer business, which was then involved in a bitter struggle for market share. I decided I would present this concept at Intelcom '77. I planned to begin my keynote address with an immediate reference to the merger of computers and communications. Meanwhile, at the exposition itself we would display our NEAX 61 digital switching system and our intelligent terminal, connected online to our ACOS system 700 mainframe at NEC's Central Research Laboratories south of Tokyo.

Unveiling C&C

I arrived in New York on October 8; a copy of my speech, which had been printed in Tokyo and sent on to New York, was brought to me by the president of our local office. Although I had gone over the speech with my staff and polished it carefully before my departure from Japan, the wording was still unclear in a few places: so I made some changes and had the local staff type up the new version, a task that went on well into the night. Still tired from jet-lag I flew to Atlanta the following morning.

The podium in the seminar hall of the recently completed Georgia World Congress Center in downtown Atlanta was decorated with the flags of the participating countries. At the beginning of the seminar immediately following that morning's opening ceremonies, I gave my thirty-minute keynote address, "Shaping a Communications Industry to Meet the Ever-Changing Needs of Society." According to plan I began my speech with the words "Today, in most developed countries, . . . communications technology is beginning to merge with computer technology, and the new terminology of computer communications is becoming popular." As I spoke these words I felt a surge of excitement at finally announcing in public this long-held conviction of mine. I went on to explain how, since its founding, NEC had worked to build the communications business in Japan, tracing the relation between the historical development of Japanese communications and actual examples of the products we had developed, right down to digital switching. I also alluded to semiconductors and computers, which were becoming inseparable from communications technology, and concluded with advice on how the developing countries should build their own communications industry.

Attending the seminar were Mohammed Mili, secretary general of the International Telecommunication Union; John D. deButts, chairman of AT&T; Scrivener of Northern Telecom; and Lundvall of Ericsson, as well as a number of other leading authorities in the communications field from around the world. But unless my memory deceives me, I was the only one to refer to the integration of communications and computers. I had chosen this great gathering of the telecommunications world attended by 8,000 visitors from eighty-three countries to unveil my concept of C&C. Now we had to actually put it into effect.

Orientation for C&C

It is not the fact that something exists that is important; awareness of its existence is what really matters. Now that I had formally announced my C&C concept to the leaders of the communications industry, other companies would soon recognize the business opportunities arising from the integration of computers and communications. There was consequently a pressing need for NEC to map out a business strategy as soon as possible. First, we would have to move rapidly ahead with systematically elaborating the C&C concept; then we needed to establish an organization within the company to build the C&C business and ensure its success.

Exactly one century earlier, in 1877, Alexander Graham Bell had made the first commercial application of the telephone, an invention so revolutionary that, notwithstanding major advances in its function and shape, essentially the same device had been in use for the past hundred years. It seemed a stroke of good fortune that in this centennial year I was able to make public the ideas about C&C that I had been mulling over ever since I became president of NEC thirteen years earlier. At the time, of course, computers and communications were thought to be two completely different types of technology, so not surprisingly the world was slow to respond to C&C. But not only did I have faith in the concept, I wanted to plan its implementation as soon as possible.

The two months after my return from Atlanta were frantically busy. Just before the end of the year, on the afternoon of December 29, I gathered together a dozen company executives and division heads at Senkaso, NEC's guest house in a quiet residential district of Tokyo. I wanted to hear the heads of NEC's leading business groups discuss their perceptions of C&C and what they expected from it so that we could formulate a more precise image of the C&C business. A review of the actual business activities of these groups soon revealed that many of their efforts to respond to market needs already involved the merger of computer and communications technologies; thus our present achievements in this area would be extremely valuable in formulating a future corporate image for our company.

The problem I put before those attending that day's meeting was this:

The expression C&C, which our company has begun to use recently, is attracting widespread interest. If we look at C&C in terms of technological trends, first, in the computer field, came the concept of distributed information-processing network architecture, which was made possible, of course, through the mediacy of communications networks. Next, in the communications area, came digital transmission and digital switching.

Digitalization has made communications technology technically the same as computer technology and has thus made it easy to integrate the two. Of course, a computer remains a computer, and communications remains communications, but an interface has been developed between them. I don't exactly understand the nature of this interface, but it should contain the seeds for new technologies. Judging from recent trends at the leading corporations in the United States, which is in the vanguard of information technology, if we don't make plans for this new area now we will be left behind. I want all of you to give your views about what direction C&C should take at NEC.

This meeting was subsequently known as the C&C Orientation Meeting. After repeated sessions the participants succeeded in laying the foundations for developing the C&C concept and promoting the C&C business. Their efforts eventually led to the establishment of the C&C Committee on June 30, 1978.

In May that year I first presented my ideas on C&C to a Japanese audience, during the keynote address at the thirtieth anniversary meeting of the Japan Electronics Industry Development Association in Tokyo. Here a chart was publicly unveiled outlining the concept in a way both striking and easy to understand. The chart was so well received that it was cited in the reports of the Subcommittee on Trade of the US House of Representative's Ways and Means Committee in 1980.

Having delivered my C&C manifesto at Atlanta, I repeated the ideas at the Third USA–Japan Computer Conference in October 1978 and at Intelcom '79 in Dallas in March 1979. With each speech I could feel that the new concept was gaining acceptance and evoking a more positive response. In particular, I threw my energies into the speech I gave to the Third USA–Japan Computer Conference in San Francisco. This bilateral conference was planned in the belief that if those attending from both countries could exchange their differing views about computers, better understanding between our two countries might result. The keynote speaker on the US side was Dr Jerome B. Wiesner, then president of the MIT. As keynote speaker on the Japanese side I gave a speech entitled "The Japanese Computer Industry: Its Roots and Development," in which I tried to clarify the standpoint of the Japanese computer industry by dispelling the notion that Japanese computers were merely imitations of US models, and discussing our indigenous efforts to develop the computer. After locating the roots of these efforts in the switching circuit theory set forth in 1935 by Akira Nakashima and Masao Hanzawa of NEC, I then traced the significant stages in the development of the computer from that date to the present, concluding with a discussion of the future prospects for C&C. The main points of my keynote address can be summed up as follows:

The Japanese computer industry has its roots in communications and has developed out of communications technology. This background is in direct contrast with the computer manufacturers of the United States and Europe, most of which grew out of office equipment, and is a special feature that should prove extremely valuable for the information-processing systems of today and tomorrow.

Judging from both their past history and the way they can be expected to develop well into the twenty-first century, computers are unmistakably and unswervingly moving in the direction of a merger with communications. If the Japanese computer industry continues to build on its technological foundations and maintains a true vision of the future, it undoubtedly will achieve greatness. The most important factor is the time required to develop this vision. We must not be too hasty, but must move steadily and deliberately toward our goal.

The creative activities of a number of different companies have contributed to the growth of the computer industry in Japan today. A major contribution has also been made by the multiplication effect resulting from the interplay of such areas of technology as telecommunications, consumer electronics, and semiconductors.

At first, computers were mutually incompatible, each run by its own software, what I call "point-oriented" computers. Later, these computers developed into computer "lines," a family series of computers in all sizes from small to large, all using the same software. Although the way lay open to extend this line upward in the direction of ever larger models, proceeding in that direction would inevitably result in increasingly complex software. Given the present advances in communications, computers can henceforth be expected to move in the direction of "area-oriented" machines, whereby the processing function is distributed to a number of computers which are connected together to form a network.

The importance of software to a computer system is increasing every day. We must raise software to the status of an industrial product and find ways to improve its quality and manufacturability. And we must also recognize the economic value of software as a product independent of and distinct from hardware.

In September 1979 at Telecom '79, the Third World Telecommunication Forum sponsored by the ITU in Geneva, I explored the general prospects for C&C in an address entitled "The Japanese Telephone Industry in the Year 2000."

During the two years since my Atlanta manifesto I watched C&C permeate the world's information and telecommunications industries like water seeping into parched earth. What exactly, then, did I mean by C&C? First, technological innovations such as the digitalization of communications methods mean that communications technology is now of the same nature as computer technology. Second, as computers come online and make use of distributed processing, they are making greater use of communications circuits. That, in turn, means that communications systems are evolving into comprehensive communications networks capable of processing and transmitting not only the human voice but also data and images. As a result, communication will cease to be simply a part of the national infrastructure and will also be widely used both in manufacturing activities and in the home to help people lead more satisfying lives.

In other words, C&C will not only remove the temporal and spatial restrictions on our ability to transmit information; *it will also reduce the quantitative, temporal, and intellectual limits on our ability to generate, process, and store information. For that reason, I considered it my duty as an industrialist to develop C&C so that it could contribute to society and the human race.*

Organizing for the "New Age"

"The high yen is the harbinger of a new age for the Japanese economy and for NEC Corporation. Now is the time to revise our thinking and lay plans to deal with this new age." These were the words I addressed to those attending the regular Executive Committee meeting on November 1, 1977, the second such meeting to be held after my return from Atlanta. Because the economy had entered a period of transition from high-level to stable growth, I was calling attention to the need to find a new direction for NEC.

NEC had three markets: (1) the government and quasi-government market centered on the NTT Public Corporation; (2) the general domestic consumer market; and (3) the overseas market. The key to determining how we should allocate our energies in each of these areas could only be found in the priorities of the "new age" I saw us entering. Back in 1965, our long-term plan had been to use "information" as the direction in which to develop our company's business. More than ten years later we had finally achieved a balance in the types of information-oriented equipment that we made, and the multiplication effect from this balance had led to the birth of C&C. Now we could – indeed, should – expect "something big" to occur. If so, then the new age for NEC was the age of C&C, which we should develop, reinforce, and implement as our corporate strategy.

Specifically, the steps we took included, first, setting up the C&C Committee mentioned above. Because the organizational functions of our existing business groups and divisions operated on the principle of autonomous vertical integration, inevitably any attempt to introduce a horizontal coordination between individual divisions or groups of divisions was bound to cause problems, both at the organizational level and in terms of corporate consciousness. The objective of the C&C Committee was to overcome these barriers by formulating and promoting specific strategies for the C&C business, which would be interdisciplinary by nature, and then evaluating their success. To fulfill these functions the committee discussed ways of strengthening our various corporate strategy divisions, regulating the authority of the group executives, and setting up an independent coordination division. But I pinned my hopes on a more loosely knit type of coordination and set up subcommittees, expert meetings, and work meetings under the main committee to work out all the details. Representative of the subcommittees set up initially were the Long-Range Strategy Subcommittee, the International Operations Strategy Subcommittee, and the Telecommunications Liberalization Counter-plan Subcommittee.

The second phase of building up the internal structure for C&C involved the formation of the C&C Systems Division and the reorganization of our Research and Development Group on July 28, 1980. The latter involved dissolving NEC's Central Research Laboratories, which had been in operation since 1965, clarifying the distinction between research functions and development functions, and establishing five new independent research laboratories – the Fundamental Research Laboratories, the Optoelectronics Research Laboratories, the C&C Systems Research Laboratories, the Software Production Research Laboratories, and the Resources and Environment Protection Research Laboratories.

No strategy, no matter how splendid it may seem, can survive unless management is flexible enough to cope with current conditions; if it is not, all efforts will be wasted. The reorganization of our R&D aimed to ensure that this essential condition was met. As the entire company began to move toward C&C, cooperative relations between the research labs and our operating divisions or groups would inevitably expand in scope and become extremely fluid. By dividing up our R&D organization and realigning it, the monolithic authority previously vested in the head of the Central Research Laboratories would be split up among the various research labs to give greater mobility to our research activities. *We might say that this was my "point to area" concept applied to research.*

The starting-point for our C&C organization on the marketing side began with the establishment of the C&C Systems Division within the Special Projects Group, also on July 28, 1980. Just as the reorganization of NEC's research system was aimed at invigorating our research activities, the objective of this new organization was to enable us to carry out dynamic marketing activities. On July 1, 1982, we expanded the C&C Systems Division into a subgroup consisting of one planning office, four divisions, and a sales outlet, thereby laying the groundwork for NEC's preeminent position in the C&C market, which is now growing rapidly.

The C&C business, it goes without saying, spans all of NEC's technological and marketing areas. This means that we could not operate smoothly and efficiently without a company-wide system of cooperation. Although it is a fundamental criterion that each operating division is self-supporting, there must be solid teamwork, both among the divisions and among the groups of divisions. The C&C Systems Subgroup plays a central role in directing this effort.

Around this time sales in the North American market accounted for about half of all NEC's overseas sales. In 1977 we had begun local production of communications equipment in the US, albeit on a small scale, and in 1978 we opened a full-sized plant in a suburb of Dallas, Texas. That year we also began production of computer peripherals on the East Coast, outside Boston, and at the end of the year bought out a medium-sized chip maker in Silicon Valley lock, stock, and barrel – employees and all – and began local production of semiconductors. For home electronics we built a production plant in Atlanta, Georgia in 1985.

I certainly believe, and it should be clear to everyone, that the US electronics market demands the most technologically advanced products and services in the world; for that reason, the weeding-out process through competition is very tough. Our efforts to develop the C&C business in the US came under sharp criticism in the July 5, 1982 issue of *Business Week*, which complained that "NEC's products do not always reflect the integrated C&C dreams of top management." After numerous attempts we established a C&C Business Promotion Division at NEC America with headquarters in a New York City suburb in November 1983.

Engineering Education and Technology Development

C&C was now steadily taking hold within the company as both a technological schema and a corporate structure. What perhaps might be called the third phase in my C&C business building program, and the most fundamental of all, was the system for training C&C-oriented personnel. The development of C&C products requires the close cooperation of computer engineers, communications engineers, and device engineers. As very-large-scale integration (VLSI) technology becomes the basis of C&C products, functional elements of all kinds are assembled on one silicon chip a few millimeters square. None of this work would be achieved without systems engineering, circuit engineering, device engineering, mechanical engineering, materials engineering, and software engineering. Thus, engineers in each field must not only be well versed in their own areas of expertise, they must also have some knowledge of adjacent and related areas. To train the type of engineer from whom we could expect this sort of scope, we set up the Institute of Technology Education on March 1, 1979 at the Tamagawa plant. It is essential to continuously upgrade the expertise of all our engineers in the rapidly changing area of electronics, and the institute's mission is accordingly to provide them, on a systematic and continuing basis, with the most up-to-date technological training. One of its basic educational policies is "to provide an education aimed at synthesizing and strengthening innovative engineering skills to keep pace with technological advances and cope with the C&C Age." The institute has revised and updated its curriculum every single year since its founding.

I myself used to gather together board members, vice presidents, the general managers in both operating divisions and head office, and other members of the corporate staff and hold brainstorming sessions twice a year in summer and in winter to discuss my own management experiences and exchange ideas about how to build the C&C business in the years ahead. The ideas and proposals brought forward during these talks, which were held from 1981 to 1983, immeasurably deepened my own convictions about the success of the C&C business and confirmed my belief in the abundant human resources possessed by NEC.

Managing Uncertainty

On July 17, 1979, NEC celebrated its eightieth anniversary. Our previous balance sheet – the consolidated performance figures for March 31, 1979 – indicated that sales were at an all-time high of 790 billion yen, with profits of 7.9 billion yen. Although this latter figure did not match our past peak of 13 billion yen, we were beginning to move steadily along the road to recovery. It seemed likely that fiscal 1979 would fulfill my dreams with a corporate performance appropriate to an anniversary year.

We still, of course, had to cope with the second oil shock. At their general meeting in Geneva in June 1979 the OPEC countries had agreed on a new price level for oil of $20 a barrel. To counter this rise the Agency of Natural Resources and Energy at the Ministry of International Trade and Industry led Japanese efforts at energy conservation and the shift away from oil. Specific plans included a movement beginning that summer to cut back on the use of oil by 5 percent, set air conditioners at 80 degrees, and encourage office workers not to wear neckties or jackets. What really made the difference, however, was that Japanese industry's experiences with energy conservation during the five years since the first oil shock had provided valuable lessons that were now beginning to pay off.

The exchange rate, which had continued to rise, reached an unprecedented high of 175.5 yen to the dollar on October 31, 1977; but on the following day – November 1 – the US government announced comprehensive plans to defend the dollar, and the yen plummeted. The cheaper yen was a blessing to the Japanese economy, which entered a period of spontaneous recovery without the need for any stimulative measures by government. The long-range planning figures worked out in fiscal 1979 by our manufacturing and marketing groups showed a strong expansion, in terms of both sales and profits, reflecting prevailing economic trends, but repeated jumps in the price of crude oil and violent fluctuations in the yen–dollar exchange rate were becoming cause for concern.

Perhaps indicative of this unsettled business climate, the Japanese translation of John Kenneth Galbraith's *The Age of Uncertainty*, published in 1978, became a phenomenal bestseller. I met Professor Galbraith in South America in the fall of 1978 at a seminar sponsored by the Colombian Management Association at Medellin, which we had both been invited to address. I also had a chance to talk with him informally at his home in Cambridge, Massachusetts in March 1979. I have vivid memories of that conversation and some of the pointed remarks that we exchanged: "Change and uncertainty force people to think"; "Uncertainty can break a deadlock because new possibilities emerge more readily from dynamic situations than from static ones."

If one stopped to think about it, an age of change was undoubtedly good for new business opportunities. Repeated hikes in oil prices, for example, had resulted in a keen interest in energy conservation and resource-saving technologies. Here was a perfect opportunity, I thought, for C&C, which was conservation-oriented since it made extensive use of resource-saving technologies to cut down on the movement of people, goods, and money. Believing that it was my management mission to build the new C&C business on the solid foundations of NEC's glorious eighty-year tradition, I regularly assembled the management staff to make my basic thinking on business operations common knowledge. Because the company directive of July 30, 1979, expresses my thoughts on these matters, I include it here despite some overlap with what I have written earlier.

Managing C&C: Flexibility and Dynamism

The NEC Tree

During our company's eighty-year history we have established businesses in a range of areas, including switching, transmission and terminals, radio, information processing, industrial electronic systems, electron devices, and household appliances. These businesses have not developed spontaneously or haphazardly. The roots of all of them lie in a superb common tradition of basic technology. The trunk and branches that have sprung from these roots, tended by wise management decisions, have grown into the large high-tech corporation that we know today. The NEC Tree has been created to explain succinctly the relationship between NEC's business areas. As this image shows, technology is at the root of all the business we do.

Each business area absorbs nourishment from the roots and sends forth buds; it receives the warmth of the sun – the market, our customers – and branches out freely, sending forth numerous new shoots – new business ventures. The role of the manager is like that of a gardener who selects the most promising young shoots and trims the shape of the tree. In this context, management and coordination should be thought of as two separate functions. Because the driving forces behind the growth of the NEC Tree are technology and the market, the function of coordination is to operate from within to provide the needed water and nourishment to maintain unlimited growth. The function of management is to consider the NEC Tree as a whole, choosing the main business opportunities, and training their shape. Both functions are indispensable to the growth of the corporation, but we must be clearly aware of the differences in their respective roles.

The Division System Matrix

Even when the same terminology is used, the nature of the division system differs widely from one company to another. In some companies the divisions each deal with a single product and act independently of one another, with little correlation in their markets or technologies. In our company, however, we have superb and richly diversified technologies in the wide-ranging areas of communications, computers, electron devices, and household appliances. As we head into the C&C era, we can expect to reap the benefits of the overall strength that will result from the intersecting and interlinking of all these business areas. For that reason, the general manager of each division must take an active interest in the technology, manufacturing, and marketing practices in areas that are adjacent to his own, and try to keep abreast of what other sectors of the company are doing.

Because our markets span the areas of government demand (especially from NTT), private domestic demand, and the overseas market, we find ourselves in the position of having to cover the whole spectrum of totally different sales methods and types of orders, from custom-made systems to products for the mass market. The "division system matrix" has been created to cope with these widely divergent circumstances. It is an organizational construct unique to our company that has been refined over the past dozen years to reflect business configurations at NEC. In order to raise corporate performance, all members of the management staff must have a thorough understanding of the framework and main purpose of this construct and be acutely aware of the need to act in accordance with it.

The top management organization in our company is composed of a business division matrix consisting of a vertical "technology" axis and a horizontal "market" axis. Each division must separately consider its product planning, sales policy, and other marketing strategies in terms of its own "technology/market segment," which exists where the horizontal and vertical axes of its business intersect. Members of the Switching Group, for example, shares the same technology, but their marketing policies will be completely different depending on whether they are supplying equipment to NTT or opening a new market in a developing country. Because NTT has outstanding systems engineering and an impeccable maintenance system, a supplier simply has to work to its specifications. When selling to a developing country, however, the manufacturer must provide not only the hardware but all the knowhow as well, from building stations to training maintenance personnel. Or take the areas of central office switching systems and private branch exchange (PBX). The design concepts here are undergoing profound change. As we approach the C&C era, central office switching systems are expected to become more and more complex, while private branch exchanges will be simpler, more compact, and more and more like an office machine, so that the distinction between PBX and customer-owned and -operated equipment will become increasingly blurred.

As these examples indicate, even when starting out from the same technology, different markets will require radically different approaches. That is one reason why our company needs the division system matrix.

If the ability to tailor plans for each technology/market segment is extremely important for our business operations, devising separate product planning programs and sales policies for each market is the central task of our marketing strategy.

Marketing and Sales

Marketing and sales are different functions. Generally speaking, marketing is handled by the head, sales by the feet. If sales is the locomotive, then the job of marketing is to lay the rails for it to run on. Without rails the locomotive cannot run; but there is no point in having rails if there is no locomotive to run on them. Both functions are equally vital.

Next in importance is the speed of marketing's response to market trends. Speed – the time element – is critical in any business operation, but it must be given special emphasis in marketing. If a response comes six months late, it becomes extremely difficult to remain competitive; a year late and the company will be forced to drop out of the field altogether. Examples of successful and unsuccessful responses are too numerous to mention and can be found both inside and outside the company.

The Relation between Operating Division and Marketing Division

In the division system matrix the functions of marketing and sales depend on the nature of the business area: In some cases the focus is on technology, in others, on sales. Government demand is an example of the former, the mass market is an example of the latter. In both cases, however, responsibility for the technology/market segment is shared jointly by the general managers of the relevant operating and marketing divisions. The reason for making the operating division a profit center is, first, to avoid the waste of energy involved in internally coordinating the distribution of profits, and second, because it allows room for efforts to bring down costs through the adoption of value engineering methods – whereby commercial products satisfying customer needs can be provided at minimal cost – and new technology such as integrated circuits, by putting them under the control of the division head. The fact that an operating division is a profit center does not mean that it ranks higher than a marketing division. The heads of both divisions hold equal responsibility; the only difference is the nature of that responsibility.

For this reason the heads of marketing divisions must also have an interest in business trends in each of the operating divisions. Similarly, in order to put in practice the lessons learned from "listening to the market," the heads of operating divisions will have to be more receptive to what those in the front lines of sales have to say.

Special Projects and Joint Strategy

The division system matrix is not a rigid system that demands that everything and anything be forced into its framework. Our Special Projects Group is an exception. In areas like the Air Traffic Control Systems Division it is more appropriate to operate the technology/market segment as an independent organization: here, therefore, the head of the project has sole responsibility for both technology and marketing. With the growth of the business and changes in the economic environment innovations may be needed to respond to actual circumstances. This is to be desired. In problem areas such as software, for example, where it is desirable to establish joint strategies, it is reasonable to think that an altogether different approach might be adopted.

The Operating Group

Although the head of an operating division has direct responsibility for business operations, because each business area in our company has deep bonds, technologically speaking, with adjacent areas, this has created the need for a smooth interface between divisions. In view of this fact, the "operating group" has been established as a kind of federation of operating divisions.

The group, however, cannot infringe the autonomy of the operating division, which is our strategic business unit (SBU). The group executive's main responsibility is to serve as the *alter ego* for the company president and to coordinate policy among the operating divisions under his control or with other groups of divisions in the company.

Because our company's business spans many different areas, it is extremely difficult for the chairman and the president to exercise constant control over what is going on in all our enterprises. The top management structure at NEC is therefore based on a division of labor, with each general manager of a division or group executive in charge of an operating group responsible for running the day-to-day business in his respective area. Under this division of labor a centrifugal force is at work as each division tries to choose the most suitable options for its particular business area independently of what would be most suitable for the entire company. If left unchecked, the interests of the division would come first, and the interests of the company as a whole would be ignored. Moreover, this centrifugal force could be expected to become stronger as the pace of divisional activities picked up, just as it does when a revolving top increases its speed. To maximize the efficiency of the technology, equipment, and capital of the company as a whole, and give maximum scope to the overall strength in the area of C&C, a countervailing centripetal force is needed. This centripetal force rests primarily in the coordination exercised by the group executives.

As business prospers, the stronger the centrifugal force the greater the need for a centripetal force to balance it. For this reason, the group executives, who are also members of the Executive Committee, will need to work even harder to strengthen their management skills.

Corporate Development

For a business to grow it must have a first-class management organization. We therefore need to consider, not what is the most appealing abstract ideal of management theory, but what is the most appropriate organization for existing circumstances. A vertical hierarchy, which is meant to deal with business matters on a sound and steady basis, is appropriate for government agencies but not for corporations, which need an organization that can expedite the evolution of dynamic marketing activities.

The leading companies of the world are already beginning to build new organizations. This requires taking into consideration the nature of the business, the stage of development that it has achieved, and the personnel needed to run it, and then building an organization that can respond flexibly.

The C&C era that will emerge from the integration of computers and communications, it is commonly acknowledged, will belong to NEC, but if we are to realize these expectations, we must coordinate our company's many-faceted technological prowess and wide-ranging sales skills and marshall them effectively to achieve overall strength.

To do so we must apply the motto "more flexible, more dynamic" to the corporate structure itself. I expect a thorough understanding of these principles and a smooth display of organizational strength from all executives.

As we completed plans to respond to the second oil shock I was becoming increasingly concerned about the state of President Tanaka's health. After some discussion Tanaka stepped down and was succeeded by Dr Tadahiro Sekimoto on 30 June 1980.

9

The Expanding Horizon: Software, Fiber Optics, and Space Technology

Man and Technology: The Evolution of Software

If we trace back the history of computers, we see that software came first – in other words, an idea occurred in someone's mind, then the hardware was built to embody it. When computers appeared on the market, however, the software was embedded in the hardware and, for a long time, was considered merely an appendage to it. Around 1970 the idea of "unbundling" software from hardware began to gain currency, mainly in America, and software came to be regarded as an independent product.

For advanced systems like C&C it would be no exaggeration to say that their ease of use is wholly dependent on the maturity and level of performance of their software. If we think in terms of the interface between C&C and the people who use it, in other words, how user-friendly C&C systems will become with the passage of time, we could divide the process into three stages: "Man in C&C," "Man on C&C," and "Man with C&C." These stages can be explained more concretely as follows:

"Man in C&C"

In this first phase, system intelligence and the man–machine interface were still inadequate, so extensive human effort was required to attain maximum performance from C&C systems and machines. The programs needed to run the computer, for example, were written in computer language. Because this was a machine language consisting of strings of numeric characters and symbols, far removed from the language human beings normally use, programming was an extremely tedious operation. In the communications field, this stage would be the equivalent of the age of manual switching and human switchboard operators.

"Man on C&C"

By this stage, system intelligence and the man–machine interface have advanced considerably. Programming has become much easier, with the development and use of assembler and compiling programs to translate from natural language into machine language.

Instead of creating data files for each program, the concept of a database has been developed so that information can be stored. As the focus shifts from the program to the data *per se*, information processing makes great strides. Input/output in the Japanese language and the use of computers in daily work become commonplace.

The equivalent of this stage in the communications sphere is the era of automatic telephone exchanges that make it possible to telephone to any part of the world and the use of satellite communications to transmit world events to our television sets.

"Man with C&C"

In this age everyone, not just experts, will be able to use C&C easily, and C&C systems will play the role of sophisticated personal assistants. Intelligent information-processing functions and automatic translation functions will be developed so that the system will be able to understand the desires and demands of the people who use it.

Programs using charts and graphs will be commonplace; databases will come equipped with built-in programs; and programming in natural language and automatic synthesis and generation systems will be in practical use. The interaction between people and terminals can be expected to become more user-friendly.

Incorporating the Human Dimension

Earlier schematic diagrams of C&C showed the three lines representing the technological development of computers, communications, and semiconductors as a two-dimensional plane surface. Now I was faced with the problem of how to express the new human element. I have always had the habit of drawing pictures in order to clarify my ideas. In most cases a picture helps to pinpoint problem areas and suggest solutions: this was no exception. I assembled a group of specialists from within the company and posed the question: "Somehow C&C is incomplete without the human dimension. Does anyone have any good ideas on how to convey this?" They came up with several suggestions.

The original two-dimensional diagram contained a vertical "communications" axis moving in the direction of digitalization and a horizontal "computer" axis moving toward systematization. The human element was added to this as a third dimension showing semiconductors moving in the direction of intelligence. The graph now showed the three lines of C&C slowly moving upward like an arrow pointing in the direction of the development of C&C. If everyone, not just experts, could really master the C&C system, it would lead to a more fulfilling way of life both culturally and economically. This would be the ultimate goal for both the developer and the user of C&C systems.

This idea was in fact an important leap forward in my C&C theory. In September 1981, at the twenty-third IEEE Computer Society International Conference held in Washington, DC, I gave a keynote address entitled "Computers, Communications and Man: The Integration of Computers and Communications with Man as an Axis – The Role of Software," in which I stressed the central importance of software for C&C. Originally this conference had dealt with both hardware and software, but one of the signs of the times was that almost all the speeches given that year were about software. As the title of my speech indicates, I started from the recognition that software was essential for the creation of a prosperous, user-friendly C&C society, then outlined current software activities at NEC, especially our quality control methods for software development and our small quality circle activities to improve the quality of software and make it more amenable to mass production. The speech seemed to be of great interest to members of the audience, especially young academics.

As I have already mentioned, the ultimate aim in considering the human element of C&C is the creation of C&C systems that people can master at will. Because software is what imparts intelligence to a C&C system, a well-thought-out approach to software – or the lack thereof – will have serious consequences. In 1980, the cost of software was said to be 60 or 70 percent of the cost of an entire system. If this trend continued, software costs would account for 90 percent of the total in ten years' time. If we did not bring the cost down significantly, C&C systems would never materialize. A prominent consulting company had predicted that in a year or two software would account for 40–45 percent of a computer company's profits. If firmware, service, and maintenance were added in, that figure would rise to 90 percent. Even if this prediction were slightly off, we at NEC would still be affected.

Software Production

Climbing Mount Fuji

What then should we do? There were two problems. The first was streamlining software production. The development of software can be compared to climbing Mount Fuji. The fifth stage of the climb is the dividing line. Up to that point climbers do not need to rely on their own legs – they can go by bus or even drive their own car. This is mountain climbing in name only. But after the fifth stage the path grows steep and can be ascended only on foot.

This analogy gave me an idea for solving the first software problem. Producing some kinds of software is as easy as the climb to the fifth stage of Mount Fuji, but other software involves the sheer drudgery of the final ascent. In terms of quantity, however, the former far exceeds the latter, perhaps by as much as ten to one. If the development of software in these areas could be standardized and modularized, as is the case for hardware production, it should be possible to adopt various production and control methods. This is an area of software that should be conducive to automation. At NEC the Software Production Technology Research Lab, established in July 1980, is in charge of research and development of mass-production techniques for software. We did not call it the Software Research Lab because we did not want researchers to be thinking in high-flown terms about the difficult things they were doing: rather we wanted to remind them that their objective was production technology.

To address the need for complex, advanced software we created the C&C Systems Research Lab at the same time. The software that is like the final ascent of Mount Fuji above the fifth stage is quantitatively small but includes such advanced revolutionary areas as intelligent information-processing systems and automatic translation programs. The development of this kind of software is *terra incognita* and not at present amenable to streamlining methods. But the segmentation of software development in itself may be one way of streamlining production.

The second problem was to equip software production with C&C. In the past, all that was used to write programs was paper and pencil and the craftsmanlike intuition and knowhow of the software engineer. When foreign journalists came to Japan to report on Japanese software production, they all had the same impression – that the number of computer terminals was far too low for the number of engineers. That time is long past, however, and now engineering work stations with more than one computer per person have been set up, especially in our advanced software divisions. At NEC this upgrading of the development environment has helped to improve our ability to produce software.

Quality Control for Software

Another idea that I was very keen to see implemented was that of adapting the quality control methods that had proved so successful for hardware production to the production of software. I have discussed NEC's development and introduction of a quality control system for the entire company, which has achieved excellent results. Because the role of software would become extremely important as we entered the C&C age, it was clear that any problems in the quality of software, especially its reliability, could cause serious problems to the development of the C&C business. I was constantly telling the people in charge of our software operations that there ought to be some way of applying quality control to software, but they did not seem too enthusiastic. "We understand what you are saying," they would tell me, "but it would be awfully difficult to do." One day I asked them, "What do you mean by this word 'debugging,' which you are always talking about?" Debugging, I was told, meant getting the bugs – defects – out of a program. When I asked why there were defects in the first place, they told me it was unavoidable because human beings make mistakes. Clearly, it would be better to make software without any bugs to start with, but how?

As the technology evolved, however, it became clear that something would have to be done. As integrated circuits evolved into large-scale integration and very-large-scale integration, software was being built into LSIs and VLSIs. How in the world would it be possible to debug software once it had been inserted in an LSI? The conclusion was clear: only by practising quality control could we produce good quality software. Around 1979, I could sense a change; people were beginning to feel that we could do it. *In undertakings such as this the right timing is essential.*

Beginning in 1979 about thirty or forty employees who participated in our Software Problem Review Committee came to the tentative conclusion that it was possible to make software without bugs. They began to consider quality control methods for software and ways to automate software production. Testing began in 1980 and on April 17, 1981, I attended the official start of NEC's Software Quality Control program at our central research complex in Kawasaki. In effect, it was a zero defects program applied to software, but to distinguish it from our long-standing company-wide ZD program aimed primarily at hardware, it was called "software quality control", or SWQC for short.

The specific aims of SWQC were, first of all, to improve the production environment. Documents that had hitherto been created by paper and pencil were now made using computers. Not only did this lead to the wholesale improvement of programming production efficiency, it made it possible to convert the process of making software from the work of an individual to that of a group. The technical knowhow and experiences contained in the minds of software engineers could now be stored in databases. Even the supervising practices were cited as an area of potential streamlining.

To bring an idea to fruition requires creating the proper atmosphere for large groups of people to work in (small groups have a different dynamic). The right atmosphere acts as a kind of stimulus that arouses the will to work. Now we had gone to the trouble of creating a lab and starting SWQC, it was only natural that people would begin asking for a formal opportunity to present their findings. Acceding to these demands, we set up a committee to select papers on software quality control. The first presentations were made in November 1981, and sessions have since been held twice a year, in the spring and in the fall. From fifty reports at the first session the number of papers put forward climbed to more than 1,300 at the fourteenth session held in June 1988. Every year I give the keynote address and am heartened to be able to experience for myself the enthusiasm that NEC employees have for SWQC.

Around 1982 NEC's software activities began to gain momentum. These included the construction of a nationwide software production map, stiffer controls on software ordered from outside the company, systematization of software education, the transplanting of experimental results to the operations line, and many others too numerous to mention.

Software Production System with Direct Links to Demand

As mentioned in chapter 7, NEC established its first software subsidiary in September 1975. The aim of NEC Software was the research and development of software engineering techniques and the design, development, and sale of software products. In 1976 we formally joined the ranks of the Japanese software industry as a corporate member in the Japan Software Industry Association (later, the Japan Information Service Industry Association) and took part in a program sponsored by the Ministry of International Trade and Industry to strengthen and develop Japanese software engineering.

In 1977, when the business began to show signs of taking off, NEC Software Kansai split off from NEC Software and became an independent company. By the end of fiscal 1979 NEC Software was the largest company specializing in software in Japan, with 650 employees and annual sales of 13 billion yen. Between 1980 and 1982 it entered a period of all-round expansion.

My software strategy seemed right on target. It was getting to the point where, not only in computers but even in communications and microelectronics, one could not hope for growth without strengthening software. We therefore set up NEC Communication Systems (software for electronic switching equipment) in January 1980; NEC IC Microcomputer Systems (software for electron devices) that May; NEC Telecom Systems (software for transmission and terminals equipment), NEC Aerospace Systems (software for aerospace electronics), and NEC Scientific Information Systems Development (software for research and development), all in October 1981.

By establishing this series of companies, NEC Software, although located in Tokyo and mainly responsible for software for our information-processing group, was able to respond thoroughly to the software needs of the entire country. Furthermore, to keep personnel in rural areas, we established software companies in or near major regional centers. By now we have established thirty-four companies from Sapporo in the north to Naha in the south and are contributing to the growth of the local economy as the influence of software on the Japanese economy becomes more and more pervasive.

Software Development to Suit National Conditions

Once the decentralization of software production was under way within Japan, we set out to produce software overseas and build a worldwide distribution network. Our aims were to supplement the inadequate supply of software engineers in Japan and improve the efficiency of software production by circulating software among centers in Japan and abroad, or among our overseas centers, and by avoiding reduplication. But these were not our only objectives. Because software reflects local language and customs, our software strategy was based on the recognition of national borders. To put it another way, software is by nature conducive to local production.

In the computer field, to keep pace with the rapid growth of our computer business abroad and to establish a true international division of labor we began developing and producing software in our overseas subsidiaries in Australia, China, Germany, Singapore, Taiwan, and the US. In Beijing we set up the China–Japan Software Center in January 1982. As I recall, in November 1979, just after NEC had completed plans to deal with the second oil shock, I discussed trends toward an information society with Vice Premier Wan Zhen (now vice president of the People's Republic of China). During the conversation I broached the subject of setting up a software center and got his approval. The Chinese contributed the building, and NEC provided the computers and the instructors. More than 1,500 Chinese students have since received training there.

In October 1982 we established a company to produce software for switching equipment in New Zealand, which has since become the New Zealand Telecommunications Systems Support Centre. In July 1985 we set up NEC Engineering (Thailand) to improve software for switching systems, which it also installs and maintains. NEC America has steadily expanded its local development system, establishing a software production center for modems in San Jose, California in

August 1983, and a switching technology center in Dallas, Texas in April 1986, which has begun developing switching equipment software.

The Power of Light: Fiber Optic Communications

In February 1985 Japanese newspapers carried the announcement that NTT Public Corporation had completed an optical fiber communications trunkline spanning the entire length of the Japanese archipelago. This splendid achievement marked the dawn of a new era of fiber optic communications in Japan.

My first encounter with the power of light dates back to a visit to Hughes Aircraft in 1960, when Lawrence A. Hyland told me that a Hughes engineer, Dr Theodore H. Maiman, had obtained the world's first pulsed laser action, using a ruby crystal. This meant that it was now possible to artificially generate coherent light – that is, light in which the electromagnetic waves maintain a fixed phase relationship with each other. In the past, radio waves had been developed to extremely high frequencies, known as millimeter waves, for use in communications; now it looked as if it would be possible to do the same thing using light. Hyland said to me, "Most important inventions usually take twenty years before they can be put to use, but lasers are so remarkable that it will be only a matter of a few years before they are operational. We at Hughes have already started organizing for research, production, and marketing." I remember taking his words as a kind of warning. Immediately realizing that this was an enormously significant discovery, I had NEC begin research in the area as soon as I returned home.

Fiber optic technology is a revolutionary means of communications that uses the ultimate radio wave resource, light, as a carrier for ordinary communications, and silica, a non-metallic conductor that exists plentifully on earth, as a transmission line. Moreover, it can be readily adapted to existing telecommunications systems. Nor has it posed any technical problems incapable of solution. When NEC started research in optic technology I used often to buttonhole researchers and ask them about the prospects for fiber optic communications. Most of them spoke optimistically.

Around 1980 we had solved the technical problems involved in using semiconductor lasers as a light source and optical fibers as a signal transmission line and both were ready to be put into actual use; the corporate structure for the optoelectronics business had been consolidated where necessary; and, last but not least, as a large-scale order from Argentina indicated, the market was showing signs of accepting the new technology. For all these reasons I think of 1980 as the start of the fiber optic communications business at NEC. Although it is tempting to give the full story of the development of our optical communications business from 1980, I will limit myself instead to writing about two or three incidents that were either ordeals or valuable learning experiences, even though not all of them postdate 1980.

Making Haste Slowly

The first problem we faced was gauging the trends in communications technology, especially with regard to high-capacity transmission lines. Around 1968 millimeter wave communications, which used a circular waveguide fifty millimeters in diameter as a transmitter, seemed a promising successor to microwave communications systems or coaxial cable systems. Most engineers, when asked what would come next, answered "fiber optic communications." Under the circumstances it made no sense to rush recklessly ahead. First, I had NEC develop a millimeter wave repeater system in cooperation with NTT's Electrical Communications Lab. Although development of the system itself proceeded smoothly, there was some difficulty in acquiring the land for the relatively straight route required for laying the circular waveguide. But the delays caused little inconvenience because the demand for video telephones, which was supposed to be the main use for this transmission method, was lower than expected. In the meantime we succeeded in developing a fiber optic communications system, which suddenly leaped into prominence as the most promising technology for the next stage of high-volume transmissions.

In 1979, when NEC was celebrating its eightieth anniversary, our technological achievements in the fiber optic communications field were reaching levels comparable to any competitors worldwide, and we were about ready to launch our system as a business venture. On March 7, I called a meeting of the Executive Committee and raised a stir by proposing to allocate management resources to the fiber optic communications business, stressing the need to reinforce our internal organization to prepare for the period ahead when the business would be a major growth area.

Up until this point our organization for fiber optics consisted of two different operating groups, each maintaining contact with its respective customers and providing them with the latest technology from our Research and Development Group. The business trend, however, was moving in the direction of a single, large market. To ride this trend successfully we would have to step up the development and coordination functions of the Fiber Optic Communications Development Committee, which had been set up in 1975. After debating the issue, we decided to take the plunge and in 1980 established the Fiber Optic Communications Development Division within the Transmission and Terminals Group. To use a favorite expression of mine, it was a classic example of a "market-oriented" business.

Countrywide Developments

On July 10, 1980, the Optoelectronic Industry and Technology Development Association came into being with backing from the Ministry of International Trade and Industry to promote information about, and the expansion of, the optoelectronics industry and optics technology. I was asked to serve as president, a position I have held ever since. By 1987 a total of well over 300 companies and institutions belonged to the association, including NTT, the Japan Machinery Federation, the Japan Electronic Industry Promotion Association, and the Japanese Electric Wire and Cable Makers Association, as well as universities, banks, electric power companies, cable makers, manufacturers of electrical household appliances, and makers of computers and communications equipment such as NEC and Fujitsu. For my part, I look forward not only to the growth of NEC's optoelectronics business but to the development of optics technology and the growth of related areas throughout Japanese industry.

Among the activities of the association that I have found especially impressive have been its efforts to promote technology exchanges with other countries. In 1981, for example, the association invited Dr Charles Kuen Kao to Japan. Dr Kao, then at Standard Telephones and Cables in England, had been the first to predict the development of low-loss optical fibers back in 1966. In 1982 the association invited Dr Maiman, now of TRW, and has since played host to several other world authorities, including Dr John E. Midwinter, head of Optical

Communications Technology at British Telecom, and Dr H. Melchior of the Swiss Federal Institute of Technology.

The October 13, 1986 issue of *Fortune* magazine contained a comparison of the strengths of various countries in a number of high-tech areas. Japan ranked first in the world in optical fibers and other forms of optoelectronics. As someone who had long been involved in fostering this technology, I was delighted.

Export and Domestic Success

As time passed, interest focused on when NEC would enter the overseas market. At the time of writing, NEC has built numerous fiber optic communications networks not only in Japan, but in Europe, North America, the Middle East, and elsewhere throughout the world, and has established a reputation as the world's top manufacturer in the field. I would like to highlight two memorable projects that date back to the beginning of our optical communications business overseas.

The first was the system we built for Vista Florida Telephone, the world's first optical circuit in ordinary use. At the beginning of 1977, the sales division of NEC America learned that Vista Florida, whose service area contains the famous amusement park, Disney World, was planning to install a new communications system. For NEC, which was about ready to launch out overseas, this seemed the perfect opportunity to create a showcase system that would attract worldwide attention. I visited Florida and proposed a fiber optic system to the company president, a former university professor: he readily agreed. This was the very first optical system NEC exported abroad; and though the area is famous for its thunderstorms, it has operated smoothly with no interruptions since it went into service in July 1978.

Less than a year later, in the spring of 1979, NEC sponsored the Argentine Digital Symposium in Buenos Aires. While attending the symposium I learned from the Empresa Nacional de Telecommunicaciones, the Argentine communications agency, that they were planning a digital communications network for Buenos Aires. At the time, Argentina's market for communications equipment seemed an impregnable stronghold for European makers, and indeed an Italian manufacturer, which had proposed a microwave coaxial cable system, was thought to have the advantage for this project.

The deadline for bids was October 1979. Knowing that success here would have an incalculable effect in stimulating the subsequent development of our fiber optic communications business, NEC submitted a bid for a system using optical fiber cable. During the microwave communications sales wars of the late 1960s and early 1970s NEC had dominated the world market by pushing up the technology to levels that rival companies were unable to provide. This time too I decided that we would have to outdo the competition by offering the most advanced technology at the most reasonable prices. We proposed a 140-megabit system that was then the fastest in the world. To demonstrate its feasibility we hurriedly put together a demonstration model, which we exhibited at the Telecom '79 exposition in Geneva and which amply displayed the power of the system in operation.

The project called for simultaneous switchover to the new system for all 1.6 million subscribers to the old telephone network. This was an unprecedented undertaking, and I felt a certain anxiety myself as I visited the site during construction to cheer on the NEC team. Yet when the new communications system went into service in 1981, the call completion rate for Buenos Aires shot up dramatically. As we had hoped, this success had a striking effect on the subsequent evolution of our overseas strategy – between 1981 and the end of 1987 we received orders from over forty countries.

Within Japan, NEC has given complete support to NTT in developing a commercial fiber optic communications system, from on-site testing of a 100-megabit system in 1978 to the completion of the optical cable trunkline throughout Japan in 1985 as well as subsequent testing of new types of equipment. Because the use of fiber optic communications will not be limited to trunklines but is expected to extend to local area networks (LANs), cable television, underwater cables, and subscriber loops, it has become essential to mass produce the optical devices that lie at the heart of these systems. NEC built a plant specializing in the mass production of fiber optic devices at Otsuki in Yamanashi Prefecture. Operations began in June 1986 at what was almost certainly the first plant of its kind in the world.

Divergence and Convergence

A major technological change occurred in the fiber optic communications business around 1977. Before then the wavelength used in optical communications was the 0.8 micron or short wavelength band because at that time the lowest loss levels for optical fibers made of silica occurred in this wavelength band. But when NTT's Electrical Communication Lab succeeded in removing all the impurities, especially the moisture, from silica glass, they were able to achieve the lowest transmission loss in the long wavelength band, first in the 1.3 micron, then in the 1.5 micron band. NEC was also hard at work in this area in the expectation that the long wavelength band appropriate for long-distance high-capacity transmissions would become the standard for fiber optic communications in the future.

Though I have focused here on the use of fiber optic technology in the communications area, optoelectronic technology soon began to take hold in other business areas too. Because I have always regarded optoelectronics as a core technology, I never thought that we would be able to cover all optics-related businesses with a single operating division: Just as each of NEC's operating groups use ICs and LSIs, so we encouraged each division to make use of optoelectronics in its own area of business as the need arose. But because we also needed to find ways to do research and development in shared basic technologies and handle technology transfers, we established the Optoelectronics Research Lab to provide centralized support for the development of everything from devices to entire systems used in communications, information processing, industrial applications, and home electronics.

The main sources of strength for NEC's fiber optic communications business lie in (1) having recognized back in 1960, at the time lasers were discovered, that optoelectronics would become an important future technology and giving it solid priority investment for more than twenty years; and (2) having consciously developed the business through close cooperation between our operating groups and our R&D group. But good luck has played its part: Although fiber optic technology requires a vigorous R&D effort, it has proved itself to be a particularly fertile technology that can promise adequate return on investment.

To make a technological breakthrough requires discovering the proper theme, motivating people, creating a free and open atmosphere, and having patience. More than twenty years ago NEC began giving priority investment to optoelectronics, built up an internal organization, motivated personnel, and developed the requisite technology. At the time I was so deeply involved in nurturing our fiber optic communications business that, looking back now, I cannot say which of these efforts has proved most fruitful in bringing NEC to the position of prominence it now enjoys in the fiber optics field.

Exploring the Frontiers of Space

In 1955 Professors Hideo Itogawa and Noboru Takagi of the University of Tokyo's Institute of Industrial Science succeeded in launching a pencil rocket, nine inches long and less than three-quarters of an inch in diameter. This was Japan's first space development project. NEC received a request from Professor Takagi to develop telemetering and guidance equipment. Because this was an area of interest to NEC, we agreed to cooperate without concern for profit. This research was primarily carried out by the team under Masatsugu Kobayashi, the director of NEC's Central Research Laboratories, so it is fair to say that NEC's corporate space development operations had the same starting-point as Japan's national space enterprise.

In 1963 the Kagoshima Space Center opened at Uchinoura in Kagoshima Prefecture, and the following year the Institute of Space and Aeronautical Science (renamed the Institute of Space and Astronautical Science in 1981) was inaugurated at the University of Tokyo and the Science and Technology Agency's Space Development Center was set up. Thus, around the time that I became president of NEC, all at once the stage had been set for Japan's entry into space development.

Japan's First Artificial Satellite

In May 1965 space development projects at NEC, which had been carried out primarily by the Communication Research Laboratory and the Radio Division, were consolidated into a single unit, overseen by the newly created Aeronautics and Space Development Laboratory, and an Artificial Satellite Section was established – the very first time, I believe, that the words "artificial satellite" had ever appeared in the title of an organization within a Japanese company. Though our space development operations have been reorganized several times since those early days, and the corporate structure has been significantly upgraded and reinforced, I still get a strong feeling of nostalgia whenever I think about them.

Japan's first satellite was launched into space on February 11, 1970. It was called the Osumi after the cape at Uchinoura from which it was launched, and it had been built by NEC. Although the launching of the Osumi was insignificant compared with the moon landing of the US Apollo 11 spacecraft the previous summer, it made us at NEC feel that we too could handle space development.

A request from Hughes Aircraft in 1969 had also had great significance for NEC's space business. Hughes, which had developed jointly with NEC the transponder used in the communications satellite Intelsat IV planned by Comsat, asked NEC to take over production. Because this was a perfect opportunity to make artificial satellites on a much larger scale than anything then being planned in Japan, I did not hesitate to agree. Thanks to this joint development project NEC later provided the transponders for Intelsat IV–A in 1970. To the great delight of our engineering staff transponders made from NEC's own design were adopted for the Intelsat VI fleet that was first launched in 1988.

In August 1968 the government established the Space Activities Commission to promote space development in Japan. The Space Activities Promotion Council had been set up in June of that year by the Federation of Economic Organizations as a support group in the private sector. In June 1970, at the Council's sixth general meeting, I was to succeed Atsuyoshi Oya, the association's first chairman. My role in this organization was to project a long-term vision for space development in Japan and to lobby the government for the budgetary allocations necessary for its achievement. Around 1973, as I recall, I proposed to the committee members that we draw up a long-term plan in order to win a national consensus and promote space development efficiently, and made the bold suggestion that the government allot 0.5 percent of the nation's GNP to space development. This plan was adopted by the Space Activities Commission, which set up the Long-Term Planning Special Committee in February 1975 and approved the Fundamental Space Policy in March 1978. Although revised in 1983, these guidelines continue to serve as the "constitution" for space development in Japan.

At NEC, Osumi was followed by the successful launch of a series of scientific satellites – Tansei in February 1971, Shinsei in September 1971, Denpa in August 1972, Tansei 2 in February 1974, and Taiyo in February 1975 – all of which were constructed totally by our company. Our space development business was finally beginning to get on track. The launch of Akebono in February 1989 took the total number of scientific satellites launched under the jurisdiction of the University of Tokyo's Institute of Space and Aeronautical Science or its successor at the Ministry of Education to eighteen: NEC has had a monopoly on the production of all of them.

The project to introduce applications satellites began with plans for weather forecasting, communications, and broadcasting satellites to be built under the direction of NASDA (Japan's National Space Development Agency), which had been founded in October 1969. In the mid-1970s a trade war developed for the rights to the weather satellite. Meanwhile, the US spaceprobe Viking 1 succeeded in making a soft landing on Mars in July 1976, followed by the Viking 2 that September. At NEC the Space Development Laboratory established in June 1967 was renamed the Space Development Division, signifying that it had at last become an independent operating division. Because NEC had virtually monopolized the development of artificial satellites in Japan, we naturally hoped to monopolize the three areas of applications satellites as well. Our partner Hughes's star was also in the ascendant, dominating the US market.

But as the saying goes, "There's many a slip 'twixt cup and lip." Hughes's star fell, and Ford won the order for the US weather satellite. Because Japan's first applications satellite was also to be a weather satellite I wanted to win that contract more than anything. Perhaps to compensate for its loss in the US, Hughes gave NEC its full support, and we succeeded in winning the order in November 1973. This satellite, called Himawari, was launched from Cape Canaveral, Florida in July 1977. NEC was also in charge of production for Himawari 2, launched in August 1981, and Himawari 3, launched in August 1984. Although we made plans at the same time to build communications and broadcasting satellites, in the event the contracts fell to Mitsubishi and Toshiba.

Toward the Industrial Use of Space

In March 1980 NEC received the order to act as the main contractor in developing the 340-pound maritime observation satellite MOS-1, Japan's first large observation satellite. I had given strict orders to those involved to win this particular contract. Because NEC had been concentrating its energies on perfecting the technology for spin stabilization, observation satellites that required three-axis stabilization presented a technological challenge that I very much wanted us to master. An additional problem I faced was that the existing production facilities at our Yokohama plant were not big enough to accommodate a satellite this size. Since one of the preconditions for the completion of the MOS-1 was the construction of facilities to assemble and test it, a proposal to build a new spacecraft factory crossed my desk at the same time as the confirmation of the contract arrived. The proposal called for an investment of 3 billion yen to construct a building five stories high. I approved it without a moment's hesitation; but if we were going to build, I wanted the building to be the most advanced in the world. I set up a Construction Preparations Committee and sent several committee members to the leading satellite makers in the US to study their facilities. Actual construction posed a new set of problems because of local zoning restrictions, but with the help of the National Space Development Agency we were able to get the plans cleared.

The new spacecraft factory opened in a corner of the Yokohama plant in June 1982. I was fully confident that the day would come when even that enormous floor space would seem crowded. On the official opening day in November the plant was shown to more than 1,300 visitors and given extensive coverage in the mass media. The MOS-1 assembled here, which was launched from the Tanegashima space center on February 19, 1987 and named Momo-1. The Sakigake and Suisei were also built here and launched as part of an international cooperative effort to observe Halley's comet, which returned to earth in 1986 after an absence of seventy-six years.

Outer space is the last frontier remaining for the human race. In May 1986, the Science and Technology Agency's Space Policy Committee published a report entitled "Toward a New Age of Space Development." It recommended that Japan, by its efforts during this century, should aim to become a major presence in world space development by the beginning of the twenty-first century, and urged that 6 trillion yen should be allotted from the national budget between now and the year 2000 to improve the space development infrastructure.

The human race must wake up to the fact that it has entered the age of space navigation. Japan's present annual budget for space development is 120 billion yen, roughly the same amount as the annual sales of the tatami mat industry. As chairman of the Space

Activities Promotion Council, in 1982 I made an appeal to Ichiro Nakagawa, who was then the head of the Science and Technology Agency, for an increase in the budget from 70 billion to 100 billion yen. Unfortunately budget allocations for space have not risen much since then.

Distinctive trends in space development have been emerging recently. Previously we have positioned satellites in space for communications, broadcasting, or observation purposes. Now we are entering an age when we will be attempting to use the space environment itself. In other words, we are approaching the dawn of the industrial use of space.

Let me give one example. At the end of 1981 the general manager of NEC's Space Development Division asked to be allowed to conduct an experiment in space. The *Asahi Shimbun* had come up with the idea of doing an experiment on board the US space shuttle and had approached NEC about developing the necessary equipment. After soliciting ideas from its readers across the country, the newspaper decided to try to grow artificial snowflakes under the conditions of weightlessness. They had asked Battelle Memorial Institute in the US to develop the equipment for them, but the Institute had declined. Several Japanese companies had also turned them down. I was sceptical whether NEC with no experience could do what a major US lab had refused to do, but the division head was very eager. I had no way of knowing whether it was feasible to grow snowflakes in space where not even clouds can form, but I told him to go ahead and try if he really wanted to. And, to be honest, two years later I had completely forgotten our conversation. On April 4, 1983, the equipment was launched into space on board the space shuttle Challenger. The results were inconclusive – artificial snow could be grown, but it was not possible to measure it. When the experiment was repeated the following September, however, it was a great success. The *Asahi Shimbun* gave extensive coverage to the experiment over several days. An experiment involving the collision of water drops and steel balls carried out on the space shuttle Discovery in April 1985 was also successful. The day is approaching when the focus of interest will fall on research into new materials and high-tech engineering using the weightless environment of outer space.

10

"C&C in Every Home": Personal Computers and Domestic Appliances

The Appearance of the Microcomputer

In July 1969, the people of the world were riveted to their television sets, watching the Apollo 11 spacecraft land on the Sea of Tranquillity and a US astronaut take mankind's first step on the surface of the moon. Ultra-small computers using large-scale integration had been used in the controls of this spacecraft. After much trial and error, the technology embodied in these micro-computers would ultimately lead to a major business opportunity for NEC.

This was the era of the electronic calculator, and in Japan, which reigned supreme in the calculator business, manufacturers needed higher levels of integration in the integrated circuits that formed the heart of the calculator in order to develop new products and beat the competition. The result was large-scale integration – where twenty ICs had once been needed for a calculator, with LSI you could make do with only three or four. To supply these LSIs, most of the Japanese calculator manufacturers were dependent on American makers of semiconductors, who at that time were technologically ahead of Japan.

The US makers of semiconductors naturally assumed that since the basic functions for all the orders they received from Japanese manufacturers were the same, with only slight differences in certain components, they could make a standardized design. The result was the concept of using LSI devices to do all the basic functions of the computer, which in turn led to the development of the micro-computer. In November 1971 the US semiconductor maker Intel succeeded in developing a four-bit microcomputer, the i4004.

Interestingly enough, it had been a Japanese manufacturer of electronic calculators for the export market that had placed the order with Intel to develop the microcomputer. I once said to the president of that calculator company, "For a small company like yours, it was quite an accomplishment to dabble in microcomputers. Why didn't you try to profit from it?" His reply was, "All I wanted to do was to get ahead." Instead of taking the traditional approach and converting the functions of the calculator to LSI, he had wanted to develop an advanced calculator that would contain the memory and programming functions of a computer. In other words, the revolutionary concept of converting the computer itself to large-scale integration lay behind the microcomputer developed by Intel.

Japan's first domestically produced microcomputer was NEC's μPD700 series, which we perfected in April 1972, six months after Intel's i4004 model. This was a P-channel MOS LSI consisting of a single LSI chip for peripheral use and a two-chip central processing unit. P-channel elements were then the world's standard, but the NEC engineering staff were so encouraged by this success that they decided to tackle N-channel elements, which, although capable of doing more rapid calculations, were so difficult to produce that hardly any companies had started work on them. In September 1973 NEC succeeded in putting on the market the world's first N-channel MOS four-bit microcomputer with parallel processing, the μCOM-4, and in 1974 we unveiled our eight-bit μCOM-8, which was compatible with the Intel model. In so doing we joined the ranks of the big manufacturers of microcomputers such as Intel, Fairchild, and Rockwell.

Outside sales of microcomputers began in 1973. At that time few people had even heard of microcomputers, which made matters quite difficult for our sales staff. When a salesman recommended a microcomputer to a sewing machine manufacturer, for example, the customer would have no idea what he was talking about. To set about overcoming this obstacle we created the Microcomputer Sales Department within the Semiconductor and IC Sales Division in February 1976, but even so we were lucky to sell 300 microcomputers a month.

The dawn of the microcomputer age arrived at just about the same time as I became chairman of NEC. The time had come to launch our microcomputer strategy. Although a microcomputer is a small LSI, it is still a computer. But when this ultra-small computer first appeared, everyone, even engineers, was an amateur as far as this new product was concerned, so in order to sell it we first had to get the user to understand something about microcomputers. As a teaching aid we put on the market an assemble-it-yourself microcomputer, the TK-80 (TK for training kit), in August 1976 for the then astoundingly low price of 88,500 yen.

The first step in our campaign to popularize the microcomputer was to open a showroom. Realizing that winning Akihabara, Tokyo's famous shopping district for consumer electronics, was a necessary condition for nationwide dominance, we joined forces with a store specializing in electron devices and decided to create a salesroom on the seventh floor of the Radio Hall in front of the Akihabara train station. We formally opened in September 1976, a month after the TK-80 had gone on sale. On the advice of one of the young engineers in the Microcomputer Sales Department, we called it "Bit-Inn."

As soon as the showroom opened, any misgivings within the company were dispelled once and for all. Young computer buffs, elementary and middle school students as well as those of high school and college age, flocked to Bit-Inn; it was such a huge success that our chief worry was providing enough staff members to answer their questions. The demonstrations given at Bit-Inn and microcomputer games widened the circle of fans until in time the showroom became a microcomputer consultation center and a place to exchange information. Later, we opened Bit-Inns in Osaka, Nagoya, and Yokohama, which we managed directly.

The Transition to the Personal Computer

The age of the microcomputer was the forerunner of the age of the personal computer. How did we make the transition from the one stage to the other? Thanks to Bit-Inn, NEC now had a direct channel of communication with computer users. Through it we were able to learn what users wanted and what the market needed. This confirmed our feeling that market demands for microcomputers were rapidly increasing. In order to meet these demands we put on sale the TK-80BS, a superior machine in kit form capable of using BASIC computer language. Riding the crest of interest in microcomputers, NEC was able to make the transition to its first personal computer, the PC-8001. As an extension of the microcomputer kit days, we put the Electron Device Group in charge of everything from development to sales of the PC-8001. The Microcomputer Applications Division was set up in May 1979 and renamed the Personal Computer Division in April 1981, but when the PC-8001 project was getting under way, microcomputers were not even a formally recognized business area within the company.

While NEC was polishing its plans for the PC-8001, Apple Computers, Tandy Corporation, and Commodore International, the big three in personal computers in the US, had begun selling their respective models. I had to make a decision: Should we enter the personal computer business or be satisfied with our line of microcomputer kits? The success of the kits, though unexpected, had led to an exchange of ideas between customers and staff at Bit-Inn that was proving fruitful in generating new and more advanced products. Because this ideal pattern was being formed, I decided to give the go-ahead to the personal computer business.

Market Leader in PCs

On May 9, 1979, around the time that the Second Microcomputer Show was being held in Tokyo, we announced to the press that we were putting on the market in August a personal computer that would offer outstanding performance at 170,000 yen per unit. We predicted sales of 2,000 sets a month. This was the birth of the PC-8001. In fact, this press release contained one glaring mistake – our estimated sales figure was way off. We had to work frantically until the middle of the following year just to ship out the sets ordered before the computer went on the market. It was a happy mistake. By the time the PC-8001 ceased production in January 1983, we had sold 250,000 sets, an unbeatable sales record for a single model in the Japanese personal computer industry. With the PC-8001, NEC acquired the top market share for domestic personal computers, a position we have continued to hold to the present day. Moreover, since the appearance of the PC-8001, domestically made personal computers have been the market leaders in Japan.

NEC's huge success with the PC-8001 was no accident. Many factors contributed to its success. The first of these was the development of applications software for the personal computer, the appearance of third parties to make it, and our efforts to maintain good relations with these third parties. Although the number of these third parties increased rapidly, the important point is that they first appeared more than two years before the unveiling of our personal computer. In other words, soon after we came out with our TK-80 kit, new companies sprang up to develop and sell electric power supplies and software products for it. When we put the PC-8001 on the market, independent third-party firms again appeared to make and sell software, peripherals, and reference manuals, creating a huge new business field almost literally overnight. For its part NEC encouraged third-party software houses to develop new products for the NEC personal computer, even to the point of releasing proprietary information, in the belief that if more software became available it would increase the popularity of the NEC PC.

Other factors contributing to the growth of NEC's personal computer business in the early days were the adoption of a new sales strategy and the creation of a new sales route. A sales route that targeted large groups of unspecified users for an item like a personal computer was something that NEC had hitherto lacked. When we thought about the future development of the business, it became clear that there were limits to the electron device route adopted for the TK-80. This led to the concept of the NEC Microcomputer Shop. We opened our very first store in Hiroshima in 1978, and the number has since grown to nearly 300 stores. The microcomputer shop is a new type of store to meet today's new needs – a specialty store providing technological expertise, it is not like any existing computer, communications, or home electronics store but overlaps with the territory of all three.

To produce the computers we placed New Nippon Electric (renamed NEC Home Electronics on July 1, 1983) in charge of our personal computer line, both to take advantage of its experience in mass production and in the belief that personal computers would in time become more like a household appliance, a decision that I believe is correct. In 1980 we added the sales channel for New Nippon Electric's home appliances to our personal computer sales route. This contributed greatly to the success of Japan's first home computer, the PC-6000 series, which went on sale in 1981.

Fortunately, the success did not end here but helped to improve sales for our home electronics goods such as television, which New Nippon Electric had traditionally handled.

Bringing the Organization Up to Date

Once NEC's personal computer business had gotten off to such a good start, my own interest in personal computers quickly began to grow. I have long held that the first step toward the integration of computers and communications is to understand the computer and master it for one's own purposes. So one day I said to Atsuyoshi Ouchi, then Senior Executive Vice President, "Now that we have this convenient device, shouldn't it be more widely used throughout the company? We can't have the shoemaker's wife go barefoot, you know. Let's have everyone learn how to use the computer, beginning with top management." The NEC Personal Computer Study Program was organized for NEC executives and division heads, who gave up their Saturdays and Sundays to attend. It began on December 6, 1980. A photograph taken on that day, which shows me tapping away uncertainly at the keyboard of the PC-8001, was given wide circulation in the press. Our own publicity efforts included a four-page corporate advertisement on personal computers for the 1982 New Year's Day issue of the *Asahi Shimbun*.

In September 1981 we announced the eight-bit PC-8801 and the PC-6001, and unveiled our sixteen-bit PC-9800 in October 1982. I will omit the technical details here, but our sixteen-bit personal computer was a superior model. Since 1983 we have released about ten new products a year in forms suited to multiple user needs.

Once the lineup of new products was perfected, we needed to reinforce the organizational side of the business. On April 28, 1982, we created the Personal Computer Subgroup within the Electron Device Group. In addition to the engineering and sales staff we established a Personal Computer Planning Office to oversee business planning and strategy. Although the Electron Device Group had been responsible for our personal computer business from the time of our microcomputer kits, the sixteen-bit computer was handled by our Information Processing Group, which is in charge of all our mainframe computers, minicomputers, and small business computers. The less powerful computers in the PC-6000 series were taken over by New Nippon Electric, although the Electron Device Group remained in charge of the PC-8000 series until December 1983, when all our eight-bit computers were transferred to NEC Home Electronics. By redrawing the battle lines in this way, we made a sharp division between sixteen-bit machines and eight-bit machines, which enabled us to clarify the philosophy behind the development of personal computers.

Although the Japanese market for personal computers went through a slump, it has subsequently picked up, thanks to investment in new products and the increasing use of the computer as a communications terminal. Already 32-bit models have appeared.

NEC's various computer strategies have continued to be successful, and we still dominate the domestic market. We are now making plans for an even wider spectrum of products, developing new models that will satisfy the needs of users who have invested in the new technology and software that will be compatible with higher levels of machines. We are also working to develop personal computer communications and other new applications areas. The personal computer is now becoming NEC's indisputable champion product.

Some ten years have passed since the personal computer was first created within the Electron Device Group. A product that a decade ago literally did not exist in any shape or form now accounts for more than 10 percent of NEC's consolidated sales. I believe the reason for this success is that the computer is the result of what Peter Drucker would call ordinary, mundane innovation. Although it is, of course, true that the computer involves innovations in advanced device technology, I think that the real source for the vitality of our computer business has been our entrepreneurial spirit, which has shown a keen sensitivity to social innovations – changes in individual values, hobbies, and lifestyles – and a faith in this business and its future prospects.

The Transformation of Home Electronics

I once wrote in an essay entitled "Corporate Management at the Turning Point," "How to achieve one's aim at all times and in all things is a difficult problem for top management." I have felt the truth of this statement especially strongly as the helmsman of NEC's household appliance – or, as we now call it, home electronics –

business. This area of our company has a long tradition, dating back to 1904 when NEC astounded everyone with the very first electrical appliance to be sold in Japan: an electric fan imported from Western Electric. We were also in the vanguard with radio, supplying NHK with its first ten-kilowatt broadcasting equipment in the mid-1920s and offering for sale a radio receiver that made use of a peanut-shaped, direct-current vacuum tube. Since the war, however, the home electronics business has been run as a separate company, New Nippon Electric, and its corporate culture seemed to be different from NEC's three other mainstays (communications, computers, and electron devices). However, viewed in the context of my vision of C&C, the integral role of this business area to the company's sphere of operations becomes clear.

If you can free yourself from the conventional view of "brown (entertainment) goods" and "white (domestic convenience) goods," NEC's advantageous position in having a home electronics business becomes clear. In my concept of C&C, the home electronics business will form the interface between C&C systems and the people that operate them. By incorporating the huge market for home appliances under the motto "C&C in every home" we will be able to respond readily to the growing role of information in the social infrastructure, trends toward knowledge- and information-intensive lifestyles, and the proliferation of values. In other words, by weaving together into one strand these two areas of NEC's business, which at first glance seem to have totally different natures and cultures, the position home electronics occupies in our company and its *raison d'être* become clear. Thanks to C&C, the cooperation between NEC and New Nippon Electric has become even closer.

The Evolution of New Nippon Electric

On that fateful day in 1964 when Toshihide Watanabe called me into his office and announced that I was to be the next president of NEC, he made the offhand observation that, though it had been his decision to go into the household appliance business, much to his dismay it had not gone as smoothly as he had hoped. He had assumed the position of first chairman of New Nippon Electric at the time of its founding in 1953 and had held that office, with interruptions, for a total of four years. After I became president of NEC I served simultaneously as president of New Nippon Electric for five and a half years beginning in November 1965, and later as chairman of the Board of Directors for nine years beginning in May 1971.

New Nippon Electric Company came into existence on June 1, 1953, when it separated off from NEC's Radio Division. It was capitalized at 200 million yen and had 1,170 employees, with its head office in Osaka. In 1955, two years after its founding, the number of Japanese households owning television sets topped the 100,000 mark. Japan had come to the "end of the postwar period," as the government's economic white paper for fiscal 1956 would aver, and was poised to enter its first golden age of household appliances. Viewed in this light, the decision to establish a new company specializing in consumer appliances reflected a correct assessment of market trends.

For several years after its founding, vacuum tubes and fluorescent light bulbs made by New Nippon Electric accounted for nearly 80 percent of its sales. Finished goods such as televisions, tape recorders, refrigerators, and air conditioners were supplied by NEC and its affiliates and sold by New Nippon Electric. Because there was some doubt whether the system of making parts and stocking finished goods was the wisest way to get ahead in the highly competitive world of household appliances, NEC decided to take a serious stab at consumer goods as a company-wide strategy. In November 1958 we made a fresh start. We renamed the Special Products Industry Division and the Special Products Sales Division, which had been established in August 1956, the Consumer Products Division and the Consumer Products Laboratory. As a result, around 1960 household appliances became NEC's second largest business area, accounting for 23 percent of our consolidated sales. (At that time our communications equipment business amounted to 53 percent of consolidated sales.)

During this period New Nippon Electric was one of twelve major manufacturers of household appliances in Japan, all of whom gave priority to marketing over manufacturing and fought furiously to increase their market share by even a single percentage point. To achieve growth for both companies under these circumstances, NEC and New Nippon Electric racked their brains for ways to unify their operations and came up with the following plan to strengthen the business. First, the head office of New Nippon Electric was moved from Osaka to Tokyo in 1961. Second, in September 1963 the Basic

Plan for Reforming New Nippon Electric's operations was adopted. The main points of this plan were (1) to establish New Nippon Electric as a division company of NEC; (2) to consolidate NEC's Consumer Products Division and the Mizonokuchi Works and put them under New Nippon Electric; and (3) to adopt a four-part operating division system consisting of the Electron Tube Division, the Radio Division, the Television Division, and the Electrical Household Appliances Division. This was the nature of NEC's consumer electronics business in November 1965 when I assumed the post of president of New Nippon Electric, which had been vacant since November 1963.

In the second half of the 1960s the "Three Cs" – color televisions, coolers (air conditioners), and cars – had come to symbolize a higher standard of living as Japan entered its second golden age of consumer appliances. At this time I was introducing a number of policies as part of my management reform program at NEC and began to introduce similar policies at New Nippon Electric as well. My first move was to launch a zero defects campaign, which got under way in October 1965 at the Tokyo plant; my next step was to introduce the "point to area" system of top management, which went into effect in July 1966. On July 1 of that year, to clarify areas of responsibility, I consolidated the business operations into two main divisions, the Electrical Household Appliances Division and the Electronic Components Division. To accommodate the trend toward solid-state parts for televisions and sound systems, the latter steadily built up its expertise in the area of solid-state components. A transistor and diode plant was built on the grounds of our Otsu plant in May 1967. This four-story building with 6,500 square feet of floor space was air conditioned and completely windowless, a rarity in Shiga Prefecture at that time. My third move was to strengthen the export system. Until that time, although all products carried the same NEC logo, communications equipment and semiconductors had been exported by NEC, household appliances by New Nippon Electric. To centralize the system, from April 1968 all exporting was carried out by NEC.

I like to think of the large-scale reorganization carried out in April 1969 as my fourth reform. To quote from the corporate history of New Nippon Electric, the purpose of this organizational reform was "to strengthen profit lines by making each division responsible for its own profits and consolidating the efforts of all employees under a new operating group system that encompasses all the existing divisions in an effort to respond to rapid developments in the nature of our business and to changes in the corporate climate both inside and outside the company." This reform program had the same aims as the division system inaugurated at NEC on May 13, 1965, and was related to the "point to area" top management structure enacted earlier.

Integration under C&C

In March 1971, just before I became chairman of the board at New Nippon Electric, and NEC senior executive vice president Yuzaburo Makino succeeded me as president, I took the first step in evolving a new information-oriented strategy for the household electronics area, one that would have been difficult – if not impossible – for any other company except NEC to emulate. I felt confident that the proper place for our "new" or "expanded" household appliance business, as some corporate analysts called it, was integrated into NEC's business sphere, along with communications equipment, semiconductors, and computers. We therefore established a new Information Equipment Division within the Electrical Household Appliances Group to sell information terminals and communications terminals such as telephones and fax machines.

In the fiscal 1976 edition of NEC's annual report in English for foreign stockholders we announced that we were changing the expression "electrical household appliances" to "consumer electronics." In the fiscal 1981 edition we changed the terminology once more to "home electronics" to reflect changes in NEC's view of this business sphere. Any discussion of this area must mention its "business culture," which is rooted in consumer values, the special features of the manufacturing process, the differences in its products (whether mass-produced, multi-use, or custom-made), and the other special characteristics of any business. It has often been said that goods for the mass market are NEC's weak point and that we have a jinx in this area. Some people feel that there are marked differences between the home electronics business and communications, computers, and electron devices. In our statement of accounts for fiscal 1978, for example, when reporting financial information by business segment as required by the US Securities and Exchange Commission, we had to divide NEC's business into C&C (communications, computers, and electron devices) and consumer electronics. "Corporate culture" is a major reason for these divisions.

The appearance of the personal computer gave new impetus to our information-oriented home electronics strategy. As noted earlier in this chapter, New Nippon Electric assumed responsibility for selling our computer for hobby use, the PC-6000, in October 1982, and in December 1983 all eight-bit computers, namely the PC-6000, the PC-8000, and the PC-8800, were added to their sales line. As a result, in the fiscal year ending 31 March 1984 domestic sales for personal computers exceeded those for color televisions. Until recently the mainstream for home electronics has been entertainment-oriented "brown goods," such as televisions, on the one hand, and convenience-oriented "white goods," such as washing machines and refrigerators, on the other. Unfortunately, other consumer electronics manufacturers in Japan are one step ahead of us in these areas; but NEC is blazing the trail in the new information-oriented area of home electronics.

To reflect this new view, we revised the NEC Tree. As you may recall from the earlier discussion, in the original version New Nippon Electric was depicted as a small sapling growing beside the larger parent tree. Now we decided to incorporate this offshoot into the parent tree and make it the fourth branch alongside communications, computers, and electron devices.

After a major organizational reform of NEC's R&D Group in July 1980, the Home Electronics Research Laboratory was created within the C&C Systems Research Laboratories to strengthen our basic research and development system in the home electronics area. New Nippon Electric responded by setting up its own R&D Laboratory on January 6, 1983. As the name implies, its basic objective is to develop new products and new technologies that have clear application potential. The aim was for NEC and New Nippon Electric to adopt a division of labor in the applied development of technology related to home electronics.

The personal computer marked a major turning-point in NEC's home electronics business. Through its traditional specialty of mass-production engineering, New Nippon Electric has made a great contribution to the manufacturing of our personal computers. On July 1, 1983 New Nippon Electric was officially renamed NEC Home Electronics and its semiconductor division was transferred to our semiconductor affiliate, NEC Kansai.

C&C: The "Home System"

On June 11, 1982, men and women from all over the world, old and young, crowded into Kresge Auditorium on the campus of Massachusetts Institute of Technology for the alumni reunion. That day I stood on the podium as special guest speaker to deliver an address on "The Future Role of 'C&C' in the Home." I proposed the idea of a multi-layered structure that could be divided, according to the nature of the market, into areas where the role of C&C technology seemed most promising. I went on to discuss the creation of a "home system" as a third area to complement "public systems" and "business systems" and analyzed its value and future prospects.

Information equipment, symbolized by personal computers, had only just begun to penetrate the home at that time, and because the situation had both its positive and negative aspects, future prospects for the home system were not easy to describe. But judging from the fact that the human race was seeking wider areas of exchange and that the advanced industrial countries were already entering the information age, it was possible to predict that the need for a home system would rapidly materialize. That was what gave me the idea for "C&C in every home." And now the future of home electronics looks more promising with every passing day.

11

Becoming a Global Corporation

The Growth of the Semiconductor Business

After the introduction of GE technology and the opening of our Tamagawa semiconductor plant, NEC's semiconductor business began to boom in the early 1960s. As use of transistors increased, demand for miniaturized, highly reliable, low-power-consuming devices spurred growth even further. Keeping pace with these demands, the levels of integration also increased. Hybrid integrated circuits that made use of thin-film and thick-film technology and micromodule technology became the standard and attracted widespread attention in 1964 when IBM used them in their computer system 360. NEC shipped its first IC computer, the NEAC-1240, in 1965 and under the leadership of NTT began joint research on digital ICs for use in electronic switching systems.

Observation of these technological trends led me to decide that our IC business would be the nucleus of growth for the entire company, and I began exploring the possibilities with the division heads in related areas. Our first step was to establish the organizational structure, and so in November 1966 we set up the IC Design Division within the newly created Semiconductor and IC Group and seconded to it engineers with knowledge and experience in systems engineering. Realizing that a manager was needed who would view the work from a broad perspective, I appointed Atsuyoshi Ouchi to head the IC Design Division.

More than fifty engineers, including the departmental managers and section managers from our product manufacturing divisions, took part in planning the merger with our component manufacturing divisions. The resulting organization concentrated the knowhow of the entire company on our IC operations, which was able to provide

great support to the C&C concept when I announced it in
1977.

From Local Sales to Local Production

In 1973 semiconductor output at NEC reached 50 billion yen, and we
were beginning to produce top-level products even by world
standards. In order to expand the business even further we began to
consider exporting. We set up sales offices in what in those days were
our main target areas – the US, Europe, and southeast Asia. In May
1973 we established NEC Electronics (Europe) in Düsseldorf as our
European sales outlet and in May 1980 we created NEC Microcomputers in America to take charge of sales for the memory devices
and microcomputers that we had finally succeeded in producing.

As our export system expanded and the volume of exports
increased, a new problem began to emerge. After the Semiconductor
Industry Association was set up in the US in 1973, it began to take a
tough stand against the Japanese semiconductor trade. Europe and
the developing countries also raised tariffs and imposed various other
restrictions on imports. For these reasons we drew up plans to begin
local production starting in southeast Asia, where NEC had first
tried its hand at doing business overseas. For the site of our first plant
we decided on Malaysia, which offered attractive incentives. I had
heard Prime Minister Tun Abdul Razak speak very enthusiastically
about the prospects there on his visit to Japan and was favorably
impressed. In 1974 we established NEC Malaysia, later to become
NEC Semiconductor (Malaysia). Although construction proved
difficult because the economy had not fully recovered from the first
oil shock, we were able to ship out our first products in September
1977. At present, in accordance with local government policies, we
are in the process of converting to local capital.

Because Europe has the highest tariffs on semiconductors, we had
to respond rapidly to counter them. Looking for a place where we
would be welcomed by the local populace and enjoy the support of the
government, we chose Ireland as our first European base for
semiconductor production. The plant opened in October 1976, and
when I visited in 1986 to celebrate its tenth anniversary I was given a
warm reception by the government and the local people.

As we began to achieve results in the European market, customer demand became more complex and more varied. Not only did we need to be able to respond more efficiently to these demands, we also faced a growing need for a through-process production system, from diffusion to assembly, to counter growing trade frictions. After examining the infrastructure we decided to build our second production plant at Livingston, Scotland, and opened the facility on July 4, 1983 – an occasion honored by the attendance of Her Majesty Queen Elizabeth II. The Livingston plant has grown steadily and by the summer of 1989 was the only Japanese facility in Europe to produce one-megabit memory devices.

The US leads the world not only in the size of the market but in the level of its technology in this area. Making corporate inroads there is no easy matter, and by the 1970s US producers, feeling the pressure from Japanese imports, were giving rise to complaints of "dumping." However, the best way to build close relations with potential users of our products and to increase sales was clearly to build factories in the US and strengthen our service organization there. As a start, in 1977 we bought Electronic Arrays, an LSI manufacturer located outside San Francisco, and began studying ways of working with Americans while producing LSIs: For after the takeover, Charles Wood, the president of Electronic Arrays, and all the employees stayed and carried on as usual.

Although this acquisition offered great opportunities to learn the American style of plant management, the costs were considerable. We had accomplished my long-cherished dream of establishing a beachhead for our semiconductor business in America, but the equipment was outmoded and unsuited to producing state-of-the-art devices. We therefore decided to build a plant of our own and set about looking for a site with the help of the California government. In October 1985 we opened a through-process plant for the production of 256K memory devices at Roseville, near Sacramento. That year friction between the US and Japan over semiconductors had once again flared up into a major political issue, causing us some concern about our local reception: But fortunately we received a warm welcome. High expectations from our customers have led to a steadily expanding business. Plans have been completed to build a second plant to produce four-megabit memory devices. In August 1989 we invited state and local officials to ground-breaking ceremonies for the plant.

Shifting to Large-scale Integration

Memory devices and microcomputers were to be core products in promoting digitalization for NEC's C&C systems business. The risks are great in this area, but we recognized its crucial significance and persisted in our drive to become world leader, despite inevitable setbacks.

Back in 1966 we had succeeded in developing the MOS memory. The paper outlining this advance was the first to be accepted from Japan by the International Solid State Circuit Conference (ISSCC), a forum with a prestigious tradition among semiconductor engineers where each year the most recent results in integrated circuit technology are made public. The response to our achievement was enormous. With each succeeding year our memory-based technology accomplished noteworthy results: we succeeded in putting on the market a 64K device in 1981, a 256K device in 1982, and a one-megabit device in 1985.

However, our microcomputer business at first suffered a series of false starts. In 1970 we designed and manufactured a microcomputer based on the design knowhow for LSIs used in electronic calculators. Microcomputers were formally established as a business around 1977, but for wider distribution we decided we needed a second-source contact with another company. We entered an agreement with Intel, then headed by Robert N. Noyce, with whom we had an existing relationship. But as NEC's competitiveness increased and we frequently found ourselves contending with each other in the same market, the tie-up became difficult to sustain. It also gradually became clear that we could not assume the lead in technology or develop personnel under a second-source agreement. So I made the decision that we should switch to an original product as soon as possible and designated Tomihiro Matsumura, who was then in charge of microcomputer development, to head the project. That was the start of our NEC V (for victory) series.

Not only is large-scale integration essential for the C&C business, its importance has increased in direct proportion to the ability to give advanced functions to LSIs. I realized that a new division was necessary for organizational as well as for technological reasons, and in 1979 we started the System LSI Development Division. The shift to large-scale integration was not the only factor underlying System LSI; we also had to plan for the growing merger of semiconductor devices and systems engineering. This meant that we needed to develop, design, and produce these devices in cooperation with our systems engineering unit. I also hoped that the formation of the new division would help to promote the C&C business. The System LSI Development Division subsequently succeeded in developing a 32-bit microcomputer. In 1989 the division employed 300 engineers, primarily on the systems side. In the Tamagawa and Sagamihara plants we have experimental manufacturing lines for MOS and bipolar devices. To date, this organization has developed more than 5,000 different types of LSIs.

Fighting for Quality

One of the benefits of integration and integrated circuits is that they make it possible to produce high-quality goods with a high degree of reliability. But it was a circuitous route we had to take before we were able to attain this objective. The semiconductors manufactured by NEC are used mainly in communications and computer-related equipment, which demand high quality and high reliability. Semiconductors used in equipment made for NTT, for example, had to pass a certification procedure that was just as stringent as the one for the US military or for NASA. Strict quality control was essential.

For a while we depended on semiconductors imported from America for part of our in-house demand, but though the failure rate on mass-produced devices from the US was 4 percent, our American suppliers responded arrogantly to our complaints. I felt strongly that we could never maintain stable operations if we were dependent on other companies for the semiconductors indispensable to C&C. We reviewed our in-house development system and decided that we had to be able to produce the world's most advanced products under a system of strict quality control. In practical terms, this meant that the production site must be free of all dust and dirt. To achieve this we would need to cut down on work done by hand and increase the level of automation.

To raise morale and improve the level of manufacturing control expertise at our plants, I set the goal that we should become the first semiconductor plant in Japan to win the Deming Application Prize. After several years of trial and error, NEC Kyushu was awarded the Deming Application Prize in 1979. Realizing that this achievement boosted morale and was useful in improving conditions within the plant, I had NEC Yamagata compete as well: It succeeded in winning in 1982. In 1987 NEC IC Microcomputer Systems, a wholly owned subsidiary specializing in IC design and software development for personal computers and microcomputers, was awarded the Deming Application Prize. This marked the first time in its 37-year history that the Deming Prize had been given to a company engaged in design activities.

Learning from Experience Overseas

Becoming a global corporation meant upgrading our technology, streamlining production, and strengthening our sales techniques through competition with the leading companies of the world. By honing our skills in the international marketplace, we learned just what foreign markets wanted and how to reflect these needs in our overseas business strategy. This was an invaluable experience for us. We acquired the knowhow to discern what levels of technology were expected, what we needed to do to be competitive, and how to win our customers' confidence. All these lessons paid dividends in what I view as NEC's "international expansion period" of the 1970s and 1980s.

Within the company the accumulation of overseas experience proved a good teacher. After many disappointing results on the profit side from our foreign contracts, a cost awareness gradually permeated our entire organization. As the number of turnkey contracts grew, and more and more of our personnel in marketing, engineering and manufacturing gained overseas experience, the circle of people within the company who understood foreign cultures continued to widen. As exports came to account for a growing proportion of our sales, all operating groups had to find ways to bring down costs in order to increase profits. In these ways, while we travelled the world making sales, we gained an accurate understanding of the strengths and weaknesses of NEC, the level of our technology, and other important business factors, and the desire to strengthen and improve our position spread to every corner of the company.

As the first part of this chapter has shown, the remarkable advances in semiconductor technology and the digitalization of communications that accompanied it gave rise to technological innovations that in turn led to new business opportunities for NEC. Semiconductors and digital communications equipment made their appearance as NEC's new strategic products on the world market. A special feature in the August 1977 issue of *Fortune* entitled "The Great World Telephone War," and a similar article in the March 1978 issue of the Japanese magazine *Soh*, described the bitter fight among the communications equipment makers of the industrialized world, including NEC, to win a share in the huge projects being planned in the Third World, especially in the oil-producing countries. NEC ranked seventh out of the world's nine major manufacturers of communications equipment (Western Electric was first, ITT second, Siemens third, Ericsson fourth, General Telephone & Electronics fifth, Northern Telecom sixth, Compagnie Générale d'Electricité eighth, and Philips ninth). The more prominent one becomes, the fiercer the competition and the sharper the criticism to which one is exposed. Fortunately, NEC's NEAX61 central office digital switching system – produced exclusively for our overseas customers – was well received, and by April 1981 we ranked first in the world with total orders for 30 million lines in the highly competitive global free market.

Balancing our Geographical Portfolio

The period of overseas expansion was naturally accompanied by several qualitative changes in NEC's business abroad. The first was the expansion of NEC products aimed at the foreign market, ranging from our traditional forte, communications equipment, to semi-conductors and other electron devices, home electronics, and computers. This diversification reflected our belief that the main way to avoid business risks was to improve the balance of the products we offered, as well as our geographical balance in North America, Europe, Asia, Oceania, the Middle East, Central and South America, and Africa (cited in the order of business performance as of fiscal 1987).

For a more detailed picture, I will look at developments in the US and Australasia; similar patterns of development occurred in other areas of the world. When NEC entered the US market, we built up experience exporting communications equipment to some of the leading US companies – an international gateway switching system to AT&T's Long Lines Department; digital microwave systems to New York Telephone Company and Data Transmission Communications; a small ground station to Satellite Business Systems; and a frame synchronizer to the National Broadcasting Company. After NEC

America opened a plant in Dallas, Texas, in 1978, however, we formally initiated a system of local production for the communications equipment we supplied to the US market. In the computer area we set up NEC Information Systems (currently NEC Technologies) in a Boston suburb in 1977 and opened our Woburn plant in 1978. In April 1984, when we began operations at our new plant in Boxborough, I made a special trip from Tokyo to attend the opening ceremonies, when I was delighted to be able to announce that since the ground-breaking ceremony two years earlier, both the number of employees and the volume of sales had tripled. NEC Home Electronics (USA) (currently NEC Technologies) was established in Chicago in 1981 to expand the sales routes for our household appliances, and in 1985 that company opened its first US plant in Atlanta, Georgia.

The Oceania region, especially Australia, accounted for 7 percent of NEC's overseas sales in the fiscal year ending March 31, 1990. Deregulation of the communications equipment market, in Australia in 1980 and in New Zealand in 1988, has led to new business opportunities there. I made my first visit to Australia in 1963, when I was senior executive vice president, to enter NEC's bid for the 930-mile microwave system planned between Brisbane, the capital of Queensland, and Cairns, in the northern part of that state. I had a very pleasant discussion with Francis P. O'Grady, director-general of the Australian Post Office, and happily NEC received the contract. I mentioned in chapter 4 that we set up NEC Australia, a communications equipment company, for which we had the encouragement of the Australian Post Office; since 1975 that company has produced transmission equipment, microwave communications systems, and private branch exchange (PBX) systems. The company received a charter from Australia Telecom, the successor to the Australian Post Office, recognizing NEC Australia as a local corporation and conferring on it the right to be an approved supplier to Australian Telecom. To accommodate the Australian government's plans to develop high-tech industries we are stepping up our R&D activities there and have already succeeded in exporting mobile radio equipment made in Australia.

In 1982 I broached the subject of C&C with the heads of Australia Telecom: The view of C&C which I outlined then is now about to be realized. Since February 1981, when we set up NEC Information Systems Australia, we have strengthened our sales system for small computers and are proceeding with plans to export UNIX software for small business computers from that company to Japan in the near future. NEC Home Electronics Australia came into being in 1983, when the joint venture Rank–NEC (founded in 1974) became a wholly owned subsidiary and changed its name. The color televisions that this company produces have become the top brand in the Australian home appliance market.

In neighboring New Zealand, NEC's foothold in the switching equipment market was the five-year supply contract we concluded in 1971 with the New Zealand Post Office. Under the terms of this agreement NEC was given a monopoly on the supply of crossbar switching equipment for use in urban and non-urban areas through-out New Zealand. A similar five-year contract was signed in July 1979 for the NEAX61, the central office digital switching system NEC had developed. New Zealand was the first foreign country to adopt a Japanese-made digital switching system as its standard equipment; I have described in chapter 9 how we set up a local software development company to develop the necessary software for it.

By considering both what foreign markets wanted and what NEC had to offer we charted the course of development for our overseas operations. In the process the overseas market for our goods expanded both geographically and in terms of the types of equipment we offered.

The second qualitative change was the emergence of the private market for communications equipment. In the United States the Carterfone decision handed down by the Federal Communications Commission (FCC) in June 1968 was a landmark event. At the time, the Bell System had overwhelming control of the US communications business, and only terminal equipment made by its sister company Western Electric could be connected to Bell telephone circuits. Thomas Carter of Carter Electronics, the inventor of an acoustic device for relaying mobile radio/telephone messages, filed suit against Bell on the grounds that end-to-end service violated US antitrust laws. The FCC ruled that any customer-provided equipment could be used as long as it did "not adversely affect the telephone company's operations or the telephone system's utility to its customers." An FCC decision in 1970 recognizing customer owned and operated private branch exchange systems gave rise to a new market for communications services. At that point I decided that NEC should enter this new US market, and in the years since then we have worked to open it up with considerable success.

Private demand for communications equipment has taken us into the other leading markets of the world as well, including that for computer-related business systems. In August 1978 we set up the Overseas Terminal Equipment Marketing Promotion Division (later renamed the International Business Systems Marketing Promotion Division) within our International Operations Group. To reflect the changes in the nature of our business overseas we made organizational reforms in August 1981 and established the Latin America Business Systems Division, the Asia Business Systems Division, and the Europe Business Systems Division to specialize in sales of PBXs, fax machines, and telephones. In June 1984 we carried out a similar reorganization of our North American Business Systems Division, setting up three separate divisions to deal with different types of communications equipment for the mass market. Although these goods first began competing with our customized communications systems in 1970, by 1980 sales for our mass-market products had moved ahead of sales for our customized systems.

NEC Technologies (UK) in Telford, England, our second British-based production center, was established in January 1987 to make consumer items such as video cassette recorders, printers, cellular telephones, and fax machines, 70 per cent of which are exported to continental Europe. At the official opening ceremonies for the Telford plant on November 2, 1988 I greeted the audience with these words: "Not only will products of the highest quality be shipped out from this plant, I am confident it will pursue the highest forms of excellence in both technology and management as well." As I spoke these words I recalled the six points that I have long regarded as the basis of a successful overseas strategy:

1 International operations require time.
2 The simplistic view that "if the domestic market is bad, go international" does not make sense.
3 Have your production and marketing facilities as close to your market as possible.
4 Take full advantage of local management resources.
5 Maintain a well-balanced global distribution of production facilities.
6 Top management must have a clear vision of international management principles and trends.

The third qualitative change has been the evolution of our business on a global scale. Following our established practice of setting up marketing and manufacturing facilities close to our customers we have strengthened our local production bases and overseas sales networks to respond to their proliferating needs. But as we expand our local business capabilities the time is coming when we will need to increase the efficiency of our overseas operations by establishing an international division of labor among all our production bases, including those in Japan. For example, instead of supplying goods and services to the markets where our plants are located, the optimum system might be to have parts made in a US plant and assembled in Singapore for sales to customers in the United States or Japan, or parts made in a Mexican plant assembled into the final product in the US. I see this sort of production method as another example of my "point to area" philosophy: The head office in Japan is the "point" to which all the other points are connected and controls business through its connections with all points on the "area," our overseas production facilities.

In the operation of our overseas business two forces pull in opposite directions. The first is a centripetal force that propels the ideas of the head office in Japan out to our local subsidiaries. Counterbalancing this is a centrifugal force pulling in the direction of complete local control summed up by the proverb "When in Rome do as the Romans." Because neither extreme alone is desirable, it is important to find the optimum balance between these two opposing forces. With this aim in view, we established in 1974 the International Education and Training Center within our International Operations Group to host trainees from abroad; and in 1982 we opened Takaido House in Tokyo, a facility that provides lodging for approximately 100. Both of these projects have been well received by our foreign employees and customers.

NEC's overseas operations are now very substantial indeed. We have twenty-six manufacturing companies in fifteen foreign countries operating twenty-nine plants; forty-five sales and service companies in twenty-three foreign countries; representative offices operated directly by the Tokyo head office in twenty-three foreign countries; and numerous local sales offices incorporated abroad. In March 1991 these overseas businesses employed 25,000 people throughout the world, of whom only a mere 3 percent – 860 people – were Japanese. NEC does business with 148 of the 168 countries that Japan officially recognizes. In fiscal 1990 our overseas sales amounted to 892 billion yen, or 26 percent of NEC's total sales. NEC at the end of the 1980s could truly claim to have attained global status.

12

Competing in a Changing World

C&C Comes of Age

Telecom '83, which took place between October 25 and November 1, 1983 in Geneva, Switzerland, reflected the groundswell of interest in C&C. Held once every four years under the sponsorship of the International Telecommunication Union, Telecom might well be called the Olympics of the telecommunications world. That year 650 groups participated, representing government communications agencies, communications businesses, and manufacturers from seventy-two countries, and an unprecedented 193,000 visitors thronged PALEXPO, the newly built Swiss national exhibition hall. Booths everywhere displayed central office digital switching equipment, PBXs, telephones, fiber optic communications systems, communications networks, office automation systems, and new media equipment: a clear sign that the trend toward the integration of computers and communications – my C&C concept – was well advanced.

Forum '83, which was held in tandem with Telecom '83, was an international symposium to discuss the various economic, technological, and legal issues surrounding telecommunications. On October 27 I spoke on the theme "Strategic Approaches to Modern Communications," taking advantage of this opportunity to expound all my hopes for C&C and set them forth clearly, if not as yet completely systematically. I reproduce here excerpts from the speech as it was originally delivered.

Strategic Approaches to Modern Communications

Man and C&C

During World Communications Year, it seems particularly fitting to examine strategic approaches to modern communications at this tele-communications forum. Methods of electronic and optical intelligent communications that make liberal use of computer technology are playing an increasingly important role in the infrastructure of human society. Many years ago I recognized and drew attention to the fact that the systems which would result from the merger of computer and communications technology constituted an important technological trend that would facilitate the transition away from agriculture and industry toward a knowledge- and information-intensive society.

As an extension of these views on what I call "C&C," I have also proposed the concept of a "Man and C&C" system based on my awareness of the importance of software technology and the need to develop more "user-friendly" machines.

Technical Features of Modern Communications

The field of modern communications can be considered from three different perspectives. First is the functional approach, which in turn can be divided according to the three main methods of information handling: (1) "information transfer," transmitting information quickly and accurately, the basic function of conventional modes of telecommunications; (2) "information generation," processing information in an easily intelligible format with the aid of computers; and (3) "information storage," filing information away for subsequent delivery.

Next, let us examine the media that form the interface between modern communications systems and the human beings who use them. These media, classified according to the human input and output organs that regulate the flow of information – speaking with the mouth, listening with the ears, writing with the hand, and reading with the eyes – include voice, data, text, and still and moving images. This classification is not rigid, however, and is likely to change as advances are made in computer technology. The first step in introducing modern communications systems will be to provide comprehensive information transfer services that can deal uniformly with all these diverse information media.

Finally, we can draw up a global overview of modern communications systems based on these ideas, with wide-range domestic transparent communications networks connected via international communications networks such as communications and broadcast satellites.

These transparent communications networks have a multilayered structure that includes public telephone networks, public packet networks, and various leased lines. This multilayered structure holds true not only for service functions but also for business operations, in the sense that a number of different operating agencies coexist and responsibility is allocated among them.

The Task of Building Global Infrastructure

What strategies should we adopt to promote and accelerate the creation of such modern communications systems? The first approach is to take the various systems for global communications – communications satellites, television broadcasting, information centers, automatic interpretation systems, and other systems that transcend national boundaries – and make them part of a global infrastructure.

Here I would like to discuss just one of these modern communications subsystems: teleconferencing. Office automation is helping to increase the efficiency of office workers, but ways of holding meetings and conferences still show room for improvement. More attention needs to be paid to teleconferencing systems to bring together people who are widely dispersed geographically. Those attending international meetings, in particular, generally spend long hours traveling huge distances: for such people international teleconferencing would be an extremely attractive alternative.

For teleconferencing to be successful, however, participants must be able to convey their ideas or thoughts to others quickly and accurately. This means the effective use not only of verbal information but also of visual information, including facial expressions and gestures.

International Cooperation and Exchange

Another strategy for developing modern communications systems on a global scale is to promote international cooperation and exchange. Examples of such cooperation would be international data flow or an international division of labor in the area of software development; the particular subject that interests me here is the joint international use of satellites.

Since initiating international commercial communications via the Early Bird satellite in 1965, the Intelsat system has made remarkable progress, developing into a global satellite communications network. It also started transponder lease services for domestic communications in 1975. Since then, the number of countries utilizing these services has risen to twenty. Plans are under way to provide further applications, such as business communications and teleconferencing. In addition, INMARSAT (International Marine Satellite Organization) began service in 1982; the Indonesian Palapa satellite is being used by the ASEAN countries; there is also ECS in Europe; and the ARABSAT regional satellite is scheduled to be launched in the near future.

Meteorological observation satellites are perhaps the best known example of international cooperation in the modern communications area. Meteorological data gathered by these satellites are not only provided to aviation and shipping but have also become part of our everyday life in the form of weather forecasts. Information from the Japanese meteorological satellite Himawari is utilized by fifteen countries in Oceania and Asia, including Australia, China, Korea, the Philippines, Singapore, and Thailand.

An Automatic Interpretation Telephone?

These are some of the strategic approaches to modern communications, which I have defined as one aspect of C&C, that is, as systems that combine computer functions in the broad sense (i.e. as electronic aids to information generation and storage) with conventional communications (i.e. information transfer). But what about the future?

Recent advances in microelectronics, optoelectronics, and computer technology have revolutionized the concept of conventional communications. And I have little doubt that the impact of modern communications on the development of human culture and the industrial economy will far exceed the influence that conventional methods of communication have had since their advent a little more than a century ago. As someone engaged in the communications field, I feel a heavy sense of responsibility whenever I think about the changes that our line of business is making in industrial and social structures.

Yet despite the enormous impact of modern communications methods, language barriers still impede mutual understanding among the peoples of the world. To overcome these barriers, I propose that we develop what I consider to be the epitome of C&C technology – an automatic interpretation telephone. Fortunately, we at NEC have at our disposal sophisticated technologies for voice recognition and voice synthesis that we have developed over the past twenty years. My hope is that by wedding these technologies to techniques of sentence analysis we will be able to fulfill the dream of an automatic interpretation system so that English spoken by you would reach me in Japanese, and my own thoughts would be interpreted and transmitted to you in English.

I am confident that an automatic interpretation telephone will be created before the year 2000; I have made it my remaining mission in life to be around to see and hear for myself when this breakthrough is made – for what greater gift could my "C&C" concept confer on mankind than an automatic interpretation system?

Six years had passed since I had announced my C&C concept in Atlanta. Then, the lack of response was almost total; now, the situation was completely different – the response was almost palpable. The audience seemed to be waiting for what I would say next.

It had been a long haul. Since 1977 I had repeatedly discussed C&C with my staff, in conversations which sometimes ran on late into the night. At the same time, as I have already mentioned, I took advantage of every opportunity to spread my C&C message throughout the world. But at Forum '83 I experienced one of the most unforgettable thrills of my life when Charles L. Brown, chairman of the board of the world's largest communications company, AT&T, referred to me and my C&C concept in his opening address on "The Future of World-Wide Integrated Communications Networks and Services." As a member of the audience I was listening attentively as he described the seemingly limitless stream of technological innovations, and the flood of new products they had produced, not as a "win–lose" situation but as a "win–win" situation, in which everyone will benefit equally from the revolution in information and communications technology. Suddenly, in the middle of this high-minded speech, I heard the words C&C. "*The driving force of this revolution, of course, is the convergence of communications and computer technology, which is literally redefining the telecommunications industry*. Various terms are used to describe the union of these two technologies. Some people in the United States refer to it as 'compunications.' In France, it's called 'telematique.' Dr Kobayashi of Japan's Nippon Electric calls it 'C&C.'"

C&C had become a globally accepted concept. Back in the days when communications were communications, computers were computers, and home electronics were home electronics, C&C had been the portent of a new direction, somewhat ahead of its time. But we had now reached the stage when everyone had to think about specific ways to enter the C&C field. Since a thorough understanding of the direction in which the information and communications industry was heading was essential for drawing up specific plans, one first had to know what was happening in America, the information capital of the world.

Structural Issues in the US: The AT&T–IBM Ruling

AT&T is the giant of the communications world, and IBM is the king of computers. Until a decade ago this was common knowledge. Around 1980, however, whenever NEC submitted bids on international communications projects in Europe, Africa, and the Middle East, so did IBM. Of course, there was no threat to its computer operations, but IBM had to do business with C&C in mind. The biggest issue was the competition between AT&T and IBM. AT&T was then the world's largest corporation with more than one million employees; IBM had cornered 60 percent of the world market for computers, with a monopoly on first place everywhere except Japan. When both these companies began to pay serious attention to the C&C market, I, of course, paid close attention to their movements in turn. In January 1981 US newspapers reported that Frank T. Cary, who was then chairman of IBM, had made a very interesting statement at a corporate presentation to a group of stock analysts. According to Cary, IBM had four important new areas. The first was robotics, an area he probably put first because he was thinking of Japan. In fact, the international industrial robot exhibition held at Harumi in Tokyo in October that year drew worldwide attention to the thriving state of Japan's robotics industry. The second was communications; the third was home electronics; and the fourth was medical electronics. All four were areas of C&C. IBM was now beginning to say the same things that I had been thinking for years.

Although I could not help feeling that my C&C manifesto had been the impetus behind these developments, the underlying idea could probably be traced back to the introduction of online services using computers linked to communications circuits at the beginning of the 1960s and the gradual blurring of the distinction between data processing and communications. Originally, under the Communications Act of 1934, in order "to make available . . . to all the people of the United States a rapid, efficient . . . service . . . at reasonable charges . . ." the Federal Communications Commission (FCC) had been set up "for the purpose of securing a more effective execution of this policy." But the waves of technological innovation symbolized by the computer had created a situation unforeseen at the time the Communications Act had gone into effect.

The Communications Act made public communications services local monopolies, but, to compensate, their operations were subject to strict regulation. On the other hand, in the computer business monopolies were not allowed, and companies were able to operate freely without regulation. Thus, if AT&T wished to introduce computers into its communications networks and broaden the definition of the communications area, it could not infringe on the computer industry. Conversely, a strict definition of communications meant that AT&T would be locked into its traditional business sphere. The merger of communications and computer technology was not simply a technical matter; it raised the whole issue of industrial structure.

In 1966 the FCC stepped in to clarify the boundaries between computers and communications. Their First Computer Inquiry formally set out the regulatory and policy issues arising from the convergence of computer and communications technologies and clearly recognized the existence of the problem. In its ruling four years later in 1970 the FCC defined the genre of "hybrid (communications/computer) services" and reached the compromise decision that only services whose primary purpose was communications were subject to regulation. But the appearance of large-scale integrated circuit technology, intelligent terminals, and distributed processing would force the FCC to reconsider its initial ruling.

The Second Computer Inquiry began in 1976, and a decision was handed down in 1980. Because drawing an artificial line around the flood of technology that I call C&C was a hopeless proposition, the FCC did not attempt to make a technological distinction and allowed complete freedom for all advanced services, leaving only basic transmission services still subject to regulation. There was one condition, however. The FCC handed down the epoch-making ruling allowing AT&T entry into the competitive, free market.

Even before the FCC's second ruling, we might say "technology sought competition." Following the Carterfone case the FCC had begun to liberalize the use of telephone lines by deregulating specialized services in 1971, domestic satellite communications in 1972, and VAN services in 1973. In the home telephone services area it deregulated the ownership of the home telephone receivers in 1977 and customer owned and operated private branch exchange equipment in 1978. The liberalization of PBXs in 1978 coincided with the opening of NEC America's Dallas plant, which began operations in July of that year: Thus NEC was able to get in at the very beginning of the rapid expansion of the American market for office automation. That year NEC also received a huge order for small ground stations for digital domestic satellite communications from Satellite Business Systems, IBM's beachhead in the communications business. NEC America set up an assembly plant in Virginia near SBS for local assembly of the required equipment.

After the FCC handed down its second ruling, the question remained how AT&T and IBM would handle basic and advanced services. On January 8, 1982, the US Department of Justice dropped its case against IBM and reached an out-of-court settlement of its antitrust suit against AT&T. AT&T's annual report for 1980 had stated: "No longer do we perceive that our business will be limited to telephony or, for that matter, telecommunications. Ours is the business of information handling, the knowledge business. And the market that we seek is global." These words had proved prophetic.

The international attention these events attracted is clear from the special article published in the January 25, 1982 issue of *Time* magazine entitled "A Guide to the Electronics Jungle." A cartoon captioned "Who's Who in the Electronic Jungle" accompanying the article depicted AT&T as a lion, IBM as a tiger, and NEC – the only non-US firm to be represented – as a crocodile. The Justice Department's consent decree, after many vicissitudes, resulted in the divestiture of the Bell System in January 1984.

The twenty-two regional Bell operating companies that separated off from AT&T as a result of the divestiture had traditionally received their equipment from Western Electric, the manufacturing arm of the Bell System. Now, however, the equipment procurement market was open to all US and foreign makers. Our NEAX2400, an information management digital PBX system that NEC began selling in the US in September 1983, is one example of the products we offered as core equipment for office information networks. The flip side of the coin was that AT&T – backed by the technological might of the Bell Lab, widely considered the best in the world – was now free to develop new markets, including those abroad.

As the wording of the consent decree makes clear, the Justice

Department's decision had been based on "the unseparability between computer and communication technologies." The leading companies of the world were now free to contend for the C&C market.

Structural Issues in Japan: Deregulated Communications

Japan in the early 1980s, spurred on by the immediate installation of telephone set upon application and countrywide direct dialling services (completed on March 14, 1979) as well as society's proliferating needs for new means of communications, was in the process of creating a communications infrastructue for an advanced information society. At just this point rapid changes began to occur in the business environment.

The first issue was NTT's procurement practices for telecommunications equipment. After January 1, 1981 the system was changed from the traditional closed tender method to an open bid system. Back in November 1977, during discussions on US–Japan trade issues, the US delegation had announced that computers and telephone equipment were among the items that the US was interested in selling to the Japanese market. US–Japanese trade frictions led to the issue being raised during negotiations on government procurement procedures at the Tokyo Round of the General Agreement on Tariffs and Trade (GATT). As a result, on December 19, 1980, Saburo Okita, the Japanese delegate for international trade issues, and Rubin Askew, the delegate for the US Commerce Department, exchanged memoranda reaching a compromise on the NTT procurement issue. Japan and the US would open their markets reciprocally to each other, and NTT would procure equipment on a competitive basis without regard to whether it was made at home or overseas. All purchases were to be classified into three groups or "tracks" – Track I for standard items, which were to be purchased on the open market; Track II for ready-made goods that had to be modified to meet NTT specifications; and Track III for products that needed to be jointly developed by NTT and the manufacturer.

The next issue was the privatization of NTT and the total deregulation of communications circuits, which went into effect on April 1, 1985. On this day three laws came into force governing the reform of Japanese communications, namely, the Telecommunications Business Law, the NTT Corporation Law, and the law on the enforcement of these two laws. Privatization had been a possibility ever since the prewar Ministry of Communications had proposed privatizing telephone services back in 1930. The issue surfaced again in 1951 in a report of a cabinet-level government advisory committee, which stated that the "telecommunications business will be a public corporate entity for the time being, on the precondition that it be privatized in the future." That was how NTT Public Corporation came into existence on August 1, 1952. By 1980, the opinion of the Ad Hoc Committee for Administrative Reform coincided with contemporary trends toward deregulation. In order to deregulate, however, it was necessary first to privatize NTT and break up its monopoly status. My own personal opinion was that once NTT's two great tasks – immediate installation of telephone set upon application and a nationwide direct dialling network – had been accomplished, it was time to begin privatization. It was a privatization that was long overdue.

The first deregulation of circuits in 1971 and the second in 1982 had been piecemeal; under the current revision of the law, deregulation would occur all at once. The interesting point was that, as in the United States, it was conducted in a way that formally recognized the development of computers. Once again it was possible to catch a glimpse of my concept of C&C at work.

Creating Value-Added Networks

In 1969, when NEC celebrated its seventieth anniversary, we had already been in the computer field for more than ten years and had acquired considerable insight into what the computer business was all about. As a result of this experience I recognized the importance that information services would one day have as a business area. Again it was a question of waiting for the right time; and the deregulation of communications opened up many opportunities.

When General Electric sold off its computer division to Honeywell in 1970 it retained its information services division and entrusted the management of this promising field to a subsidiary, GEISCO. Software specialists within the company had advised GE's top management to keep the software and information services division because it was certain to be a future source of revenue. Sharing that view, and thinking that a tie-up with a foreign company might be one way of expediting NEC's entry into the information services field, I explored the possibilities of an affiliation with GE. I also spent some time trying to come to an agreement with Dentsu, which was also in contact with GE at that time. In the end both explorations fell through, and I decided we should enter the field on our own. (Ironically, sometime later GEISCO began to use a powerful NEC mainframe computer for its information services business.) At the beginning of 1971 I gave the go-ahead to proceed with laying the groundwork for this new business venture.

As mentioned in chapter 7, NEC Information Service was founded in September 1974 with its main offices in Tokyo. I consider the founding of this new company to be NEC's first real step into the information services field. Because the information environment in Japan was on the verge of changing from batch processing to online production, at first we encountered many difficulties of one kind or another. But, although I heard grumblings from some members of staff that they didn't understand what information services were all about, or that we didn't have enough personnel for it, everyone cooperated with me in laying the foundations and developing the new business.

At the 147th regular general meeting of NEC shareholders held on June 28, 1985, the articles of incorporation were changed, and these words "to provide telecommunications, data base, and other information services" were added under the Object of the Company. From October 1 of that year NEC began offering value-added network (VAN) services as a special Type 2 telecommunications carrier. Our PC-VAN communications services for personal computers, inaugurated in April 1986, have shown rapid growth. Parallel with this, as part of our efforts to enter the international VAN business, in August 1985 we founded C&C International, a joint venture with GE to set up leased line service between the US and Japan and open an international network covering 750 cities in fifty countries throughout the world. Although at first there were legal restrictions on the service areas, after the revision of the Telecommunications Business Law, NEC was registered as a special Type 2 international carrier in September 1987 and formally entered the market as an international VAN service provider. Since then the service area has expanded to eighty-three countries.

The VAN business is an area of great promise, but it cannot be established overnight. There are many management problems: For example, the initial investment is enormous, but the fees received from customers are small. For that reason, I have always believed that for a value-added network business to blossom, it is vitally important to have both a long-term perspective – one that looks ahead to the twenty-first century – and an efficient policy for investing the company's resources based on such long-term views.

Computers Take the Lead

Having entered the computer business in 1954, and after encountering many difficulties along the way, we were finally within sight of our goal some twenty years later in 1975, when it seemed likely that our computer operations would soon be the same size as our communications business – or, to put in another way, when one C was no longer so much bigger than the other that it was hard to speak in terms of C&C. Once I felt confident that we had achieved an even balance between the two, I publicly announced my C&C concept. The changes in the global information environment since then are reflected in the discussion of the United States and Japan earlier in this chapter; as for NEC's computer business, sales on a consolidated basis have risen at an annual rate of more than 30 percent over the past five years. In 1980 we ranked third in Japan for computer sales; by 1984 we had seized second place. Within the company itself, computer sales rose from 23 percent of our total sales in fiscal 1982 to 44 percent in fiscal 1990, taking the number one spot in fiscal 1985 of all our major business sectors.

Fortunately, as I had predicted, computers have moved in the direction of distributed processing, a good direction for NEC, and we lead the domestic market in personal computers, small business computers, and small main-frame computers. In the area of large computers we have occasionally been able to beat our rivals in announcing new products such as our ACOS system 1000 in September 1980, followed by the system 1500 in February 1985, the system 2000 in February 1986, and our supercomputer in April 1983. Furthermore, we have succeeded in marketing an automatic fingerprint identification system that utilizes artificial intelligence technology; supplied optical character recognition technology to Burroughs in the US in 1981; and were an original equipment manufacturer of a system 1000 for Honeywell in 1983 and for Groupe Bull in France in 1984. With Honeywell we set up a company to sell supercomputers in 1986 and formed a company with Honeywell and Bull in 1987 to manufacture and sell large main-frame computers. As these moves indicate, our overseas strategy is proceeding smoothly.

The expansion of our computer business affects the business dependence structure of our entire company. From the mid-1950s to the mid-1960s, when NEC finally began to grow after the war, communications equipment had been the company workhorse; in the late 1970s semiconductors took over the leading role. Now the computer business occupies the central position in NEC's total business operations.

The Evolving Shape of the NEC Group

Led by the NEC head office in Tokyo, the NEC Group does business on a global scale. In May 1991 the group consisted of 202 companies, including NEC Corporation itself, and employed about 170,000 people. Two-thirds of these companies, 130 in all, are located in Japan; the remaining one-third, seventy-one companies, are incorporated abroad.

These companies could be said to be built on a common foundation of C&C technology and to share a fundamental management philosophy of mutual prosperity, autonomous management, mutual trust, and the principle of fair market value in all intercompany dealings. For management purposes group members have been classified into three categories according to their capital holdings, personnel, and relationship to the business of the parent company. (These three categories – subsidiaries, partially controlled companies, and independent companies – apply only to group members within Japan.)

Subsidiary companies can be divided into three types: Manufacturing subsidiaries, service and sales subsidiaries, and software subsidiaries. Our first manufacturing subsidiaries were founded in the late 1960s; they now number twenty-nine. Service and sales subsidiaries began at around the same time, and at present thirty-five companies have been independently incorporated either to perform staff functions within line divisions or to undertake line responsibilities within staff divisions. Our software subsidiaries have developed regionally since the late 1970s and now number thirty-four. (See chapter 9 for detailed discussion of these companies.)

Our partially controlled companies include firms that do business in areas that supplement NEC's own business operations. The earliest of these affiliations dates back to the late 1940s, the most recent to the early 1970s. The eighteen companies in this category differ widely in their capital participation, types of business, and personnel. Our fourteen independent companies are mainly businesses of an independent nature from the parent company, many of which are listed on the stock exchange. These companies might be considered partners in conducting NEC's business.

Although methods of guidance, direction-setting, and support need to be coordinated to accommodate each of these categories, I welcome the diversity the group members bring to the development of competitive products. It is this competitiveness that strengthens the NEC Group as a whole.

R&D: The Company's Lifeblood

However finely tuned the organizational structure of a company, if its business is in technology its creative heart is its research base. Japanese industry as a whole has realized that one must be ahead to compete, and recently the rush has been on to build new research facilities or expand old ones. The old adage popular during the period of high-level growth that "you can sell anything you make" no longer applies, and Japanese industry is beginning to invest heavily in research and development to improve its long-term prospects. Gone are the days of the "catch-up" period when Japanese companies scoured the industrialized world for technological models to follow; now we can expect just the opposite – that these countries will have to learn something from Japan. In fact, probably the primary reason for Japan's heavy emphasis on research and development is the need to develop state-of-the-art technologies by our own efforts.

The second reason is one that I have alluded to earlier. To deal with industrialization in the developing countries we are being forced to transfer the technologies we can pass on and acquire more advanced technologies for ourselves, ones that have no superiors.

This strategy is one that must be considered seriously as a response to the newly industrializing economies of Asia.

The third reason is that *the time is coming when a company's R&D strength will determine its growth or even its very survival.* To prepare for the demands of such an age, NEC decided to build its new Tsukuba Laboratories on the site of Tsukuba EXPO '85, Japan's highly successful scientific world fair. The laboratories, which opened in July 1989, will provide the impetus for basic research with long-term prospects that will come to fruition in the twenty-first century. In the belief that cooperation among industry, government, and academia will be indispensable for Japan's future R&D system, national research institutes and universities have already begun to gather at the Tsukuba site, generating an optimum environment for basic research. There are also plans to hold international scientific conferences there on a regular basis. Thus the idea that the site may one day grow into a Japanese mecca for research and development is no idle fancy. By having a research facility here NEC can fully expect to improve its image. In addition, on July 30, 1988, NEC established its first basic research center abroad: the NEC Research Institute in Warren, New Jersey.

NEC has traditionally prided itself on its commitment to technological progress. Over the years, we have stressed the importance of R&D and have committed many of our most capable personnel to this sector. This has been particularly true since I became president in 1964. I immediately threw my energy behind efforts to improve the efficiency of our R&D organization, strengthen and perfect our technology development strategy, and foster original and independent technologies. Around 1970 nearly 70 percent of NEC's total annual consolidated sales was accounted for by new products developed within the previous five years; in some divisions, the rate exceeded 90 percent.

Managing R&D: Divergence and Convergence

The R&D system at NEC which has produced these new technologies and new products has an organizational structure that distributes responsibility for R&D throughout the entire company to ensure that research activities are carried out in close association with our operating divisions. Here as elsewhere, however, the principle of "divergence" is balanced by the principle of "convergence"; in other words, the direction-setting for our diverse research activities is centralized to make them easier to control.

In my book *Management Problems for the Seventies* I wrote:

because there is no hard and fast method of achieving technological development, the wisest course of action is to try to fashion approaches that will make it easier to obtain results. *Since technology is a means of satisfying human desires, we should try to avoid areas for which there is little immediate need.* Traditionally, most research and development has sprung from the interests or concerns of the researchers themselves. From now on, however, it will be important to lay down an order of priority and set objectives based on degrees of social utility . . . There is a tendency to regard the development of independent and original technology as being only of academic interest . . . but its *raison d'être* lies in the fact that it is the source of a company's future profits. In this sense, we might say that *the ultimate aim of R&D rests not with new products* per se *but with products that satisfy customers and make them want to buy*.

This strategy underlies the three-tiered decentralized system of R&D activity NEC inaugurated in May 1965. To bring R&D closer in line with corporate objectives our Research and Development Group was detached from the central corporate staff and placed on a par with our line operating groups, each of which contains several divisions. Since each division acts as the profit center for its own business operations, it has direct ties with the marketplace and, in order to ensure its profits, must develop products that the market wants. Because the division is most sensitive to current market needs, its engineering unit has the responsibility for developing technology for "today." At the next level, the development laboratories within each operating group have the responsibility for R&D into technology for "tomorrow," nurturing the seeds of what will eventually grow into new business ventures. Finally, primary responsibility for research and development for the "day after tomorrow" belongs to our Research and Development Group, an organization that is not constrained by current market needs. Thus my R&D philosophy is to divide research and development into strategic areas, from basic research into the technologies that will be important for the future, to applied research and basic development, right up to leading-edge research into the basic technologies needed to establish or revise today's corporate strategy.

As this R&D system put down roots, it became necessary to modernize and upgrade our research facilities. In 1973 we began construction of our new Central Research Laboratories on a fourteen-acre site in the Tama Hills in Kawasaki. The new facilities, with almost 400,000 square feet of floor space, replaced the original Central Research Laboratories at our Tamagawa plant, which had begun to show their age. Right after the ground-breaking ceremonies we were hit by the first oil shock; yet despite both a recession and difficulties in obtaining the materials we needed, construction was completed in the spring of 1975, and by that July the Central Research Laboratories had moved into their new premises. In August 1976 they became host to the VLSI Technology Research Association's joint research lab. This was a national project with a total budget of 70 billion yen, sponsored by Japanese electronics manufacturers, including NEC, and the Ministry of International Trade and Industry's Agency of Industrial Science and Technology, to develop the world's first very-large-scale integrated circuit. The group worked from fiscal 1976 to fiscal 1979 and was disbanded in March 1980 when basic research was completed.

R&D Reorganization for Future Success

In July 1980 NEC carried out a major organizational reform of its R&D system, the first such reshuffling since May 1965. My public pronouncement in 1977 about the integration of computers and communications had taken hold in industries throughout the world, and market needs were beginning to reflect the trend toward C&C. To accommodate our R&D plans to our new business strategies we decided to model the structure of our research activities on the concept of distributed processing that had proved so successful in the computer field and decentralize even further to enhance our maneuverability. Accordingly, the various laboratories that had belonged to our Central Research Laboratories were consolidated or reorganized, and five independent labs were created: the Fundamental Research Laboratories, the Optoelectronics Research Laboratories, the C&C Systems Research Laboratories, the Software Production Research Laboratory, and the Resources and Environment Protection Research Laboratories. In June 1982 the Microelectronics Research Laboratories split off from the Fundamental Research Laboratories; and the C&C Information Technology Research Laboratories split off from the C&C Systems Research Laboratories in July 1986.

The new system reflects the future strategies targeted by NEC. No other company, for example, has an equivalent to our C&C Systems Research Laboratories: these form the core of our R&D into the basic technology for the systems that will support C&C products. Because it requires enormous capital resources to do basic research in all areas, we have put special emphasis on those where the lack of adequate technological foundations within the company might impede future business – technology for communications, computers, and terminals, for example. The newly created C&C Information Technology Research Laboratories conduct necessary research into creating the technological foundations for the information services area, such as the VAN business; research activities there extend from basic research to applied research in areas such as home electronics, media technology, and pattern recognition.

The Optoelectronics Research Laboratories point in yet another direction. When we originally set up an independent laboratory in this field, it was probably the first of its kind in the world. The practical applications of optoelectronics are centered primarily on fiber optic communications, which has developed rapidly over the past few years, but optical information processing and the applied use of optics in energy, industry, and home electronics are also being explored. I believe that each of our operating groups will one day consider optoelectronics a basic technology in their respective fields.

The Software Production Research Laboratory is another example of a new venture with few precedents. What gave me the idea for this experiment was the fact that although advances in microelectronics technology had led to wholesale improvements in hardware functions, software had not proved amenable to automation. Every company has had to make a huge commitment of personnel in this area, and a cost analysis of electronics products showed that the percentage of the software component was rising. My feeling that something had to be done about software production resulted in the creation of a research center dedicated to developing the necessary tools to improve the productivity of software. The C&C Software Development Group grew out of this laboratory in September 1987.

The Production Engineering Development Group developed from our Production Engineering Laboratory, which had been founded in May 1965. Product engineering and production engineering are two sides of the same coin and share a common matrix. Although each division has total responsibility for its own production R&D, in order to make the most efficient use of technology, the development of basic production engineering methods and manufacturing equipment that can be used throughout the entire company is carried out in a centralized fashion by the Production Engineering Development Group. The organization of this group underwent major reinforcement in July 1988.

How Far Off is the Future?

In my experience it takes at least twenty years for an invention that shows promise of making a technological breakthrough to establish a firm enough footing to become a viable commercial venture. In 1945, for example, British science-fiction writer Arthur C. Clarke proposed "extra-terrestrial relays" using man-made satellites from which to beam television broadcasts throughout the world. Twenty years later Dr Harold A. Rosen of Hughes Aircraft was able to translate this idea into reality. NEC cooperated with Hughes from the very beginning of that project to develop a satellite communications system using synchronous satellites. Another example is the pulse code modulation (PCM) method of digital communications developed in 1937 by the young British engineer A. H. Reeves, which was made praticable by transistor technology in 1957. Here too NEC began at an early date to experiment with this technology and develop it into a viable commercial product.

If this rule of thumb continues to apply, we will have to identify today the technology that will be needed the "day after tomorrow" – twenty years from now – or face disastrous consequences. If we take this timespan as our temporal axis, we must also think in terms of a spatial axis. For example, if we analyze market needs and the technology required to develop the new products that will satisfy those needs and draw up a market/technology matrix, many of these products will be seen to share several basic technologies. By bringing together basic technologies that closely resemble one another, we can define groups of core technologies that will continue to be the focus of R&D efforts over the long term. Because these core or quasi-core technologies will remain unchanged for the next ten or twenty years, if we divide them up among the relevant research laboratories, then the laboratories – or the groups of specialists to whom these assignments have been distributed – will not be distracted by superficial changes in new products but will be able to respond flexibly to the task of refining and developing these basic technologies.

A core technology program such as this requires that the core technologies be carefully coordinated every year and that major reappraisals be made every ten years. Moreover, setting up strategic technology domains (STD) that bring together several core technologies will increase efficiency, make collaboration easier, and promote cooperation and the exchange of research information vertically across the entire company.

Another idea is that of conducting special R&D projects. Because new systems or new products can be developed by adding one's own creative imagination to composite technologies or products or to the germs of previously known basic principles or technologies, we should not limit the work of research and development to putting the finishing touches to ideas or products developed within a particular organization. For example, when one research division has to decide whether or not a basic technology it has been working with has reached the level of actual usefulness, it needs the cooperation of many other divisions. In a case like this a research laboratory and its related division might choose an area where the basic technology seems to show the most promise and cooperate to develop a new product using it. This is what I call a project. The project system underscores the sense of mutual cooperation between operating divisions and research laboratories. When the system is put into practice, divisions become more eager to assess the basic technologies that the research labs have been exploring, while the research labs develop a sense of responsibility and a better appreciation of timing. Another merit that should not be overlooked is that such cooperation reduces the "not-invented-here" factor.

Over the past five years NEC's investment in R&D has been more than 10 percent of sales on a consolidated basis. I am well aware that these figures by themselves mean nothing, and that if we do not make the proper moves now in the area of research and development, not only will we fail overseas, we will not even be able to survive in the highly competitive Japanese market. Whether prevailing market conditions are good or bad, I believe a company's survival depends on aggressive investment in R&D.

In February 1985 we opened the NEC C&C Hall of Technological History on the site of our Tamagawa plant. The exhibits display the achievements of the world's pioneers in computers and communications – men like Dr Yasujiro Niwa and Dr Akira Nakashima, who sparked the technological innovations at NEC in the 1930s; Dr Jack

A. Morton of Bell Laboratories; and Dr Lawrence A. Hyland of Hughes Aircraft. The exhibits also trace the technological development of each of NEC's business areas. Again and again my steps have brought me back to this hall.

Afterword

As I wrote the "Afterword" to the Japanese edition of this book from my office on the twenty-second floor of the NEC Building, I could look out of the huge window on that level and see the entire expanse of the construction site one block away where NEC's new headquarters was being built. In January 1990 that building – forty-three stories high with four floors underground – was completed and I moved into my new office on the forty-second floor. The construction of our new headquarters was a fitting celebration of the ninetieth anniversary of the company's foundation; on July 17, 1990 NEC marked its ninety-first anniversary by unveiling a less tangible but every bit as significant a construction: its new corporate philosophy, pointing to the twenty-first century.

As the new building rose, story after story, I watched it grow; and every time I looked out of the window at the foundations being laid, the steel girders being put into place, the walls going up, I was filled with an inexpressible emotion. My mind went back to November 28, 1964, the day when President Toshihide Watanabe called me into his office and suddenly announced: "Kobayashi, you're our next president." At that time NEC had sales of 70 billion yen, or 81.4 billion yen on a consolidated basis. Today, a quarter of a century later, sales have grown nearly forty-fold to 2.8 trillion yen (3.4 trillion on a consolidated basis). When I became president in 1964, I spent day and night thinking of ways to make the company grow. This book has been a record, as accurate as my memory allows, of the process by which one corporate manager physically came to grips with the task before him. I would like to think that some of the readers of this book are young people, the leaders of the business world in the twenty-first century. I know of no greater happiness than to think that this account of my management ideas and my actual business experiences may be of some use to them.

On May 25, 1988, I became chairman emeritus and representative director of NEC Corporation. I would like to conclude here with my "Ten Pointers for Executives," which have served as a touchstone for me throughout the long period of my stewardship and which I have passed on to others to serve as guidelines to the next generation.

1. *Make a picture of your thoughts.* Maps and sketches will provide guidance for attaining your next objective.
2. To grasp the situation in which you are now placed, *take account of a coordinate axis of both time and space.*
3. *Recognize that a seemingly stable corporation contains instability* while a seemingly unstable corporation can be stable.
4. *Teamwork multiplies individual abilities.* Don't forget the proverb, "Two heads are better than one."
5. Do not follow a one-way, single track in your thinking. *Set up feedback loops as a means of rectifying your own one-sided judgements.*
6. In any undertaking, *things develop from points to lines, and from lines to dimensions.* Keep in mind, for example, that marketing and technology form a matrix.
7. Divergence vs. convergence, the part vs. the whole – consider the advantages and disadvantages of both sides and always *cultivate a sense of balance.*
8. *Do not let yourself be swamped by the rising tide of information and knowledge.* Be selective. Remember that the most important information is not always the most obvious.
9. *Self-help is the mainstay of development* for both the individual and society.
10. *Cultivate the strong points and potentials of an individual or an enterprise and nurture them like a gardener.* It may take ten or twenty years for them to mature.

I pray from the bottom of my heart for the happiness and venture-mindedness of all who come after me, especially the young people of the next generation who bear the future hopes of the world on their shoulders.

Further Reading

The following list includes books referred to in the text of this edition.

Ralph J. Cordiner, *New Frontiers for Professional Managers*, McGraw-Hill, 1956.

Peter F. Drucker, *The Practice of Management*, Harper & Row, 1954.

——*Managing for Results – Economic Tasks and Risk-Taking Decisions*, Harper & Row, 1964.

Dennis Gabor, *Inventing the Future*, Secker & Warburg, 1964.

——*The Mature Society*, Secker & Warburg, 1972.

John Kenneth Galbraith, *The Age of Uncertainty*, Houghton Mifflin, 1977.

Frederick R. Kapell, *Vitality in a Business Enterprise*, McGraw-Hill, 1960.

Koji Kobayashi, *Meeting the Challenge of the Computer Age*, Jitsugyo-no-Nihonsha, 1968.

——*Management Problems for the Seventies*, Diamond, Inc., 1971.

——*Quality-Oriented Management*, Diamond, Inc., 1976.

——*C&C is Japan's Wisdom*, Simul Press, 1980.

——*C&C: The Software Challenge – A Human Perspective*, Simul Press, 1982.

——*C&C: Modern Communications – Development of Global Information Media*, Simul Press, 1985.

Fritz Machlup, *The Production and Distribution of Knowledge in the United States*, Princeton University Press, 1962.

Chie Nakane, *Personal Relations in a Vertical Society*, Chuokoronsha, 1967.

Alfred P. Sloan, Jr, *My Years with General Motors*, Doubleday, 1963.

Thomas J. Watson, Jr, *A Business and Its Beliefs*, Trustees of Columbia University, 1963.

Index

Developmental Management

The following titles have now been published in this exciting and innovative series:

Ronnie Lessem: *Developmental Management* 0 631 16844 3 ☐
Charles Hampden-Turner: *Charting the Corporate Mind** 0 631 17735 3 ☐
Yoneji Masuda: *Managing in the Information Society* 0 631 17575 X ☐
Ivan Alexander: *Foundations of Business* 0 631 17718 3 ☐
Henry Ford: *Ford on Management** 0 631 17061 8 ☐
Bernard Lievegoed: *Managing the Developing Organization* 0 631 17025 1 ☐
Jerry Rhodes: *Conceptual Toolmaking* 0 631 17489 3 ☐
Jagdish Parikh: *Managing Your Self* 0 631 17764 7 ☐
John Davis: *Greening Business* 0 631 17202 5 ☐
Ronnie Lessem: *Total Quality Learning* 0 631 16828 1 ☐
Pauline Graham: *Integrative Management* 0 631 17391 9 ☐
Alain Minc: *The Great European Illusion* 0 631 17695 0 ☐
Albert Koopman: *Transcultural Management* 0 631 17804 X ☐
Elliott Jaques: *Executive Leadership* 1 55786 257 5 ☐
Koji Kobayashi: *The Rise of NEC* 1 55786 277 X ☐

* Not available in the USA   All titles are £18.95 each

You can order through your local bookseller or, in case of difficulty, direct from the publisher using this order form. Please indicate the quantity of books you require in the boxes above and complete the details form below. NB. The publisher would be willing to negotiate a discount for orders of more than 20 copies of one title.

Payment
Please add £2.50 to payment to cover p&p.

☐ Please charge my Mastercard/Visa/American Express account
card number ☐☐☐☐☐☐☐☐☐☐☐☐☐☐☐☐

Expiry date _____
Signature _____
   (credit card orders must be signed to be valid)

☐ I enclose a cheque for £_____ made payable to **Marston Book Services Ltd**
(PLEASE PRINT)

Name _____
Address _____
_____
_____ Postcode _____
Tel No _____
Signature _____ Date _____

Please return the completed form with remittance to:
Department DM, Basil Blackwell Ltd
108 Cowley Road, Oxford OX4 1JF, UK
or telephone your credit card order on 0865 791155.

Goods will be despatched within 14 days of receipt of order. Data supplied may be used to inform you about other Basil Blackwell publications in relevant fields.
Registered in England No. 180277 Basil Blackwell Ltd.